THE
CULTURE CLASH

Jean Donaldson

James & Kenneth
PUBLISHERS

The Culture Clash
by Jean Donaldson

Published in the USA by:

James & Kenneth Publishers
2140 Shattuck Avenue #2406
Berkeley, California 94704
(800) 784-5531

James & Kenneth - Canada
2353 Belyea Street
Oakville, Ontario L6L 1N8
(905) 469-1555 ext 3

James & Kenneth - UK
P O Box 111, Harpenden
Hertfordshire, AL5 2GD
01582 715765

ISBN 1-888047-05-4

For Lassie

Acknowledgments

I would like to express my deepest gratitude to Ian Dunbar for his advice, encouragement, influence and inspiration, and to Martin Coles for his support and advice as well as for editing the manuscript, shooting the photo and coming up with the cover concept and art.

Thanks also to the following: Carolyn Clark, Irene & Bill Donaldson, Susan Gillett, Bun Hong, Kin Hong, Delva Howell, Joan McCordick, Cathy McNaughton, Judy Miller, Kathy Pickel and Diana Shannon.

FOREWORD

The Culture Clash is special. Jean Donaldson's first book is quite simply the very best dog book I have ever read. It is utterly unique, fascinating to the extreme, and literally overflowing with information that is so new it virtually redefines the state of the art in dog behavior and training. Written in Jean's inimitably informal yet precise lecture style, the book races along on par with a good thriller. In fact, I read the manuscript three times in a row before it was even published.

The Culture Clash depicts dogs as they really are - stripped of their Hollywood fluff, with their loveable 'can I eat it, chew it, urinate on it, what's in it for me' philosophy. Jean's tremendous affection for dogs shines through at all times, as does her keen insight into the dog's mind. Relentlessly, she champions the dog's point of view, always showing concern for their education and well being.

The Culture Clash joins a very distinctive group of books and it runs at the head of the pack. Like Karen Pryor's Don't Shoot the Dog, The Culture Clash has a refreshingly original perspective. Like Gwen Bohnenkamp's books, The Culture Clash cuts to the chase - no if's and no but's - here's the story - now educate your dog! Without a doubt, Jean's book is the hottest doggy item on the market - the quintessential book for dog owners and dog trainers alike - a very definite two paws up! Do yourself and your dogs a big favor: Give it a read! And let's look forward to many more books by Jean Donaldson.

Ian Dunbar
Berkeley, California
31st May 1996

Contents

1. Getting the Dog's Perspective

Walt Disney vs. B.F. Skinner

A book which was recently published refers to the "moral code" of dogs. It became a bestseller. It seems that most people still buy into the Walt Disney dog: he is very intelligent, he has morals, is capable of seeking revenge and planning, he solves complex problems, he understands the value of the artifacts in Walt's home. Nobody wants B.F. Skinner's dog, the black input-output box who is so obviously not the furry member of your family. It's been marketed all wrong, I think. Skinner was right but has gotten bad press. The truth must be presented in a way which people will start to buy into. They have to, because not getting it has led to the death of countless dogs. Here is an example to illustrate the difference:

A dog has been reprimanded every time he has been caught chewing furniture. Now the dog refrains from chewing furniture when the owner is home but becomes destructive when left alone. When the owner comes home and discovers the damage, the dog slinks around, ears back and head down.

Walt's view: The dog learns from the reprimand that chewing furniture is wrong. The dog resents being left alone and, to get back at the owner, chews the furniture when the owner leaves. He deliberately, in other words, engages in an act he knows to be wrong. When the owner comes home the dog feels guilty about what he has done.

BF's view: The dog learns that chewing furniture is dangerous when the owner is present but safe when the owner is gone. The dog is slightly anxious when left alone and feels better when he chews. Later, when the owner comes home, the dog behaves appeasingly in an attempt to avoid or turn off the punishment he has learned often happens at this time. The owner's arrival home and/or pre-punishment demeanor have become a predictor: The dog knows he's about to be punished. He doesn't know why.

There is little question that the second view is correct. The question is really no longer which interpretation is the truth but rather why is it that we are even still arguing the point? Amazingly, this information has been around for decades, yet most people who own dogs haven't gotten it down yet. How is it that this can even be up for discussion in 1996? It would seem no amount of proof can make a behaviorist model politically correct. The implications of this are really important.

The staying power of the fuzzy-wuzzy warm-hearted, distorted view of dogs has to do with how much we like them. We want them to be smart, morally "good." We see dogs as superior to people in their loyalty and trustworthiness in today's society. The behaviorist model, however inescapably verifiable, hasn't caught on in the mainstream because it seems to reduce dogs to input-output machines. I think our fear is that if we accept this viewpoint, we strip dogs of their status as honorary humans. The logical extension of this is that it would make it harder for some people to use dogs as surrogate children and that there would be negative ramifications for the welfare of dogs. Humans, like most animals, are tribal: our compassion and consideration for other beings is strongly correlated with our perception of how similar they are to us. Huge ethical questions were immediately raised when evidence of language acquisition in chimps appeared. Without their capacity for language, it is somehow more okay to accept a utilitarian attitude towards them. This is mainly because intelligencism is still an acceptable prejudice. Our species has a long history of incredible violence and horror perpetrated, essentially, because the victims were too far outside our perceived tribe. The current tribal boundaries have a lot to do with IQ and moral integrity. Our bond with dogs is obviously strong. To explain the emotion, we exaggerate how much they resemble us in the areas of intelligence and morality.

I think we may be ready to accept the real species though. We are now living in a culture that is much more aware of the importance of tolerance and validation. Dogs are not like us, not nearly as much as we thought. But that's okay. We can still bond with them, share our lives with them, use them as surrogate children without apology. We don't have to renovate their natures to legitimize how we feel about them. They are valuable and fascinating as they really are. They don't need to be promoted in intelligence or morality to merit fair treatment or places in our families.

Facing up to the reality becomes important, not just because the anthropomorphic view has outlived its usefulness: it has always had a very real down-side for dogs. Although at one time it may have been worth buying into, I don't think it's necessary to use this shield any more. There's a law of diminishing returns going on here. The greatest gains for the welfare of dogs are now to be found in abandoning the Lassie myth and replacing it with information from two sources: dog behavior and the science of animal learning. The prevailing winds, in fact, would make it our responsibility to have a clue about the basic needs of the species we are trying to live with as well as a clue about how to modify their behavior, with as little wear and tear on them as possible so that they fit into our society without totally subjugating their nature.

Lemon-Brains but We Can Still Like Them

The two areas in which there is the greatest amount of myth and knowledge void are:

1) dog behavior, i.e. the genetic endowment and constraints or "hard-wiring" the dog comes with, and
2) animal learning, i.e. the nuts and bolts about how experience affects the behavior of dogs and other animals, including us.

Humans do learn through operant and classical conditioning. In this respect, we are like dogs. However we, unlike dogs, are also masterful at learning through observation and insight. We have language to mediate our thoughts, we can move mentally from past to present to future and think abstractly. We internalize values taught to us through reward and punishment, most of us developing qualities like compassion and a conscience, a sense of right and wrong. Behaving congruently with our values gives us self-esteem, a feeling of integrity. This whole area swishes dogs completely. They are completely and innocently selfish. The extreme likelihood is that dogs learn almost exclusively through operant and classical conditioning. Although some of their behaviors are socially facilitated, there is little evidence that they learn by observation or imitation. This doesn't make them stupid or any less valuable than they were when we thought they could think like us. This point is so important. Dogs are great learners. They can discriminate extremely fine differences in their environment. They have incredible olfactory powers. They can deal with complex social environments. They have a rich emotional life. But they do not think abstractly. They are amoral. They cannot move mentally forward and backward through time. Although they can learn to discriminate the relevance of certain words, they do not understand language.

This shouldn't be such a hard pill to swallow but I think that the societal discrimination based on intelligence I alluded to earlier undermines any realistic assessment of dogs. We all, officially at least, denounce discrimination based on race, sex, age or body-size, but the tyranny of brain power remains and is ever so subtle. It's institutional intelligencism. Ponder for a minute how you would feel about using rats in experiments to test drugs if it was discovered that rats were sophisticated, pacifist, psychic beings with IQ's greater than the average human. We still have the might to perpetrate anything we want on them, but our internal justification has less to do with our might than the fact that, well, they're not very smart, are they.

Dogs are multi-talented, but they simply aren't very smart the way humans are. A recent book, devoted to the intelligence of dogs, is 250+ pages long. We are obviously fascinated by the notion that dogs might, just might, be really, really smart. Why do we keep referring to this particular yardstick, intelligence, to evaluate another species? The reason, of course, is that it's our strong suit. When will we start to see that there's so much that's truly fascinating about dogs, it makes intelligence a red herring. The discriminative ability of dogs in classical conditioning, the ability of dogs to use their noses, the ability of dogs to deal with a complex social environment, their feelings and bonding are all mind-bogglingly vast topics, but "intelligence" merits a pretty thin volume. At least as thin as a book on the ability of humans to sniff for bombs or echo-locate.

We crave anecdotes about genius dogs and these abound. Everyone knows a story which illustrates how "smart" dogs are. But a fundamental question has never been answered by proponents of reasoning in dogs: if dogs are capable of these feats of brain power at all, why are they not performing them *all the time?* Why never in controlled conditions? What bugs me the most about these claims is the lack of rigor in evaluating them. The whole thing reminds me of people who leap to unlikely conclusions about things like circles in English wheat fields. Before theorizing that the circles were made by extra-terrestrials, more likely explanations have to be ruled out, such as sophisticated pranksters. The latter turned out to be the case, but not before a huge amount of interest was generated by extra-terrestrial theories. Likewise, before jumping to the conclusion that the dog thinks abstractly and moralizes, first rule out an explanation based on learning theory. I find it disturbing that my dogs' value is based on myth and exaggeration, as though their reality wasn't good enough. Their value comes from their real beings, their dogginess. They don't need mental upgrading. They are worthy and wonderful as they are.

So what is the fallout for dogs of the Walt Disney myth? As soon as you bestow intelligence and morality, you bestow the responsibility that goes along with them. In other words, if the dog knows it's wrong to destroy furniture yet deliberately and maliciously does it, remembers the wrong he did and feels guilt, it feels like he merits a punishment, doesn't it? Well, that's just what dogs have been getting - a lot of punishment. We set them up for all kinds of punishment by overestimating their ability to think. Interestingly, it's the so-called "cold" behaviorist model that ends up giving dogs a much better crack at meeting the demands we make of them. The fuzzy-wuzzy model gives dogs problems that they cannot solve and then punishes them for failing. And the saddest thing is that the main association most dogs have with punishment is the presence of their owner. This puts a pretty twisted spin on what's supposed to be about loooving dogs 'cause they're so smart, doesn't it?

Learning theory, i.e. behaviorism, is the best means we have to understand and modify the behavior of our dogs. It is best both in terms of effectiveness and therefore, by extension, in terms of minimizing wear and tear on the dog and on the dog-human relationship. The large-scale unwillingness to accept and develop our expertise in applying learning theory is defended on grounds that don't hold up when scrutinized. The basis in science leaves people cold yet the warm model, as we've seen, lays the foundation for endless punishments of these brilliant, moral yet law-breaking beings. My argument is that dogs aren't demeaned or reduced to the status of laboratory rats by applying what has been learned by behavioral science. I'm incensed, in fact, by the incredible irony that zillions of rats AND dogs lived pretty awful lives in laboratories and were subjected to zillions of rotten experiments in order to come up with basic principles of how animals learn. One of the most obvious applications of the knowledge so gained would be dog training, no? Kind of a double whammy for your species to be used in the experiments and then have the mass public ignore the results and continue to punish you because you're soooooo smart. Of all the windows which exist to communicate with dogs, operant conditioning is the window which is open the widest. We should start using it.

The Eager-to-Please Fallacy

The anthropomorphic spin on dog behavior is not limited to exaggerations of their intelligence. We also misinterpret their regard for us. When are we going to put to bed once and for all the concept that dogs have a "desire to please"? What a vacuous, dangerous idea. I'm still waiting to meet this dog who wants to please his owner. Indeed, where is this dog who is interested at all in the internal state of his owner except with regard to how manifestations of this state impact events of relevance to the dog. Although praise works as a reinforcer for some individuals in the total absence of any competing motivation, this effect is limited and casts some pretty extreme doubt on a "desire to please" gene.

Closer scrutiny makes the case even weaker. Rule out, for starters, that the praise functions as a safety cue - a predictor of extremely low likelihood of aversives. This is evident in traditional obedience classes. The primary motivation is said to be praise. The primary motivation is actually avoidance of aversives, called "leash corrections." If the trainer is any good, the dog learns that if a response is praised, a correction has been avoided, and so the praise acquires meaning and relevance. Also, high pitched and staccato noises, often used in praising dogs, are intrinsically attractive to dogs as evidenced by the use of these noises by humans in their interactions with animals across virtually all cultures. But does this mean the dog is employing this sound as evidence of some internal state of the maker of the sound? This is unlikely.

Praise can also acquire some "charge" as a secondary reinforcer in the day-to-day life of a dog. People tend to praise dogs more when doling out cookies, attention, walkies and games. This all is more evidence of what we already knew and should be exploiting with a tad more sophistication: *dogs learn by the immediate results of their actions and the association of events which occur closely together in time.*

I once spoke to a traditional trainer who poured scorn on the use of food as a motivator. The line he trotted out, which still makes me wretch even to this day, was "if you use food to train, the dog is doing it for the food and not for you." This is still a surprisingly common attitude, especially among green owners and trainers. This man's dog, trained by avoidance with a strangle collar, was supposedly doing it for him because the only positive reinforcer was praise. Trainers who make claims about dogs working "to please" or strictly for praise seem oblivious to the main motivator they employ: pain. The first task in training any animal is finding out what motivates it. No motivation, no training. All animals are motivated by food, water, sex and avoiding aversives. A lot of animals can be motivated by play, attention, opportunity to socialize or get control of coveted resources. All animals can be motivated by signals which represent one of these primary reinforcers, provided the relationship between the signal and the primary is kept adequately strong. This is mostly where praise comes in, as a sort of imprecise marker which tells the animal the chances of a primary happening have improved. If you opt to not use positive reinforcement, you end up, like they all do, using aversives and announcing that your dog is doing it for you. Pathetic.

None of this is to say praise isn't good or important. I personally praise my dogs an embarrassing amount, because I like them and I like doing it. They like it when I'm in a good mood because Bad Things Don't Happen to Dogs when She's in a Good Mood. I personally love it when someone like my Kung Fu instructor, who has power over me, is in a good mood, but not because I'm genetically wired with a desire to please him. My interest in my teacher's mood is pretty selfish, and *I'm* supposed to be a morally advanced Human. Any interest your dog has in your mood is based on what it means for him. And that's, as the saying goes, okay.

Praise does work as a primary reinforcer for some dogs. They like it enough to work for it. But this is weak grounds on which to marginalize those dogs for whom praise does not work as a primary. A lot of dogs kind of like praise but won't really work for it. This is fine. There's a difference between expressing affection to the dog, for what it's definitely worth to the human and for whatever it may be worth to the dog, and relying on praise as a principal means of motivating an animal in training or behavior modification. In other words, don't confuse bonding activities with training and behavior mod. For the latter, heavier artillery is usually needed. People feel disappointed to discover the necessity of using heavier artillery, like food, access to fun and games and other primaries in order to condition their animal. They feel like their particular dog is a lemon because he "listens when he wants to," "only does it when I have a cookie," in short, has little or no desire to please. *Generations of dogs have been labelled lemons for requiring actual motivation when all along, they were normal.* I'm still waiting to meet the desire to please dog. If it shows up, I'll send it for psychotherapy.

The desire to please thing has been fed, largely, by the misreading of certain dog behaviors. Dogs get excited when we come home, solicit attention and patting from us and lick us. They are very compulsive about their greeting rituals. They often shadow us around when we're available and become anxious when we leave. They are highly social and genetically underprepared for the degree of absence from family members they experience in a human environment. They also bounce back amazingly well, to a point, from the immense amount of punishment we mete out at them. I can see how this could be interpreted as worship. They monitor our every movement. It's important not to get a big ego about this though. *They are monitoring our every movement for signs that something might happen for dogs.* My dogs' brains are continuously and expertly checking out the behavior of humans, working out to eight decimal places the probability at any given second of cookies, walks, attention, Frisbee and endless hours of deliriously orgasmic games with the latex hedgehog. They appear devoted to me because I throw a mean Frisbee and have opposable thumbs which open cans. Not to say we don't have a bond. My bond with my dogs is not up for discussion. It is psychopathological in intensity. I know they love me back. But they don't worship me. I'm not sure they have a concept of worship. Their love is also not grounds for doing whatever I say. It is, in fact, irrelevant to the training thing. To control their behavior, I must constantly manipulate the consequences of their actions. Some of the most sophisticated training jobs are done where no love and little bond is present. This is not to say that training is not one of the best ways around to foster a bond. It is. But it's not a prerequisite of training. Humans fall down on this one all the time and not just in our dog relationships.

The Dominance Panacea

The other model which has been put forth as a quasi-justification for the use of aversives in training is pack theory. Ever since the linear hierarchy was discovered in wolves, dog people have gone cuckoo in their efforts to explain every conceivable dog behavior and human-dog interaction in terms of "dominance." We really latched onto that one. Dogs misbehave or are disobedient because they haven't been shown who's boss. You must be the "alpha" in your pack. Aside from amounting to yet another justification for punishment-oriented training methods - the dog is supposedly staying up nights thinking up ways to stage a coup so you'd better keep him in his place with plenty of coercion - dominance has provided a panacea-like explanation for dog behaviors. For the owner, this simple explanation makes the work of boning up on a myriad of other topics, like learning theory, unnecessary. Notions like dogs rushing through doors ahead of their owners or pulling on leash to exert dominance over their owners are too stupid for words. Some poor people have it so backwards that they view submissive moves like jumping up or pawing as dominance plays and thus, fair game for aversive training. The whole dominance thing is, once again, a case of leaping to a conclusion before ruling out more obvious explanations. Dogs chew furniture because what else could furniture possibly be for? They are disobedient because they have no idea what the command means, are undermotivated to comply or something else has won the behavioral gambit at that moment in time, like a fleeing squirrel. Rank is not on their minds.

So, a separation has to be made between a dog feeling submissive and a dog being under aversive control. If you apply continuous shock to an animal after giving the recall command and turn it off when the dog makes contact with you, and the dog understands he can escape and even altogether avoid the shock by coming as soon as you give the command, you have aversive control. You can do the same thing more clumsily, and many do, by using strangle collars or rolled up newspapers. This is not a dominance maneuver, however. How it impacts rank is up for grabs. Big fallacy, this one.

Likewise, if a dog knows that he has a 1 in 5 chance for a reward if he comes and that the great likelihood is that he will be able to return to what he is doing if he comes immediately and will in fact lose a few minutes' freedom if he fails to comply, he's also going to exhibit a strong recall. This is control without aversives. What's important is not what brand of motivation, avoidance or positive reinforcement, you use, but the near total absence of bearing this has on the whole question of dominance. When most people say they have a dominance problem, usually they mean one of two things: they have a compliance problem or else the dog is biting or threatening them. It may very well be that in both cases the dog's self-perception is that he is dominant over the owner. It could also be the case that the dog's self-perception is that he is second-to-last in rank of all organic matter on the planet yet is still undermotivated to comply with commands and/or bites people. You could have a dog whose self-perception is that he is very dominant yet be a world-class obedience dog and never bite or want to bite anyone.

If the problem is compliance, the dog must be trained to comply, using, you guessed it, operant conditioning. This is the direct-access means to modifying behavior. Using concepts like dominance to explain that a dog doesn't want to come when he has not been conditioned to do so and had the behavior proofed against competing motivation is needlessly muddying the water. You can flip him on his back all you want, he will still fail to come if he's untrained and unproofed. And you can flip him on his back and hold him down all night (and precede him through doorways), and he's still going to bite you if you set up conditions which push him past his bite threshold.

Top Ten Behaviors
People Attribute to a Dominance Problem

1) biting/aggression, especially towards family members
2) pulling on leash
3) house-soiling, especially when accidents occur on beds, shoes etc.
4) chewing valuable owner possessions
5) jumping up to greet and pawing
6) failing to come when called
7) begging at table
8) going through doorways first
9) sleeping on forbidden furniture
10) food/laundry stealing

My favorite myth is the going through doorways first thing. What deranged mind came up with the notion that a dog would understand, let alone exert dominance by preceding his owner out the front door? When dogs are rushing through doors, they are trying to close distance between themselves and whatever is out there, as quickly as possible, because they are excited, because they are dogs, because they have never been presented with a reason not to. Whenever there's this desperate grasp for "whywhywhy" a dog does something, rather than being taken by a red herring like "pack theory," first rule out:

1) because it's being reinforced somewhere in the environment
2) because no one ever made a case to do otherwise (i.e., why NOT?)

The whole dominance idea is so out of proportion that entire schools of training are based on the premise that if you can just exert adequate dominance over the dog, everything else falls into place. This is dangerous. Not only does it mean that incredible amounts of abuse are going to be perpetrated against any given dog, probably exacerbating problems like recalls and biting, but also the real issues, like well-executed conditioning and the provision of an adequate environment, are going to go unaddressed, resulting in a still-untrained dog, perpetuating the stupid dominance program.

None of this is to say that dogs are not one of those species which forms hierarchies. They do. They also see well at night, but no one is proposing retinal surgery to address their non-compliance or biting behavior. Pack theory is simply not the most useful model for explaining or, especially, for treating problems like disobedience, misbehavior or aggression. People who use aversives to train with a dominance model in mind would get a better result with less wear and tear on the dog using aversives with a more thorough understanding of learning theory, or, better yet, forgoing aversives altogether and going with the other tools in the learning theory tool box. The dominance concept is simply unnecessary.

So, what do we know about real dogs? Here are the top ten things:

Top Ten Things We Know About Real Dogs

1) It's all chew toys to them (no concept of artifacts, tokens or symbols)

2) Amoral (no right vs. wrong, only safe vs. dangerous)

3) Self-interested (no desire to please)

4) Lemon-brains (i.e., small & relatively unconvoluted brains which learn only through operant and classical conditioning)

5) Predators (search, chase, grab & hold, dissect, chew all strongly wired)

6) Highly social (bond strongly & don't cope well with isolation)

7) Finite socialization period (fight or flee anything they're not socialized to)

8) Opportunistic & keen scavengers (if it's edible, eat it, NOW)

9) Resolve conflicts through ritualized aggression (never write letters to editor, never sue)

10) Well-developed olfactory system

2. Hard-Wiring:
What the Dog Comes With

If you had to boil the preceding top ten list down to two things which really captured the essence of dogs, it would be numbers 5 and 6: they are social predators. The bulk of dog behavior can be traced to their identity as predators and as beings who are programmed to be constantly around others to survive. It is true that dogs are not exclusively carnivorous; they can eat and digest a lot of vegetable matter and are keen scavengers. But there's a reason gerbils and ponies don't reflexively chase moving objects whereas puppies and kittens do. Behaviors pertaining to food acquisition are, understandably, pretty deeply imbedded. Even hundreds of generations of selective breeding which ignored, stylized or even actively sought to eliminate predatory behavior in various dog breeds have failed, in the vast majority of individuals, to stop dogs visually tracking, chasing and biting moving objects. Those same hundreds of generations of selective breeding also preserved the strong tendency to form social bonds.

Predatory Behavior and Its Offshoots in Dogs

The sequence of behaviors which seems pretty hard-wired in most dogs is:

Search (find prey, mainly using nose)
Stalk (sneak up as closely as possible to prey)
Rush (move suddenly towards prey, hopefully making it turn and flee)
Chase (run after fleeing prey)
Bite/hold/shake/kill (the prey)
Dissect and eat (the prey)

The other two behaviors which are in the food-acquisition constellation are not found in fixed sequence: chewing and food-guarding. Both are sufficiently adaptive to ensure their presence in the repertoire of many dogs. Chewing keeps the crucial equipment,

21

jaws, in good working order through isometric exercise. Object guarding needs to be selected for in social carnivores because of the relative scarcity of food.

By contrast to dogs, consider that if you're a herbivore and must consume vegetation 10 hours a day in order to extract enough nutrition and there's grass as far as the eye can see, you're going to expend very little energy guarding your acres for today from your confrere. Carnivores, on the other hand, have invested an immense amount of energy finding, catching and hauling down some ungulate, a dense source of protein, and may not eat again for days. If you're one of these predators, you're going to make sure you don't lose your hard-won chunk of carcass, hence the strong propensity in dogs to resource-guard.

It's compulsive behavior: no matter how plentiful resources are made to appear - continuous kibble in the bowl for instance - the dog's genetic program says "guard," so the dog guards. Not to say it's not modifiable: it is. Modification, however, requires active intervention in the form of prophylactic or treatment exercises, rather than simply feeding to the point of obesity. The other reason dogs could afford to engage in behavior like object-guarding is that animals like dogs, who are physically able to maim each other and yet who depend so heavily on each other to acquire food, have evolved highly ritualized forms of aggression. They are capable of aggressing without fatal force. They have, in fact, a huge spectrum of threat levels and means of solving disputes which, although spectacularly scary looking to humans, result in minimal damage to the dogs themselves. This is also why possessiveness has spread, in many instances, to other things besides food, like valued toys and bones, sleeping locations, Kleenexes or stolen socks from the laundry basket. There has been insufficient selective pressure against this.

Dog Play

There is one other dimension worth discussing before delving into the predatory sequence and that's the rehearsal of some of these behaviors during play - the sparring and jaw-wrestling dogs engage in endlessly with other dogs if given the chance. One function of this rough play is to keep the skills for killing polished. This behavior is normal, healthy and adaptive, with the important fringe benefits of firstly, minimizing the chances of a regular player ever developing a hard mouth and secondly, of his ever getting into serious dog fights. The social skills are kept well oiled, and the dog associates the close proximity of other dogs with extreme pleasure.

Owners of dogs usually identify dog play as a problem for one of three reasons:

1) normal play is extremely rough and therefore frightening for some owners to witness, so they want to curb it in case the dog "becomes aggressive"

2) the owner can't compete with the attractiveness of other dogs as playmates and has obedience problems in the presence of other dogs

3) the play is directed at humans

The logic behind #1 is back-to-front. Dogs who do not regularly play with other dogs have the poorest social skills. These naive animals are tense, asocial or antisocial and can't read other dogs as easily as their more experienced colleagues. They are, consequently, at highest risk for dog-dog aggression as well as fear reactions like flight or barking. They chronically engage in annoying, overly gross appeasement like wriggling, pawing, rolling and peeing when they meet another dog, not to mention overly gross ranking maneuvers which often end in skirmish. Regular play builds confidence, improves the dog's repertoire of intraspecific communications and maintains the dog's soft-mouth. The more dogs he interacts with the more slick his social skills grow to be, culminating in a dog who is a veritable doggy-diplomat, able to coax even worried or asocial dogs into play, appease tough guys and defuse potential fights with mind-bogglingly subtle body language.

At the other end of the spectrum is the two-sided coin of fear and aggression - dogs who are basically unsocialized to their own species. This is pretty much a travesty, considering the genetic predisposition dogs have to become socialized to and even form bonds with any living thing they have sufficient contact with before 4 months of age. Moving towards the middle of the spectrum, we find naive dogs who are not desperately undersocialized but extremely inexperienced nevertheless. They tend to offer the overly large appeasement gestures mentioned above or else are a little stiff and growly when making social contact. Owners of these naive animals often say things like "he's dominant with other dogs" and "I can't bring him around other dogs, he gets too excited..." What they don't realize is that they will never make the dog blasé by restricting his access. It reminds me of the guy in the desert getting all excited when he sees water. The same guy living next to a mountain stream might manage to contain his glee at the sight of water. ("Water!! Water!!"..."A dog!! A dog!!")

There is no question that a well-socialized dog will be extremely attracted to and enjoy playing with other dogs. Obedience which is near-perfect when there is no competing motivation frequently falls apart in the presence of other dogs. It's important to not go overboard in labeling failure to comply as disobedience or insubordination when commands conflict with enjoyable things like dog-play. *The dog is always perfectly obedient to the contingencies in the environment.* If the dog is not coming or sitting when there are other dogs around, it is because:

1) coming/sitting has never been necessary to obtain the reward of dog-access

2) coming/sitting has proven to be mutually exclusive to dog-access (it actually ends the fun, so other behaviors which compete have therefore been rewarded)

3) other rewards employed by the owner are below dog-access on the reward hierarchy

4) the owner has sufficient leverage but the command is undergeneralized (dog doesn't read "come" in that context; strange but true that dogs are susceptible to this)

This is the most useful way of looking at the problem of competing motivation. Coming when called, for example, is simply more weakly conditioned (trained) than playing with dogs. I'll get into more detail about training in the presence of competing motivation later. The point is that limiting dog play or failing to socialize a dog in order to avoid this distraction is shooting yourself in the foot. You still don't know how to train against competing motivation, and you have an undersocialized, underexercised, understimulated dog. You're in the flames now.

The third dog-play problem is an example of the culture clash. Normal dog play directed at humans is both annoying and potentially dangerous. It is essential that the dog be quickly brought up to speed regarding the social norms in a human environment. The rules the dog must assimilate regarding his play behavior *vis a vis* humans are:

1) keep your extremely soft mouth off human flesh or clothing at all times
2) when people walk, run and ride bikes, don't chase them
3) paws off at all times

Understand that our having these rules essentially means that the dog must never engage in its pre-programmed play behaviors. That's quite the clash. If you look at dog-to-dog play, there is virtually none of it that we humans would like directed at us. It's important to inform the dog about this and to provide alternative outlets in the form of regular access to other dogs and/or interactive games with humans that we can live with, usually involving toys as an intermediary.

Predatory Sequence Behaviors

A great way to develop outlets for your dog is to come up with stylized games involving behaviors in the search, stalk, chase, grab and hold sequence. Doing so is not just being an enlightened owner who meets his dog's needs. Providing this kind of stimulation on a regular basis is the first line of defense against behavior problems. What follows are suggested games that owners can play with their pets to burn off that predatory energy. The choice of games would depend on the individual dog and the owner's preferences. Simply experiment and come up with a selection which best suits.

Hide & Seek

Put the dog on a sit-stay out of visual contact with the room where you plan to hide the object (for details on teaching sit-stay, see chapter 6). If the dog doesn't do stays, here is an opportunity to teach him. Alternatively, you can simply shut the dog in another room to prevent him from peeking. Hide the object and then initiate the search by releasing him from the room (or the sit-stay) and asking him excitedly "where's your toy????" Then start encouraging him to search. The object can be a cookie, a stuffed chew-toy, a ball or a tug-of-war toy. There must be some motivation for the find. If the dog is a maniacal retriever, a ball or other retrieve toy is a good choice: when the dog makes a find, you may celebrate with a few intense retrieves before setting up another search. Likewise, if the dog is a tug-of-war addict, give him a nice dose or two as reward for a find.

Start off with easy finds and big celebrations to get the dog hooked on the game. It only takes a few rounds for the dog to learn that he is supposed to be looking for something of great interest to him. As he gets into it, go for tougher hiding places. As soon as possible, stop helping him to make finds, so that he gains confidence in his own ability. If you constantly bail the dog out, he will learn that giving up is the most effective strategy, rather than persevering. Most dogs will naturally begin to use their nose to make the find. This is magical to watch. At this point, they can find objects buried deeply into sofa cushions or anywhere else you might try to stump them.

Another variation of this game involves the owner him or herself hiding somewhere in the house. The disadvantages of this version are that it is more labor intensive for you and also somewhat limiting as far as hiding places, whereas there are virtually limitless places you can hide a squeaky toy. The main benefits of this game are:

1) predatory energy burner: both by making the dog use his nose to find and by working in some retrieve and/or tug-of-war
2) teaches the dog to actively search for his own chew-toys (!)
3) multiple rehearsals of sit-stay with excited dog
4) fun, of which there is too little in life

You can also use this finding skill to help the dog kill time when you're away. Before leaving, plant cookies, stuffed chew-toys, stuffed chew-toys wrapped in dissectible rags with multiple knots, stuffed chew toys wrapped in rags enclosed in old margarine containers; even the dog's meal in installments can be hidden all over the house, while the dog waits behind closed doors. Good sniffer dogs will get virtually any hiding place you cook up. This provides constructive activity for the dog when he's alone and is a blow-softener for him and guilt-reducer for you, given that you're about to leave him alone. Please note that if your dog has an existing destructiveness problem, refer to the section on chew-training as well.

Retrieving

It has been long held that there are dogs who like retrieving and dogs who have no natural inclination. More likely dogs who are strong natural retrievers have the inclination closer to the surface, whereas other dogs have it in them but it's buried deeper: they simply need to have it awakened. Their apparent reluctance could be due to any combination of things: they are laid back individuals in general, they have early histories of being punished or reprimanded for chasing and/or putting anything in their mouths, they have histories of lots of coercive training and are globally inhibited, they have a history of understimulation and have a hard time relaxing and focusing when anything interesting starts happening, or something in the immediate environment when training is attempted is stressing or distracting them. In formal training, most methods would use force to teach these dogs to retrieve. In fact, in formal training, some methods would force the natural retrievers too. My point is that not only can reluctant dogs be reward-trained to retrieve, but also they will at some point, as though triggered, start to get into it, and it will become inherently enjoyable to them. I've seen this time and time again. In fact, I've never seen it not happen, given enough time and an adequate approach.

With a dog who is not interested in retrieving, it's important to obtain that first little spark of interest and nurse it along until it develops into a flame. The first spark of interest is likely to be visual tracking - following the movement with the eyes, rather than actual pursuit. This is fine: get excited when the dog watches the movement, tease him with the object, make it retreat rapidly from him, play peek-a-boo. The sudden disappearance may trigger some movement from the dog. Again, this is to be encouraged. If you get any actual pouncing or attempts to bite the object, praise enthusiastically and try to get the dog to follow it as it moves, like a kitten follows a piece of string. Do as many repetitions as possible. The limiting factors are your own patience, how long the dog is in the room and interested in the game itself and the rewards you are offering for nice responses.

In dogs who are inhibited about chasing or picking up objects, it's a big risk for them to actually try doing this, so it is extremely important that you give unambiguous and enthusiastic approval when you see the first tentative experiment. In fact, the first time the dog tries anything is always a critical juncture. It's as though a behavioral imprint will be made. The implications of behavioral imprints, of course, extend to prevention of undesired behaviors: if the dog's first experiment with the sofa results in an enjoyable chewing session, subsequent reprimanding will have much less impact than it would have had if you had caught the initiation of the first act. Most dog owners intervene too late in the lifetime of behaviors they wish to end. None of this has to do with stubbornness on the part of the dog. It's perfectly predictable that any behavior with a reinforcement history in the dozens or scores or even hundreds of trials will not simply roll over and die. More about this later.

Many dogs' behavioral imprint of retrieving may have been negative: they picked up something the owner would rather they didn't touch and were told off. It is only much later, after innumerable punishments for chasing kids, bikes, feet and picking up shoes, Kleenexes and garbage that the owner tries to teach retrieving. A lot of chasing and object holding have been drummed out of the dog by then. A much better policy with young puppies, who will quite naturally chase anything that moves and bite all matter, is to redirect this behavior towards predatory outlets from the start. Remember that if you are going to slam one door with punishment (say, the shoes door), you must open another with positive reinforcement (the Frisbee door).

With all this baggage, it may take time for the dog to loosen up enough for him to risk chasing and biting, so persevere. Once the dog starts blossoming, you can start shaping the desired chain of behaviors. An informal retrieve consists of a chase, pick up, carry and presentation (putting it in your hand or dropping it nearby). In reluctant retrievers, each of these behaviors needs to be perfected separately, like pieces of a puzzle before you combine them in the customary order. Shaping is a technique which involves rewarding the dog's best efforts and then gradually raising the standard until the behavior is as you wish. Most people's downfall when employing shaping is that they arbitrarily set too high a standard for reward, and ignore behaviors which are on the right track. For chasing, this means initially you will reward even visual tracking if necessary. The foundation of shaping lies in the fact that behavior is always variable. The dog's average behavior in a given context will cluster around a median response, but there will be variations which the trainer may ignore or select with the reward. Over time, this will change the median and so new variations clustering around the new median will be occasionally offered and if rewarded by the astute trainer, will inch the process along a little further again. Let me give you an example.

Kurt

Kurt, a Golden Retriever, is totally disinterested in retrieving. In his first training session, out of thirty trials consisting of the trainer teasing him and making an object move and disappear etc., eighteen of his responses consist of watching with little interest and not moving. This is his median response. Twelve responses are different. Of those twelve, seven consist of him not even looking at the object, sometimes even scratching, yawning or walking away. These are below average. But five of his responses are little nuggets of brilliance. One time he watched with greater interest, his ears going up, his head cocking. Four times he actually moved. Three times he moved tentatively in the direction of the object, and once he actually moved a bit quicker and tried to paw it. These responses are all rewardable. If the trainer is smart, he or she will reward all of them differentially: a small reward for the orientation, a bigger reward for the movement and a quite substantial reward for the time he pawed. The actual selection of responses is made using a clicker: a cricket-noise-making device which informs the dog he has won a treat. Much more on clicker training later.

In the next training session of 30 trials, two consist of him not looking, six consist of him looking with some interest, 13 times he follows, five times he follows and paws, twice he follows, paws and mouths, and twice he pounces with some vigor. The median response now would probably be following the object. But the astute trainer may reward this several times and then see there are bigger fish to fry. The new reward standard becomes pawing and/or mouthing. A couple of sessions later, this dog was, with Border Collie-like intensity, exploding after every throw with a median response of fast chase and grab and a pick up and carry about two thirds of the way back. The rewardable response was a perfect retrieve, all the way into the trainer's hands.

What's amazing is not that this dog learned to retrieve and to love it, but that most people would have given up on him after that first session or else failed to reward the mild interest and achieved a training stalemate in subsequent sessions. The behavior would have remained clustered around that initial average and may have even deteriorated. In any session, there are always going to be variations in the responses the dog gives. The trainer's job is to identify those which are rewardable: not those which meet some arbitrary standard the trainer has in mind (perfect retrieving), but those sufficiently above average for that dog on that day. Individual judgment calls about whether to reward a given response at any moment is part of the art of training.

All training with positive reinforcement is greatly facilitated by using some signal that tells the dog that he has just made the grade and won a reward. Most sophisticated dog trainers use clickers, cricket toys, which have been pre-associated scores of times with food rewards. Timing is absolutely everything in training: if the dog does a rewardable pick up and carry, it's critical that this behavior be marked for reward instantly and not seconds later. Delivering food rewards to dogs is not feasible in those kinds of time envelopes so the click tells the dog he just won and may now come to collect his reward. The same system is used in marine mammal shows: the animals have been shaped to perform tricks and the whistle the trainer blows tells them they have scored a mackerel. Clicker training will be covered in detail in chapter 5.

Improving Presentation

Many dogs will chase with gusto and either fail to pick up or pick up and horde, rather than bring the object to the trainer. Improving presentation in retrieving stymies many people, but the principles are the same. In any series of carries, there will be variation. Sometimes the dog will chase and not pick up at all. Sometimes the dog will pick up and run the other way. Sometimes the dog will pick up, turn and drop. Occasionally, the dog will pick up, turn and take any number of steps in your direction. Whatever is above average is rewardable and will, if rewarded enough, become the new average, enabling you to set a higher standard. There is no limit to how tightly you can crank the standard provided you do it gradually and follow the rules. These rules have been well laid out in Karen Pryor's outstanding book "Don't Shoot The Dog" (Sunshine books). This book is worth multiple reads.

With a dog who is a natural chaser but who actively wants to play keep-away/chase-me, it's doubly valuable to cultivate a nice retrieve and presentation. Things are stacked slightly more against you in this case than when there is simple non-behavior because the dog actively wants to avoid you when he gets control of the object. This could be the dog choosing another game (keep-away), or it could be more serious object-guarding or a bit of both. With these dogs, never show any interest in the object. In fact, you're not interested in the object: you are controlling both the food rewards and the ability to make the object come to life again with your throw, so relax, watch and shape. Your refusal to notice his attempts to get you to chase him will give that behavior a bit of a jostle and hopefully give you a few more rewardable approaches. When you teach a dog to bring something to you rather than play keep-away, it is an example of counterconditioning: teaching a behavior which is mutually exclusive to the one you're trying to get rid of in a given context.

Any behavior that's occurring with such annoying regularity as the one you're trying to eliminate has a payoff already from somewhere in the dog's environment, usually from you, the owner. The payoff is the chase. The dog is ignored for lying quietly, picking up or chewing his own toys but becomes the immediate center of attention as soon as he picks up a piece of laundry or runs off with the ball in a retrieve-training session. This is a very potent reward and usually happens on the first trial, getting the old imprint effect. So, in the context of objects and dogs, retrieving is the Ferrari counterconditioning exercise against grabbing and running, and object guarding. Savvy owners will do a number of things:

1) provide reinforcement in the form of attention to the dog for playing with his own toys
2) actively teach some predatory outlets to channel the energy
3) ignore the dog's initial experiments at picking up forbidden objects, or keep forbidden objects out of reach until #'s 1 and 2 have been well installed
4) make the dog a maniac retriever to countercondition keep-away
5) put keep-away on cue

Putting keep-away on cue is one more line of defence against spontaneous keep-away as well as another fun game to play with the dog. Putting any behavior on cue simply means that you take charge of the time and place the dog may engage in the behavior: the dog knows that he's going to get a regular enough dose of the activity he likes but that the game only "works" when you give the cue. A cue is simply a politically correct word for command. In the case of keep-away, teach him that when you give a certain command, it predicts that you will actively and gleefully start chasing him ("I'm gonna GET you!!!") and he must pick up the nearest dog toy and run. Try heading him off, tackling, any variation you like. When you've had enough, sit down wherever you are and watch what happens. The dog, having had a thrilling time, will try to solicit the chase from you. You refuse to bite until he actually brings you the toy and drops it. When he does, flip it to him and start another round by saying "I'm gonna get you!!" The piece of information we want the dog to assimilate is that nothing on his part can make you play. The one predictor of your chasing him is the cue "I'm gonna get you" and your wiggling outstretched fingers. The only way he can influence your decision is by relinquishing the object.

Practise initiating and ending the game over and over. The dog learns that when you stop wiggling your fingers at him and saying

"I'm gonna get you..." you never chase him, so he may as well wait for the next time you say those magic words. Better still, alternate keep-away rounds with retrieve or tug-of-war rounds. This way the dog is rewarded both for running away on cue and for presenting on cue. There is an important maxim in training: control the games, control the dog.

For the duration of the training period, keep laundry and other grabables out of reach. When the game has become a strong habit, start leaving the laundry around again. The first time he tries out a piece of laundry, ignore him completely. Not even a blip. Even if you have to sacrifice that item, don't even cast a glance his way. Later that same day, play the game with a toy, giving the cue first. What we're after now is discrimination learning, as though the dog were saying to himself "oh, it only works when she says 'I'm gonna get you' first and only when it's the squeaky hedgehog or rubber ring. I get it now." This renders laundry stealing a useless waste of energy.

My dog, Lassie, has quite possibly the worst genetic predisposition on the planet for search and destroy and for object guarding, all kept at bay by regular bouts of "I'm gonna get you," regular object exchange exercises (discussed later) and regular predatory fixes. If, out of the blue, I say "I'm gonna get you" she will immediately pick up the nearest object and start maneuvering briskly around just out of reach until I stop chasing. There is nothing cuter.

One of the saddest comments on dog-human relations is the continued popularity of forced-retrieve training. This is part of the package deal of traditional obedience training which relies very heavily on coercion as principle motivation. You can recognize traditional obedience training by the following signs: 1) some sort of avoidance collar is usually put on the dog, 2) praise is considered adequate reinforcement, and 3) the pack theory mumbo jumbo gets thrown around a lot. This style of training has, in spite of an evolution in its trappings and rhetoric, remained essentially unchanged since the 1950's.

Today It's Not Sitting: Can Taking Over the Pack Be Far Behind?

"He knows; he's just stubborn" or "He knows; he's trying to be dominant" are extremely common attitudes. There is a true epidemic of people who witness several correct responses by their dog, presume learning is accomplished and then hunt around for reasons to explain subsequent wrong responses. It's no wonder people are clinging to stuff like pack theory. There's a serious knowledge void. In actual fact, a correct response, provided it has been reinforced, is merely like one more grain of sand on a scale: it increases the probability of the same response occurring in the same context in the future. A steady history of reinforcement is necessary to tip the scale in favor of that behavior occurring. It will become highly probable given a sufficient volume of training. Most people do not have a good understanding of how animals learn, and dog owners are no exception. Many would also dearly love to avoid having to spend a lot of time installing responses through "a sufficient volume" of training. Many are also near their rope's end, emotionally, in their own hectic lives: coping with the normal behavior of another species is breaking the camel's back. This all makes for fertile soil for explanations like dominance and stubbornness and training methods which employ aversives.

Where a behaviorist or marine mammal trainer might see a simple shaping of some behavior as the task, anyone schooled in traditional dog training typically sees either an ethology brain-buster or a battle of wills. What traditional trainers always fail to rule out when a dog does not obey a command are: 1) WHAT: does he know what that command means and is the command generalized to the context in which it's currently being given, 2) WHY: has the trainer supplied motivation, i.e., is there a strong history of rewarded responses to that command, and 3) OTHER OPTIONS: is the command proofed against distraction and competing motivation. If all these have not been well covered, the dog is undertrained. Period. No hidden agenda, no rebellion, no spite, no mule-headed stubbornness, simply an undertrained response. If you're taking tango lessons and make a mistake, or your kid gets 76% on the math quiz, there's no BIG reason. You got it wrong because you need more practice. Your kid needs more study. The dog needs more training. It's sad to think of all the astounding reasons obedience hobbyists and pet owners come up with to explain undertrained or poorly trained responses.

Top Ten Smoke Screens for Noncompliance in Undertrained/Undermotivated Dog

1) Dominance play by dog

2) Dog spiteful because of some recent event

3) Dog stubborn

4) Dog too excited

5) Dog tired, bored or in wrong mood

6) Dog over-trained (!)

7) Particular breed-related difficulty

8) Dog underexercised

9) Dog recently boarded

10) Life-phase-related difficulty (too young or too old)

My personal favorite on the list remains "overtrained." Behavioral scientists often measure conditioning histories for simple behaviors by animals in the tens of thousands of trials, so it staggers the mind to see a dog owner announce that his dog "knows" something after having witnessed a few correct responses. As soon as the assumption of learning is made ("he knows but he's...": choose your favorite from the list), people quite naturally need an explanation for subsequent incorrect responses, hence the top-ten list. Presuming learning on the basis of a few right responses is dangerous. Undertrained is a fairer assumption, especially given the huge variety of contexts in which dogs are expected to respond to cues. I have yet to meet the mythical "overtrained" domestic dog. Over-punishment-trained is, of course, a different story. The lethargy and freezing up which characterizes some competitive obedience dogs is the result of the installation of behavior through avoidance. This is almost always accomplished by means of some sort of collar. Entire methods of training are founded on specific types of collars. It must seem like bad science-fiction to dogs that their owners' choice of training methods was, until quite recently, a choice of hardware around their necks.

Ear Pinching

Another application of avoidance learning in dog obedience is the routine use of ear-pinching to train retrieving. Done correctly, it's an example of negative reinforcement: the dog learns first to turn off the ongoing pinch and later to avoid it altogether by taking a dumbbell quickly enough. The nuts and bolts of perfecting this technique are laid out by trainers whose main focus is competitive obedience. Some of these trainers have great hands-on skills (training "chops"), and most are disciplined and diligent. What is frightening is the matter of fact way they use avoidance training to obtain and perfect stylized behaviors like heeling and retrieving. They have done it for so long on so many dogs, associate only with people who do likewise and are so often rewarded for it with wins in obedience that they have lost all perspective. If this weren't sci-fi enough, the technique inevitably trickles down to less skilled trainers, people with no chops. In the hands of someone who has poor timing and little understanding of negative reinforcement, ear-pinching is basically animal abuse.

If there were any justification for the use of aversive methods in dog training, the dogs' own well-being might qualify. Might we use any means necessary to install commands which could realistically be expected to one day save his life or which improve his quality of life? It's an arguable point. And, use such aversives only on condition that you know what you're doing and have sufficient chops that wear and tear on the dog is minimized. Forcing recalls after sufficient inducive groundwork has been laid is a case in point. But a formal retrieve? A formal retrieve is of use only in an obedience routine or field trial, to receive a qualifying score and maybe win a trophy. This is good for the handler, and if avoidance trained, pretty yucky for the dog. Dogs regularly scream when ear pinches are done to them. It amazes me to this day that anyone can attend a seminar, watch an "expert" make dogs scream in the name of winning a competition and not dial the local humane society. How important are these little ribbons and plaques?

There is no question that a strong avoidance response might improve the probability of the command being carried out. You've increased motivation. The Spanish Inquisition got innocent people to admit they were supernatural demons by using torture. They increased motivation. Obedience junkies argue that a dog who is not avoidance trained might - horror of horrors - refuse a retrieve in the ring. They make this sound like the dog could be squashed by a car. I would argue that if a dog is skillfully shaped, using positive reinforcement to do the retrieve exercises in obedience, the reliability will be excellent. But it'll be less reliable than if you added avoidance. So what. You lose an occasional ribbon and keep your soul.

I once heard a competitive trainer characterize the use of force as a justifiable means to reduce the dog's perception of choice. But this doesn't even work in theory: the dog always has a choice, even if it's between two pretty scary options, one of them cooked up by the trainer. Training is merely the setting up of context-driven contingencies: "if you do this, this happens; if you do that, this other thing happens." The animal can always opt for the aversive. The choice for the trainer is a simple one: train with positive reinforcement or aversive techniques or some of both. I know trainers who have never avoidance trained a retrieve on any breed and are, to date, refusal free in the ring. By contrast I have seen avoidance-trained dogs crack up in trials and fail to retrieve. So even the increased reliability argument is weak. No one will ever convince me that it's okay to coerce behaviors like retrieves. It's morally bankrupt.

Tug of War

Dog owners have been admonished for decades to never play tug of war with their dogs because of the risk of it increasing aggression and/or dominance in the dog. Even many dog resource people such as breeders, amateur trainers and veterinarians caution against this game. This is partly a failure to discriminate between agonistic behavior (conflict resolution and defensive aggression) and predatory behavior. Played with rules, tug-of-war is a tremendous predatory energy burner and good exercise for both dog and owner. It serves as a good barometer of the kind of control you have over the dog, most importantly over his jaws. The game doesn't make the dog a predator: he already is one. The game is an outlet.

Tug of war, or any vigorous activity for that matter, played without rules or functioning human brain cells is potentially dangerous. But the baby has been thrown out with the bath water in this case: why deprive dogs and owners of one of the best energy burners and outlets there is? It's good because it's intense, increases dog focus and confidence and plugs into something very deep inside dogs. The big payoff is in lowered incidence of behavior problems due to understimulation. It's also extremely efficient for the owner in terms of space and time requirements, and it can be used as a convenient reward option in obedience.

I've personally never bought the dominance argument here either. Neither dogs nor wolves ascertain rank by grabbing the ends of an object and tugging to see who "wins." If anything, it is co-operative behavior. When you're playing tug of war with a dog and he "wins," i.e. you let go, he will try to get you to re-engage in the game rather than leaving and hoarding. And, when dogs do leave and hoard, it's often because the owner has made simple tactical errors. With a dog who tends to run the other way after getting control of the tug object, playing hard to get is an infinitely smarter owner strategy than chasing the dog. Avoid battles with dogs involving speed and agility - you cannot win. Psyche-outs are much better. Pretend you couldn't care less, and usually the object will be brought back much more quickly.

Any informal sampling I've done has never yielded a correlation between regular tug of war games and an increased incidence of aggression. I will definitely come to full alert if anyone comes up with some hard, well-controlled data, but so far all there has been is the attitude that, well, it must be bad because the dog gets so revved up. People have such a hard time witnessing real dog behavior.

Tug of war intensity is similar to the gusto seen in dogs engaging in Flyball, lure coursing, herding, field and den trials, all activities which plug into the predator in the dog. When dogs are playing tug of war, they are not playing against you,, they are cooperating with you to make a kill. It's not you vs. the dog. It's you and the dog vs. the tug-of-war toy. Watch footage of wolves or African Wild Dogs killing large prey animals. A few pack members will have hold of the animal at the same time, maybe one on the tail, one on a hamstring and one with a nose hold. They are all pulling like mad. Rank is not on their minds at that moment. This portion of the hunting sequence in social carnivores is virtually indistinguishable from a dog pulling on a rag with its owner. Tugging on Mr. Squeaky Dinosaur is not about dominance, it's about lunch. Competitiveness and even rank issues can also result in two animals yanking on the same object. But this never reaches the proportion of tugs performed in the context of cooperative kills. The latter is the root of the behavior.

I would even go so far as to say that this cooperative "killing" is a bonding experience for pack members. It's an intense, pleasurable experience the dog will intimately associate with you. That said, it is absolutely critical that tug of war games with pet dogs incorporate the following rules:

Tug of War Rules

1) Dog "Outs" on Command

Have a release command such as "out," "give" or "let go." Before revving the dog up to pull on the object for the first time, practice some low-key exchanges with him. The sequence is 1) your command to out, 2) the dog releases, 3) a food reward from your pocket and 4) your command to re-take. If the dog doesn't take the object in his mouth in the first place, practice the exchanges anyway, simply by giving the object to the dog (put it down right in front of him) and then taking it back, giving the reward and then replacing it. Rehearse dozens of exchanges for reward. We want the "give" part strongly primed before anything else happens.

If the dog takes the object and runs away, practice exchanges without completely releasing the object, so that the dog experiences

39

having something taken away, obtaining a reward and then having it presented to him again. Possessive types stand to benefit enormously from the exchange practise (much like object exchanges for object guarders which I'll talk about later) and from learning that it's more fun to play interactively with an object than to have it to themselves. Object guarders must be loosened up with a solid history of exchanges before proceeding with the actual game.

If the dog hangs on and will not out with a bit of encouragement, try first having him sniff the treat he will win for outing. This is most definitely bribery (reward making behavior appear) rather than rewarding (behavior making reward appear) but will get the ball rolling. Once the dog has done a few, hide the reward so that the dog is doing his part of the bargain first, on faith. If the dog is a reluctant outer, you will reward every exchange until he 1) outs without hesitation on the first command every time and 2) knows and enjoys the tug game. The re-take will eventually become the reward for outing on command, but provide the food fringe-benefit in early training to defuse the focus on the object.

If the dog still hangs on despite freeze-dried liver in his nostrils, try the following: with an abrupt, disgusted flourish, let go of the object, whirl around and walk away in a black cloud. Do a 2 minute time-out and then try again. If there's no softening up of his attitude and you feel confident of your ability to handle your dog (this is an important clause), you may force the out: say "out" once and with one hand on the object, use the other hand to jam the inside of the dog's lips into his canine teeth. When he outs, say "thank you," give him his food reward, then try again. If he outs on command this time, give him a double food reward and continue with more rewarded repetitions. Some dogs will hang on a second time - you will force a second out - but almost none will go for a third.

It's important to understand that using punishment like this buys you only a temporary fix. The dog will sooner or later go back to hanging on if you don't install a voluntary out with reward-training. In other words, the temporary effect gained by the punishment is enough to get your foot in the door so that you can reward some outs with the food and the re-take. This is ultimately about building up the dog's confidence that outing won't end the world but will get him a food reward and another re-take. To teach him this, you must manufacture the first few outs to get the ball rolling.

When the out is rehearsed and you are engaged in actual tug of war games, any failure to out will immediately end the game. This policy is carved in stone: his breaking of a (sacred) rule wrecked the game for himself. When the dog knows, loves and is hooked on the game, ending it abruptly is by far the most effective way to get your point across that failure to out is unacceptable.

2) Dog May Not Take or Re-Take Until Invited to Do So

This rule prevents the dog from initiating the game whenever he wants to. The easiest way to get this rule installed is to practise while playing. Have a take command like "GET THAT ROPE" or "MAKE A KILL" and present the one and only designated tug-toy to the dog at the same time. Having two ingredients to the "take" (the verbal command and the designated object presentation) is insurance against the dog ever misfiring in day-to-day life: you don't want someone innocently picking up the tug toy and being enthusiastically jumped by your dog, and you don't want to have your dog grab some other object you're holding because he thought he heard the command. The likelihood of someone presenting the right object and mistakenly saying "make a kill" are pretty remote. So, have one and one only tug-toy, reserved especially for that use. It can double up as a retrieve object or hide and seek target too, but have no other things with which you play tug of war. Limit this activity to one target.

Play as usual when the dog takes on invitation. If the dog goes for a re-take before you've invited him to do so, reprimand him and have a time-out or long obedience break. Then invite him to take. This rule infraction is extremely common in tug-of-war games, so don't sweep it under the rug. If he goes for another re-take before being invited, i.e., makes the same mistake twice in a row, end the game. There must be clear consequences to rule breaking, otherwise your rules are unclear and thus valueless.

3) Frequent Obedience Breaks

Tug of war is one of the great recyclable rewards for obedience training. Alternate back and forth between tug games and obedience to spot check control during the game and to obtain obedience from the dog when he's in Excitement Mode. Every initiation of the tug game is a potent reward which you can use to select a particularly nice obedience response he gives you during the ob-break. The dog will try fanatically hard to improve his obedience to get you to restart the game. Through their repeated association over time, the two activities will blur in the dog's mind, eventually making the dog love obedience training.

4) Zero Tolerance of Accidents

When taking the object or re-adjusting their take, dogs will sometimes make contact with your hand or other part of you by mistake. Don't let this go unnoticed. Screech "OUCH!" even if it didn't hurt, and abruptly end the game. Dogs are capable of controlling their jaws with great precision if you give them a reason to do so. The obvious fringe benefits to this rule are that you remind the dog of the sensitivity of human skin and the great necessity to keep their jaws off people at all times, and you've installed this while the dog is in Excitement Mode, which is most often where sloppy jaws are a problem.

If the dog is not breaking any of the rules, allow him to get as excited as he wants. This includes head shakes, strong tugging and growling. Once these rules are established, they need to be maintained by constant practice and testing. When things go wrong, it's inevitably because the human slacked off on enforcing the rules.

At the other end of the spectrum from overzealous dogs, who need scores of priming to teach them to "out" reliably and constant rule checks, are dogs who are hard to engage in the game at all. These reluctant dogs, very much like reluctant retrievers, are typically inhibited, worried types who are apologetic by nature or have histories of punishment for touching or picking up objects. These guys must be built up. They are reluctant to take, hold and hang on. Go for each of these in turn, praising enthusiastically any move in the right direction. The praise, in these cases, functions mostly as a safety cue. You are giving the dog permission to loosen up and act like a dog without fear of reprisal. Reluctant tuggers can be turned around. My dog Meggie was quite a dismal tug-of-war prospect initially but now hangs on like it was the Last Bison on Earth.

Dissections & Chewing

There was a time when chewing in domestic dogs was viewed as either a stage that "teething" puppies went through or else a sign of a neurotic, screwed up dog. Now we know better. Chewing is a normal canine pastime which is both enjoyable for the dog and keeps the jaws and teeth in good shape. Dogs get into chew toys the way humans get into spy novels or an absorbing movie. The problem is simply one of choice of chew object: we would like the dog to discriminate between dog chew toys and all the other items in the house, indeed the universe. This is an easy discrimination for us but not at all obvious to the dog. Remember, dogs have no concept of things in your house being "worth" anything apart from their obvious suitability as chew-objects. They also have no concept of right and wrong, only safe and dangerous. They also don't particularly care what your opinion is of their actions unless there is some impact on them.

With all this in mind, the urgency of installing a chew-toy addiction becomes clear. Under no circumstances should a dog of any age or breed be given access to anything but his chew toys unless he is actively, and I mean actively, supervised. This prevents experimentation which might result in the dog finding out he likes leather loafers or Lazy-Boy chairs. Because, once he finds out these things are mighty fine chew toys, subsequent punishments will likely teach him to wait until you are gone to employ them. This goes for regressions too. If the dog has been perfect for 3 months or 3 years but then conducts an experiment on the suitability of antique tables as chew toys, restrict his access until you've renewed his focus on his own toys and done a few set-ups to rule out the heirlooms.

People are often incapable of taking these obvious steps because they endlessly muddy the water with their tedious refrain of "whywhywhy..." trying to get into the depths of the dog's psyche to discover what Big Agenda is making a dog chew a piece of wood. They paralyze themselves against effective action. As so often is the case in dog training, "the reason why" is an interesting chat over coffee, but the solution is the same, regardless of the coffee discussion: immediate action to: 1) stock up on suitable chew toys and get the dog hooked on them, 2) prevent the dog acquiring an addiction to any wrong objects by careful dog-proofing or confinement, especially when he's not supervised and 3) after these measures have been in place for a while, start giving the dog full access (i.e. out of confinement) under close supervision and redirect him to a chew toy whenever he guesses wrong. This is accomplished through sting operations: you repeatedly set the dog up to make the mistake when you are good and ready (i.e. spying) to catch the initiation of the act and immediately redirect him to his own chewies.

Order of Events in Chew Training

The preceding order of events is very important. The third step, when you do actually reprimand the dog for touching the chair or shoe, would have yielded the "fine, I'll wait till you're gone" syndrome if implemented alone. The dog has to chew something. You must establish legal and attractive chew objects before interrupting and redirecting his chewing. An excellent model to conceptualize this is called the hydraulic model. Think of the dog's total behavioral output as being fuel in a tank. The tank has X amount of fuel in it every day. The fuel will be drained every day into several reservoirs (fuel burners), which represent the dog's various behavioral outlets. One outlet is likely labelled "chewing" (others might include "chase and grab" "bark at mailman" etc.). If you plug the hole (by punishing) leading to one of the reservoirs, there will be a backlog of fuel which will still have to drain. Thus, you might get more barking or chasing but the likelihood is that you'll get the drainage into the chewing reservoir at times when the plug (you) are not there to block the behavior. Only if you have already opened up another reservoir ("chewing chewtoys") does your punishment have a chance of plugging "furniture chewing" more permanently. Dogs must have outlets for their natural behavior. If you can't or don't want to provide for the basic behavioral needs of a dog, do not own one. Subjugating natural dog behavior through punishment and morbid obesity is no longer acceptable.

Another way to view the whole chewing issue is to consider the sheer number of things you consider wrong for the dog to chew. Remember? Virtually all matter in the universe is prohibited except for the half dozen items you have decided are dog chew toys. The chances of the dog guessing right every time are astronomical. It is neither feasible nor advisable to try and punish each and every wrong item. Each punishment makes you the bad guy and increases the likelihood that the dog will delay his entire day's chewing for when you are gone, so he can behave normally in peace. Direct the bulk of your efforts at getting the dog chewing chew toys in your presence and absence by: 1) making the chew toys really attractive and interesting, 2) giving the dog no other choices and 3) playing interactive games incorporating the toys.

The Art of Chew Toy Stuffing

Individual dogs will demonstrate individual preferences for what they like in a chew toy, but most will go for things like rawhides, pigs' ears and so on. The drawback of these items is that 1) not all dogs will go for them and 2) they don't last very long so you are forced to constantly buy more to keep the dog supplied. The creme de la creme of chew objects are hollow bones, Kong toys and Buster Cubes. Hollow bones are made of actual cow bone and are available in various incarnations like smoked, sterilized and pre-stuffed with marrow. The great thing about them is that they are safe, relatively indestructible and hollow. Every day you can fill the hollow inside with a new taste sensation for the dog. If you stuff the inside artfully enough, the dog will extract the stuffing near the ends with great ease but have to work harder to get out the goodies in the middle. Every minute he spends on this project is draining the chewing reservoir for that day. Yippee.

Some people can put the same old stuff (e.g. canned dog food and raw carrots) in the bone every day, and the dog is thrilled. Other people, by choice or necessity, vary the contents. Most dogs love some novelty in their diet. Anything that is reasonably nutritious is okay with the exception of chocolate which is potentially lethal to dogs. The stand-bys are cheese cubes, cream cheese, cheese-wiz, canned dog or cat food, peanut-butter, leftovers and commercial dog treats. Into hollow Kong Toys can go the above or variable sized pieces of dog cookie. The small pieces will tumble out easily, the medium sized pieces will come out with some effort and the large pieces will require massive labor to extract. Another variation is to put the dog's dinner or part of his dinner into a few Kongs, each with something more attractive, a piece of freeze-dried liver for instance, at the back. The dog works through the kibble to get to dessert. Buster Cubes are the next generation of "puzzle toys" for dogs. Dry food is inserted and shaken into the various compartments. The dog must roll the cube around to get pieces to fall out. Chew ropes and rawhides can also be spruced up by dipping them in soup stock and letting them dry.

Dogs love doing dissections, i.e. tearing things apart rather than simply gnawing on them. It becomes expensive to keep the dog supplied with dissectible toys like dog dollies and stuffed animals so if you want to give your dog a dissection project once in a while, wrap up a prize like a cookie or piece of liver in an old rag. Tie many knots as tightly as you can so that the goodie is deeply nested. Present it to the dog and behold a predator in action. I personally can watch dogs doing dissections for hours.

A case can definitely be made for making the dog work for much of, if not all, his food ration by putting it into Kongs, bones and rags and even hiding these around the house, so the dog has to first play hide and seek to get the toy before unpacking it. It is very unlikely you will ever overchallenge your dog. The vast majority of dogs are severely underchallenged in their day to day life. Free food in a bowl plays against the genetic legacy of dogs. The search, chase, bite and hold and dissect urge is perhaps best met around mealtime. So, even if you choose to continue giving food in a bowl, why not precede each meal with a couple of minutes of predatory sequence games?

Many zoos and research institutions have been criticized, and rightly so, for providing unstimulating environments for their animal prisoners. Behavioral enrichment, usually taking the form of housing in social groups and making the animals work to acquire their food in order to better simulate their natural environment, has improved the quality of life for many animals. These institutions wouldn't get away with the impoverished, unchallenging environment that many pet dogs are given.

Organized Dog Sports

Ten or 20 years ago, if you wanted to participate in an organized, structured activity with your dog, you were pretty much limited to competitive obedience, tracking and Schutzhund. Competitive obedience is a more stylized, rule-intensive version of behaviors like heel, stay, come, find my lost glove etc. Most cities and towns where there are dogs will have one or more obedience clubs. Schutzhund is a stylized simulation of police dog training, incorporating obedience, tracking and protection/suspect disarming. It is usually organized by clubs but, unlike obedience where any dog can join, is somewhat limited to the larger breeds of dog. Schutzhund is a great predatory energy burner as a lot of tug-toy style motivation is employed by the more progressive organizations and the tracking and protection portions are terrific, predatory fun for the dog. In both obedience and Schutzhund, there's a real lottery regarding how the training is accomplished from club to club. Be wary of traditional "you must come with a choke collar" style mentality. All leading-edge training methods make virtually exclusive use of positive reinforcement these days, so there is no reason to hammer obedience into the dog using aversives anymore.

Tracking can be done independently of Schutzhund training. The dog is taught to follow the path of the track-layer. In tracking, the goal is not to teach the dog to scent - he already knows how to do that - but to motivate him to want to keep tracking the layer's scent, indicate articles the layer has dropped and discriminate between the layer and other people who cross the layer's track. The scenting ability of dogs is truly amazing. Experienced tracking dogs can re-trace your path, footstep for footstep, six or more hours after you have walked through an area, make multiple turns, cross a road, go through changes of vegetation, indicate personal articles you drop along the way and ignore other, fresher tracks which cross yours. It's a time-intensive sport but truly satisfying if you like witnessing dogs employing their natural gifts. Motivation tends to be positive in tracking: the vast majority of tracking courses now food-train rather than force-track, though I don't doubt that there are remaining pockets of force enthusiasts around.

Flyball is a relay race between teams of four dogs who must, in turn, jump over four hurdles, paw a trigger release mechanism called a Flyball Box, catch the tennis ball which flies out and then come back to their handler over the four hurdles with the tennis ball. The first team to complete successful runs with their four dogs wins the race. This is an extremely predatory, addictive activity for dog and an exciting spectator sport. Flyball is overseen by the North American Flyball Association which makes the rules and sanctions official tournaments. Unlike obedience and tracking, which are limited to registered purebred dogs, sanctioned Flyball is open to all dogs, including mixed breeds. Many Flyball participants play just for fun and exercise and never enter a tournament. Some obedience clubs offer Flyball courses now, and Flyball clubs are growing as awareness of this sport increases among dog owners.

Agility is an obstacle course for dogs, consisting of things like jumps, tunnels, climbing frames, teeter-totters and weave-poles which the dog must negotiate in the order specified by his or her handler. It's great fun for the dogs and good for developing timing for the trainer and dog-trainer rapport. Because it is so equipment intensive, it isn't yet widely offered but is definitely on the rise. It is sanctioned by the United States Dog Agility Association who will grant titles to both mixed breeds as well as purebreds, like Flyball. The elitism (purebreds only at the official level) in dog sports like obedience and tracking is sad and a relic of the control of the Kennel Clubs who have a vested interest, through collection of registration fees and income from dog shows, in promoting purebred dogs. This doesn't mean anyone can't participate; they just can't compete in American or Canadian Kennel Club sanctioned obedience or tracking trials.

Lure coursing is a flat-out chase in a large open field of an artificial prey object ("bunny") which is moved ahead of the dog by a mechanical pulley. The course is planned in advance; the dogs each take a turn and are judged on their speed, agility, keenness and style. At the official level, it is usually restricted to sight hounds but is open to all dogs at places such as dog camps. Watching a dog with no prior experience click into coursing mode can take your breath away. The focus and intensity of the dog makes a believer out of any owner who doubted their dog was a predator. People who attend dog camps regularly rate lure coursing as their favorite activity, above the many others offered.

Dog Social Behavior and Its Implications

One of the reasons we have such a long-standing and strong relationship with dogs is that they form strong social bonds, just as we do. In this respect, we are alike. Dogs take this one step further, however. As group hunters and rearers of young, they are highly motivated to stay with their social group at all times. Separation from other group members typically is followed by behaviors which help reunite: increased agitation & exploratory activity, distress vocalizations and if physical barriers are present, scratching, digging and chewing at points of entry. The manifestation of this genetic programming in a domestic situation is owner-absent behavior "problems" like barking, whining and howling, destruction of property and increased frequency of urination and defecation due to increased stress level.

It's no surprise then, that there is an exaggeration of certain behaviors, like chewing, in a good many dogs: they frequently find themselves socially isolated. Dogs are an intensely social species. They are genetically not very well prepared to be alone for any length of time, let alone all day every day as is frequently the norm in our society. This is not to say that the dog can't be taught to tolerate periods of isolation. It simply means that because it is against the genetic grain, it is unlikely to come naturally, so deliberate steps must be taken to make the dog alone-proof.

Alone Training

To improve alone-training in puppies, newly adopted dogs without severe separation anxiety problems or even in an established companion, here are the things you can do. First, if it's a new dog or puppy in your house, set the precedent right away. The tendency with a newcomer is to be constantly with him because he's novel and fascinating and you want to make him feel at home and secure. However, if you are constantly available and heaping attention on the dog, you are setting him up for a terrific letdown when normal life resumes. He will have to face The Void of Aloneness. So, right off the bat, leave baby dog or newly adopted dog alone for brief durations, over and over. With dozens of trials, he will learn that: 1) people are not always going to be available and 2) when people leave, they always come back again. Leave him in a dog-proofed area or comfy dog-crate with stuffed chew-toys so that he won't guess wrong about what to chew. And, be sure he is getting nice predatory fixes on a daily basis. Fetch, tug and hide and seek are the first lines of defense in all cases.

So, you will come and go continually, all without hellos and good-byes so the puppy or dog becomes somewhat less attentive to all these departures and arrivals. It is absolutely normal that puppies and dogs will distress vocalize when you leave them alone, even for these brief practice periods. It's in the programming, remember. Luckily, it is modifiable. It can be made stronger through reinforcement or weakened and killed through the withholding of reinforcement. This is known as extinction. Punishment will temporarily stun the behavior, rarely kill it. The reinforcement in question is your return. If noise-making is ever, even by chance, reinforced by the arrival of a human, it will become a stronger response. The rule, therefore, with distress-vocalizing dogs is: wait for a lull before going to them, at whatever cost. Resist thoughts like "what if he needs to go out" or some other vital communication from dog to human, and worry about the potent behavior modifying influence of your arrival chez dog. Always ask yourself what behavior you want to reinforce. If you like the noise, respond to it. If you don't, wait however long it takes for a lull before going to the dog. It is not that you're not going to meet your dog's needs: it's just that you're not going to train in noise-making in the process.

Keep all your departures and arrivals low-key. The gushing hellos and long-winded good-byes with tons of cuddling and begging ("pleeeeeeeze be good while I'm gone") are not only useless but serve only to increase the contrast between when you're home (Bliss) and when you're gone (The Void). Employ every conceivable strategy to reduce this contrast. Incorporate lots of toys into your interactions with your dog, even into greeting ceremonies (celebratory fetch or tug rather than just gushing). This helps to reduce dependence. Get the dog out into the outside world so he has novel sights, sounds and experiences to process every day. This increases mental fatigue.

If you must leave the dog alone all day, consider hiring a dog walker at lunch time to break up the time. Eight or ten hours is a very long stretch, especially if you have limited time in the morning getting ready to go to work (dog walked, fast fetch and tug game, fed then ignored). It used to be thought that dogs needed mainly space, that it was the ideal life to be "on a farm" with "plenty of room to run." Now we know better. *Dogs are not space-intensive; they are time-intensive.* Given a choice between your time and a yard, virtually every dog on this earth will opt for more time hanging out with living beings.

Preventing mistakes through dog-proofing is not a frill to alone-training. This goes for any behavior problem: if you're correcting a chewing problem, the dog is enclosed in an absolutely dog-proofed room, crate or pen with nothing but chew toys whenever you're not supervising. If housetraining is the issue, the dog should be crated when not watched. If jumping up is the problem, try to have a visitor-free period between your troubleshooting sessions, or shut the dog away in a room when you're expecting people, until he's trained.

Think of establishing a new behavior or outlet as cutting a new path through dense jungle with a machete: the more times you go up and down that path, clearing as you go, the easier it is to walk. Think of the undesired behavior or outlet you're trying to get rid of as an established trail you'd like to abandon so that it overgrows: any journeys along that path will keep it clear and usable that little bit longer. Every time the dog gets a crack at the undesired behavior, he's keeping that old path alive. Therefore nipping embryonic problems is a good idea, before they become worn paths. If your "trained" dog suddenly chews furniture one day, don't let there be a second day: refresh chew training rather than waiting for a history of misbehavior to develop. I'm always astounded at how people wait for weeks or months to address their dogs' chewing problem because "well, he doesn't do it everyday" or some other lame excuse.

Separation Anxiety

In dogs who already have considerable anxiety about being left alone, simply crating or confining them isn't enough. For one thing, they may set records for distress vocalizing and ignore chew toys, going for points of entry, bloodying paws in their effort to dig through the front door. It's a pretty miserable state to be in on a daily basis. Even if the dog isn't ruining your house or annoying the neighbors with incessant screaming, reducing anxiety is the decent thing to do. Separation Anxiety is an overused term, by the way, often applied to explain any and all owner-absent chewing or barking. In truth, bona-fide cases are pretty much the minority. The majority of chewers and barkers are dogs just being dogs, in that safe-to-act-like-a-dog period when the witch (you) is not home. These cases need simple chew-training or extinction of barking by failure to respond, already discussed. Most of them also need more challenge in their life in the form of predatory games on a daily basis.

Under no circumstances should you attempt to punish any chewing or noise-making already committed while alone, hours or even minutes earlier. If well-timed punishment is a slippery technique, late punishment is abuse, and late punishment to a dog, who is already anxious, blenderizes the dog's remaining brain. In these cases, the overall anxiety level of the dog is exacerbated by the punishment which is predicted by the owner's arrival home. Now the dog has two reasons to be upset. He's alone (genetic programming he can't control), and he will be attacked when his owner returns home (human idiopathic aggression that he can't control). It is no wonder that so many dogs are mentally ill. If you've ascertained that your dog is severely anxious about being left on his own, the treatment of choice is systematic desensitization.

Systematic Desensitization

Systematic desensitization is the same technique used on people who are excessively afraid of spiders or flying in airplanes. The subject is first taught to relax and then introduced to the fearful stimulus at whatever level he or she can tolerate without anxiety while practising the relaxation exercise. Then the stimulus is gradually intensified at whatever rate the subject can handle, always building on success. A spider phobic might only be able to tolerate pictures of spiders at 30 feet in initial training but if a hierarchy of difficulty is made gradual enough, can be made to eventually tolerate the proverbial tarantula on the arm. The same can be done with dogs who are phobic or who experience separation anxiety. Usually the program cannot be taken as far as it can be with human phobias because it is prohibitively difficult to avoid re-exposure to overly high stimulus levels between desensitization sessions. In other words, the real-life necessity of leaving the dog alone undermines the training program. If the owner can arrange for the dog to be not left alone for the duration of the treatment period, he can take the procedure all the way.

Another potential way around the inter-session exposure problem is to use a safety cue, like the radio, during training sessions. The radio becomes a signal to the dog that only short, non-anxiety producing absences are in store. It is important to understand that it is not the radio, per se, which relaxes the dog but it's reliable pairing with tolerable levels of aloneness which establish it as relaxing. This effect can be quickly decimated by putting the radio on and leaving for longer than the dog can handle. Radios are frequently used without any desensitization procedure, usually to no avail. This is because when owners put the radio on to mimic the ambiance when people are present or to "keep the dog company" it immediately loses any power it had by coming to predict anxiety-producing lengths of absence. This is a classic example of mistaking the building of a tool with its use. Unskilled owners are notorious for trying to use tools without taking the time to build them first. So, whenever you're doing exercises, have the radio on. When you're leaving for real and therefore distressing the dog, leave the radio off.

In training sessions, start by reward-training a sit or down stay. Then begin gradually increasing the distance between you and the dog, rewarding a lot at each new distance achieved without anxiety or breaking the stay (refer to the chapter 6 for details on teaching commands like stay). Switch to intermittent rewards over a number of repetitions at the same distance before again increasing the distance. Do not punish broken stays but rather mark them with a "no-reward" cue like "Oh! Too bad!" Under no circumstances should stay be trained using aversives (i.e. punishments for breaking) in anxious dogs. To do so is to give the dog a lose-lose choice: he experiences anxiety or is punished. Keep the training sessions short, 5 or 10 minutes at the most. If the dog falls apart, go back to whatever level he can succeed at for a final rep or two before ending the training session. End on a positive note.

In almost no time, the owner will be able to leave the room briefly while the dog holds the stay. When you're at this point, practise leaving the dog on a stay while you get your keys and go out the front door. Close the door behind you and stay out a couple of seconds. Practise going in and out, gradually increasing the time you remain outside. The operative word here is gradually. Abrupt jumps in level of difficulty are famous for blowing desensitization programs out of the water.

Adjuncts to Alone-training

There are peripheral things you can do to help the cause. Practise semi-absences by closing the dog in various rooms of the house for different lengths of time when you're at home so he can't shadow you around. Increase regular, vigorous exercise, predatory stimulation and walks so the dog has some novel sights, sounds and experiences to process every day.

You can even reduce the overall tendency of the dog to use barking as a strategy. Put the dog behind a barrier like a baby-gate or fence so he can see you but can't get at you. Get very excited and dangle something interesting, like a food reward or new toy just out of reach, encouraging him to try to get to you. If he barks, blast it with a no-reward cue or reprimand him. Repeat this procedure until he temporarily abandons barking as a strategy. You will recognize the strategy shift when you first see him doing anything else, such as lying down and sulking. If he does this for more than a few seconds, mark this behavior with a reward cue, and go in and give him a piece of bait. Go back out of reach again and repeat. (This is, by the way, the technique of choice to teach bark on command. Instead of using a no-reward mark when the dog barks, use a reward-mark: click and treat. When it's happening with regularity, put it on cue and get rid of the frustration prompt.)

When the dog catches on and refuses to bark, it's time to change the set-up. Dogs don't generalize well, so context changes are important to solidify any exercise. Try tethering him and doing the same thing. Try a different room. Try yourself in the closet or behind a door and doing the same thing, always hitting the first bark with a no-reward mark and rewarding another strategy. When the dog knows the game pretty well, practise with you on the other side of the front door and him inside the house. Do this after you have done a couple of sessions using room-to-room doors in your house. Remember though, this affects barking behavior only and not necessarily the underlying anxiety. Do this only in conjunction with desensitizing him to being home alone.

Shadowing you around the house is par for the course in fact, and not necessarily an indicator of unbearable amounts of anxiety. Many people think it's Their Dog or only anxious dogs who follow them all over the house, including into the bathroom, but judging from my informal sampling, it is Most Dogs.

One excellent trend I see emerging is double dog households. Be advised: having two dogs doubles your food, medical and accessories expenses. It also doubles the amount of hair in the house and on your clothing and time and money spent grooming, time and training, not to mention double the likelihood of a dog regurgitating grass and bile onto the wall-to-wall carpet and double the number of eyes following you into the bathroom. Double dogs also frequently bond more strongly to each other than to anyone else, especially if the two dogs are littermates. You will need to spend quality time with them individually if you wish to minimize this.

In terms of quality of life for the dogs though, given that both dogs are socialized to their own species, things are much better. They are never alone. They have a target for a lot of their doggie behavior, a built-in playmate. They have the opportunity to develop a richer percentage of their doggie communication and interaction patterns. Their day to day life is more complex: even the inevitable conflicts and disappointments which come with being one of two rather than an Only Dog help in the never-ending war against understimulation.

I am in no way suggesting that getting a second dog is a quick fix for existing behavior problems. Life is never that simple. Indeed, it may have no impact at all. It merely shifts the odds more in your favor and improves your dog's quality of life. Interview people who own two dogs. Most will tell you that their dogs hang out together all the time and play with each other vigorously "every day." I often wonder where all this energy is going in single dogs.

3. Socialization, Conflict Resolution, Fear & Aggression

Aggressive behavior in domestic dogs is an issue that has long needed to come out of the closet. There is incredible stigma attached to dogs who bite, as though they have character flaws and are qualitatively different from dogs who have never bitten. They are not. There are not two kinds of dogs: nice dogs who would never bite and less nice dogs who do. *Biting is natural, normal dog behavior.* This is why it is so prevalent. Biting and threat displays (which are simply the indication of intention to bite) are how dogs settle both minor and major disputes and defend themselves from any perceived threat they cannot or opt not to flee from. In dog culture there are no letters to the editor, slanderous gossip and backstabbing, guilty feelings, democratic institutions or litigation lawyers. There are growls, snarls, snaps and bites. Aggressive behavior does not fracture relationships in dog society. It's all taken very much in stride. The problem is that aggression often changes things a great deal in dog-human relationships. We routinely execute dogs who bite. That's quite the culture clash.

The domestication of dogs has made it easier to socialize them, but it has not provided any guarantee against anti-social behavior. Dog bites can be extremely damaging, and serious attacks can be lethal. This, coupled with the very normalcy of the behavior, is what makes it so important to address biting more openly and actively. Dog owners tend to have an extreme head-in-the-sand attitude regarding the potential for biting in their own dogs. They have never done any active anti-aggression training. Most would agree with the statement "my dog would bite only with extreme provocation." What's insidious is that almost all owners of dogs who inflict serious bites seemingly "without provocation" believed their own dog to be safe the day before or the minute before the dog bit for the first time. All dogs must be acknowledged as potential biters.

Dogs are unaware that they've been adopted into a culture where biting is considered a betrayal of trust and a capital offense. Incredibly little is actively, consciously done to reduce the probability of biting. It is left to "good character" or the breeding of "good temperament." People seem to feel that active biting prophylaxis shouldn't be necessary if the genetics are in good order. This is a huge fallacy. Normal dog genetics should produce an animal with "bite-or-flight" as the wired in program both for conflict resolution and for increasing the distance between themselves and anything that spooks them. Dogs, like most animals, are extremely aware of and constantly manipulating social distance. There are only two ways to do this: move yourself away or get the other guy to move away, plan A or plan B. Getting the other guy to move away is the function of aggression.

Which plan an individual dog chooses first (threaten or run) is a function of his genetic predisposition and learning history. Dogs will do what tends to have been successful in the past. They will also, if plan A is not working, switch without hesitation to plan B. Cornered dogs switch to threat display. Spooked growlers and lungers will turn and run, if you keep approaching. It is a matter of great urgency when the "increase distance" alarm goes off in a dog's head. Genetic predisposition simply makes one plan or the other more likely and influences how likely the dog is to spook in the first place, all other things, such as how well socialized he is, being equal. Many of the guarding breeds, for instance, are wired up as more difficult to socialize and with plan A being threat display. This is logical if you think about it. What good is a guard dog whose plan A is threat display but who never spooks? Or, who spooks more easily but runs away when spooked? Humans must come to grips with the seemingly innocuous events and contexts which elicit spooking in domestic dogs.

To accept biting as normal behavior would require a fundamental shift in our view of domestic dogs. The potential payoff is that we could, starting today, reduce the number and severity of dog bites by facing up to the problem: dogs are animals, and animals bite. It would simply take a large-scale initiation of routine preventive intervention to minimize risk. There are things whose safety we take for granted: books, pillows, hats, flowers. We don't have safety programs for these things. There are also things we see as potentially dangerous - safe only if knowledge and care go into their management or use: kitchen knives, electrical outlets, swimming pools, chainsaws, matches, bleach. We put dogs in the safe category when they belong in the dangerous category. Dogs are seen by many as being dangerous only if really pushed, like a pillow is dangerous only if you really go out of your way to cook up a smothering scene. Dogs, like other animals, are dangerous unless you actively intervene to make them otherwise. Dog bites are the number one cause of facial disfigurement in children.

The Hidden Epidemic

When a dog bites, it is stigmatized, often killed. Yet the reputation of dogs in general goes relatively unhurt because the individual biter is blamed and labelled deviant. From a dog's perspective, however, allowing a decrease in social distance between himself and anyone to whom he's not habituated or socialized would more likely qualify as deviant behavior. So why aren't dog bites a daily occurrence? For one thing, they are. Statistics in Western countries where the number of bites is recorded are mind-boggling. And these are the reported bites. A much larger number go unreported. Many other dogs simply never meet up with the particular combination of elements which would cause them to bite, but this is a stroke of luck. There is no qualitative difference, or even necessarily a quantitative difference, between their temperament and that of the repeat-biter next door.

Just as it's inherently clear to dogs that a good proportion of matter is chew toys, it's equally obvious that you should threaten to bite or bite anyone who is spooky and comes too close or who tries to obtain important resources in your possession. The mental hurdle people seem to have is accepting that the dog decides what is spooky or threatening. This is a dangerous place to be anthropomorphic. We humans had better start to pay attention to what these things are or we will be left with the tired refrain of "I don't understand it. Suddenly and without warning and with no provocation blah blah blah."

So, a major element of the culture clash between dogs and humans is differing perceptions of what constitutes a threat. The most commonly uttered phrase following a dog bite is that the dog bit "unprovoked" or "suddenly, for no reason." This is because the number one bite provoker in domestic dogs is some variation on a behavior we humans consider non-provocative or even friendly: approaching or reaching out with a hand. We are mired in the belief that the friendly intention behind this gesture is read and understood by all dogs. We've been reinforced in this belief by the dogs who tolerate patting and handling. For sure, some dogs actively enjoy and solicit patting from people. Many dogs, however, barely tolerate it or actively dislike it. And, for a dog who is not socialized to, say, men, the mere presence of a man is provocative. What's important to understand is that bites are rarely cases of something going awry such as abuse or trauma but failures of omission: not enough was done to get the dog prepared for life in a human environment. Desensitizing dogs to humans, approach and handling must be actively installed to proof against spooking. Dogs who bite people or are afraid of people are usually behaving like normal animals. To understand why dogs bite for reasons indiscernible to most owners, it is first necessary to understand socialization.

Socialization: What Is It Anyway?

Socialization is a term which means habituation or getting used to environmental elements through exposure. In a natural setting, it is highly adaptive to increase distance between yourself and anything unusual and then to proceed with extreme caution when approaching. This is because unusual things are potentially very bad news. (They certainly aren't necessary for survival because you've made it this far without them.) Animals are very into social distance. So are we, if you think about it. We tolerate someone standing right against us in a crowded elevator but would be instantly spooked by the same person standing that close if we were the only two in the elevator. Someone can walk up and stand right behind you if you're in a line-up at the grocery store, but someone doing exactly the same thing when you're in the driveway washing your car is a whole other story. We can also, like animals, be very weird about people touching us.

In animals, curiosity is antagonistic to fear and usually less pronounced. While it is potentially adaptive to explore novel things in case they yield some advantage (especially in the case of predators), excessive curiosity would eventually result in exposure to danger and hence reproductive disadvantage. You can't pass on those curious genes if you're dead or injured. Consider, for instance, what you'd think about any wild animal in the forest who didn't flee from you or didn't put on an aggressive display if you cornered it. Would you think he was a "nice" animal, or would you think he was, say, sick? Avoidance of novelty is the default setting for animals. All these truths about animals are pretty self-evident. And, pound this into your brain: dogs are animals.

Because it would not be adaptive for animals to be continuously spooking at rocks and trees and bird song, a mechanism is wired in to ensure the animal habituates to normal environmental features. This is the socialization period, a finite time when young animals are much less fearful and are much more likely to approach and investigate novel things. Adult animals can habituate to novel things too. It simply takes much longer. The socialization window cannot remain open forever however. If it did, then you would have animals trotting up to you in the forest. Every species of animal has acquired, through natural selection, an average time to assimilate and accept things in their environment. After this period, they will behave to increase distance, through the mechanisms of flight or aggression, from anything to which they have not been socialized. There is also a "use it or lose it" clause: animals will become increasingly fearful of things they may have encountered in the critical period but see too seldom thereafter.

Notice that the pressure is always in the direction of increasing fearfulness and avoidance, never the other way. Artificial pressure needs to be constantly exerted to get animals to behave tolerantly. It must be installed in the socialization period and diligently maintained thereafter. As soon as there is any weakness in this system, the animal starts leaning towards fight/flight. By definition, the socialization period, be it one day or several months, is what works well for that species in the environment in which it evolved. In the case of domestic dogs, the socialization window closes at between 3 and 5 months of age, depending on the breed and individual make-up, with easy habituation drying up at around 4 and a half months of age in the majority of cases.

What this means is, if a puppy doesn't get sufficient exposure to men with beards before the socialization clock runs out, the risk for fear responses and aggression directed at men with beards runs higher for that dog as an adult. It's particularly wrinkly because dogs are expert discriminators and adequate socialization to women or six year-old kids does not guarantee a generalization to men or two year-old kids. Therefore, it's advisable to go way overboard covering all the bases before the socialization window closes, especially for sensitive, reactive breeds or individuals. This means exposing the puppy to as wide a social sphere as possible in terms of human age-groups, sexes, sizes, shapes, colors and gaits. The experiences should be positive (play, treats, nothing scary) and include a wide variety of patting, handling and movement by the humans. It also means getting the puppy used to anything it may have to encounter in later life, such as car-rides, veterinary exams, cats, traffic, soccer games, elevators and pointy sticks.

Pumped Up Socialization

There is a dual benefit to heavy socialization. One is obvious: the more you socialize the puppy, the fewer things you'll miss. The second advantage is a more global effect: the more the puppy encounters novel situations in which it initially is reluctant or spooky and then gets over it and habituates (as puppies do so well), the more the underlying trait of stability or "bounce-back" is developed. The puppy's overall confidence grows. The more puppyhood experiences a dog has to draw on, the more resilient the character. The mild stresses of regular novelty in early life are like inoculations. So, provided the puppy had really thorough socialization and developed good bounce-back, individual elements that were missed during socialization will be handled more easily by the adult animal. The passive approach ("get the puppy out to a few shopping malls and dog shows") is inadequate for some individuals. Aim for a systematic, continual, assault style program. Not only do you end up with a dog who is at reduced risk for fearfulness and biting, but is under much less chronic stress as an adult.

The puppy who has had actively positive experiences is less likely as an adult to spook in a challenging situation than the dog who had only neutral experiences. So, why not improve your odds of getting a relaxed, confident, solid adult temperament by actively increasing the number of strongly positive experiences? This is like putting money in the bank. (Also note, if the puppy has a negative experience on the first trial of exposure to something, a full-blown phobia can be acquired.) Why go for a dog who's more or less habituated to screaming toddlers or teenagers on roller blades when you can end up with one who actively likes them?

In socialization to any category of people, the single best way to obtain this cushion is through hand feeding. Rather than simply getting the puppy around young children, have young children hand feed the puppy small tasty treats. Each treat builds up a little more money in the bank for young children. Another method, suitable for predatory types who are addicted to games with toys or balls, is to have people in the category you're trying to cover engage in favorite games with the puppy.

Socialization Hit List

CATEGORY	NEUTRAL	POSITIVE
Women	Meets in corridor	Hand-fed by
Men	Visit house	Hand-fed by
Teenagers	Sees on street	Hand-fed by
Children	Patted by in park	Hand-fed by
Toddlers	Visit house	Hand-fed by (assisted)
Babies	Sees one on street	Rewarded when sniffs
Hats	Sees on pedestrians	Hand-fed by
Peculiar Gaits	Sees drunks in park	Hand-fed by clowns
All Races	Sees occasionally	Hand-fed by
Crowds	Attends event	Liver given by people
Uniforms	Meets mailman	Hand-fed by
Bikes	Sees on street	Treated by owner
Traffic	Walks near	Walks near to fun place
Car-Rides	Around block	To fun place
Cats/Livestock	Sees and sniffs	Treats from owner
Other Dogs	Meets & greets	Off-leash play

This list is not exhaustive. *You cannot overdo socialization.* The payoff is enormous. I have often thought that owners who are inclined to leave their dogs' socialization to everyday life (i.e., chance) should meet families of biters or dogs with world-class phobias of innocuous environmental elements. They would hear a lot of "if only," many of these dogs appeared fine as puppies. They reacted well to what they were exposed to, but it wasn't enough, either in volume or range. Experiences were neutral, rarely positive. They saw people but not up close. They saw women but rarely men. They saw plenty of people but were never manhandled. There was an omission. Doing remedial socialization on an adult dog is a slow, labor-intensive undertaking, if it is doable at all. It is infinitely easier to work on puppies because of that open window of the socialization period.

IF YOU HAVE A PUPPY, BITE THE BULLET AND SOCIALIZE IT NOW

The effort put in comes back a thousandfold, especially for dogs at higher risk through genetics. It's criminal to not put massive effort into a dog like a Kuvasz who we already know is hard-wired to be spookier. Excuses and smokescreens like "reserved with strangers" or "takes a while to warm up to people" or "great with the family" or "protective" mean one thing and one thing only: undersocialized. Period. There is no longer any excuse for dogs to reach adulthood emotionally crippled and at risk for execution after they bite someone because their feeble owners failed to socialize them. The information has been out there for years. Dog owners have just kept buying into the myth that genetics is solely responsible for temperament and that biting is highly abnormal behavior. Dog bites continue to be common, despite all the information on how to prevent them. This is disgraceful. Perhaps there's a late feedback effect: the punishing results of failing to adequately socialize a dog appear too late to modify owners' behavior. Heavy socialization is the single smartest investment that you can make in a dog.

Socialization Case History

The Campbell family consists of Mom, Dad and three kids, aged 17, 15 and 11. They recently put to sleep their 10-year-old German

Shepherd due to illness. Their other Shepherd, aged 7, has always lived with another dog, so the Campbells bought a new Shepherd puppy a few months after the death of their older dog. The puppy, Bruce, was bright and naturally very compliant, got along well with the other dog and fitted into the family easily. It was much easier raising this puppy than previous puppies because the family was better off financially than years earlier, had a house in the suburbs with a fenced yard for the dogs to play in and the kids were older and able to take more responsibility for feeding, training and clean-up. The family was shocked and appalled when Bruce, at age 8 months, bit a visiting 6-year-old girl when she tried to pat the dog.

This story is so common it makes me want to scream. The owners are experienced German Shepherd owners. Their first two dogs never bit anyone, never threatened anyone. One was reserved around strangers but simply retreated when one approached and never in its life felt cornered enough to switch to plan B: biting. The Campbells bought from the same breeder and are at a loss to explain Bruce's biting because they raised him the same way. What they don't realize is that they got away with no active socialization with the first two dogs for a number of reasons. They were raised in a household with young children which partially covered that base. At the time, the family lived in an apartment so the dogs had regular walks which exposed them to sights and sounds in a busy city. And their Shepherd who avoided strangers was simply a time bomb that never went off.

Time Bomb Dogs

Bruce experienced the same passive socialization but with a couple of differences. The kids were older when he was a puppy, so the occasional kids he saw felt to him like aliens from Mars. The yard offered exercise and elimination which was more convenient than taking him out on leash, so he missed out on regular walks. No walks = no meeting people. The other difference is that his response when spooked was a threat display rather than flight like their previous Shepherd, even though his motives were the same as the other dog: to increase distance between himself and the child who tried to touch him.

It's important to understand that this is not a case of the Campbells doing a good job on the first two dogs and then failing on the third dog. They never actively socialized any of their dogs but got away with it with the first two. Their timid Shepherd would likely have resorted to threat if flight had been unavailable when encountering strangers (plan B). It just never happened. These owners never considered what they were doing to be insufficient until, inevitably, one of their time bombs went off. Many people raise time bomb dogs who, because of some combination of passive socialization, absence of sufficient challenge and that individual dog's reaction style (flight being plan A), don't explode and bite during their lifetimes. So generations of dog owners continue to gamble unknowingly. Heavy socialization, although it does not provide a guarantee against biting, vastly improves your odds.

So, socialization can be upgraded from neutral to positive experiences and from passive to active. It's far better to actively seek out those categories of people and things than to hope that enough bases will be covered by whatever experiences happen to come up in the pup's day to day life. This is especially important for puppies who are at greater risk. These are: puppies of certain breeds (notably herding breeds), any puppy observed to already be reserved, timid, reactive or sensitive, puppies from litters not whelped and raised in a human-infested home (i.e. litters whelped in kennels, barns etc.), puppies belonging to owners who live in rural or quiet suburban areas, puppies whose owners have yards, puppies of small breeds with overprotective owners, puppies raised in multi-dog households (including dog exhibitors) and puppies of large or scary-looking breeds which strangers may avoid.

Puppy Classes

A marvelous innovation has been the introduction of quality puppy kindergarten classes. Although puppy classes have been offered in the past, these were barely distinguishable from traditional jerk 'n' praise obedience classes and often did more harm than good, especially in the case of puppies. This may be the reason behind the admonition by vets and other dog resource people to not begin formal training until a dog is at least six months old. The puppies couldn't withstand the "training." Pioneering puppy trainers like Dr. Ian Dunbar turned it all around with gentle, amazingly effective, puppy-friendly methods which teach compliance while improving temperament and level of socialization all at the same time. There's little limit to what young puppies are capable of learning if the method is right. It's a tragic lost opportunity to delay taking a dog to class till he's an adolescent. Puppy classes are the way of the future.

Another benefit of puppy classes is the instant provision of age-mates for the developing pup. The problem of dog-dog socialization is virtually obliterated simply by showing up to class. This assumes that the class in question is a true puppy class, limited to vaccinated puppies under the age of 18 weeks rather than a beginner level obedience course masquerading as a "puppy" class. All training in a good puppy class should use positive reinforcement as motivation rather than some form or other of "training collar." There should also be frequent puppy play sessions. Aside from the dog-dog social repertoire development, play is one forum for the acquisition of bite-inhibition.

Bite Inhibition

Dogs are animals who are able to kill, tear apart carcasses and crack bone with their jaws. They are also highly social. If they are to live among others with this kind of weaponry as standard issue, they need some means of preventing serious injury to each other during altercations. This is where ritualization comes in. A key ingredient to ritualized aggression is bite inhibition. Dogs are not born with soft mouths, but they are wired up to easily acquire the ability to bite softly, if conditions are right. The right conditions means: plenty of feedback about bite strength. To ensure that puppies get plenty of feedback about bite strength, nature has made puppies into veritable biting machines with needle-like teeth. Normal puppies can and should play-bite continually in social interactions. Play is an extremely interesting behavior. It encompasses rehearsal, bonding, opportunities for feedback and sheer fun. Of high concern to dog owners is the fact that puppies are removed from their litters early in life and often placed in a relative social vacuum. This is greatly compounded if the puppy is forbidden from play-biting its owners.

67

Suppressing puppy biting too early means the puppy doesn't get the repeated doses of feedback on his jaw strength; the puppy grows up with a hard mouth. This is a serious squandering of a critical line of defense against dog bites.

So, smart puppy owners allow some puppy biting in order to give the puppy information on his own strength. Puppy biting is such a valuable thing, in fact, that puppies who do not play bite should be actively encouraged to do so in order to develop a soft mouth. Start off by targeting harder bites. Let the puppy chomp away on your hands, and monitor the level of pressure. Although puppy teeth are sharp, puppy jaws are undeveloped, so this will not be unbearable. As soon as the puppy bears down a little harder, screech "OUCH!" as though it hurt much more than it did, look at the puppy like he's a little ax-murderer and leave the room for a minute or two. This time-out is a clear refusal-to-play consequence with the "OUCH!" as the conditioned stimulus. Many puppies also have an innate understanding of the screech, making the system work even better. After the minute or two has passed, return and resume play. He may be more prudent temporarily, and he may not. Be prepared to repeat this procedure over and over, so the trend emerges. Puppy learns that if puppy bites too hard, puppy plays by himself.

It's beneficial from a generalization standpoint if more than one person implements these same rules. The exception is young children. Young kids and puppies are an extremely dangerous combination. Kids do all the wrong things around dogs: they scream, flap, move a lot, fall down and react in a fun (for the puppy) way when the puppy bites them. They expertly simulate wounded animals and bring out the predatory rehearsal repertoire in the dog all too well. They are not good candidates to install soft mouth in excitable puppies. Young kids should be around puppies and well-socialized adult dogs for that matter, only when actively supervised by an adult. All their interactions should be carefully refereed. When the puppy starts to rev up, the kids must exit, so the adults may do the soft mouth exercises or redirect the puppy's energy. Kids should never, ever, ever be allowed to go up to strange dogs. The "kids and dogs" as wonderful playmates is an overblown and highly dangerous myth.

When the puppy has consistently demonstrated some greater self-control, you may start targeting even moderate pressure bites. The reason for doing it in stages is that the puppy will be unable to comply if you set too high an initial criteria. He's got to be able to manage the task you set for him. Little biting-maniac puppies can and do learn to hold back on the hard bites, but they are simply unable to hold back on all or even most bites too early on (unless you obliterate the puppy with harsh punishments). You're teaching him self-control in manageable chunks. When he is mouthing you with very little pressure, you may then teach him a "don't touch" command (using NRM's) and redirect him to appropriate bitable objects like his toys. He now knows that he may not bite humans at all, and you've got the critically important fringe benefit of acquired bite inhibition.

Bite inhibition needs to be checked and maintained in grown-up dogs, too. The best way to do this is to hand feed the dog. You'll be doing a lot of hand feeding anyway if you use food rewards in training. Rather than letting the dog eat out of your flat hand, hold food morsels in your fingers. If you feel incisors on your fingers, screech "OUCH!" and withhold the reward. Only relinquish rewards, regardless of the brilliance of the behavior you are rewarding, if the dog is demonstrably prudent with his jaws and you feel no pressure on your fingers. Dogs need these constant reminders, so they don't get rusty. Another good way to get your hands into the dog's mouth is to regularly brush his teeth. This is a good idea anyway and super, palatable dog toothpastes exist now. Regular dental maintenance like this gives you opportunities to remind the dog to be gentle with his mouth as well as giving the dog nice breath and tartar-free teeth. Yet another opportunity to fine-tune bite inhibition is during tug and fetch games. Without exception, screech in pain and end the game if the dog makes a grabbing error and nicks or bites you instead of the toy.

Timid Puppies
What we most like to see is a puppy who is outgoing: who readily and confidently, with a wagging tail, approaches any person, who play bites feverishly. This is a puppy who actively seeks to close distance

and is diametrically opposed to flight-or-bite puppies who work to increase social distance. Note that the continuum of temperament is not one with fear and aggression at opposite ends of the spectrum and normal in the middle. Rather, at one extreme there is relaxed, confident, highly socialized behavior and at the other end the two-headed coin of fear and aggression. Fear and aggression are considered flip sides of the lack of confidence coin because they are really just strategies to accomplish the same end: to keep the fearful stimulus far enough away. Dogs readily switch strategy if their usual style doesn't work. So, the opposite of a fearful dog is a relaxed, confident dog. And, the opposite of an aggressive dog is, you guessed it, a relaxed, confident dog. This is why lack of confidence in a puppy is such a major emergency. If we don't see outgoingness in a puppy, the race begins to see how much we can install before the socialization period comes to an end.

If puppies who exhibit no spookiness around strangers benefit from being socialized, puppies who already are uncomfortable around strangers urgently need intervention. Whatever the puppy seems afraid of or growls at should be the target of a massive effort to get the puppy very comfortable and confident about. The goal is a puppy who willingly chooses to approach and make contact. Socializing frightened, insecure or suspicious puppies is easier than you might think, if you go slowly enough. When dealing with a timid or anti-social puppy, it's important that the pace be set by the puppy. The handler must find whatever medication or Zen-like mood is necessary to make him abstain from ever forcing the puppy to socialize, as is many people's inclination.

It's critically important that when working with timid puppies (or undersocialized adults or biters for that matter) that it be puppy's choice whether to approach and at what speed. If the puppy wants to keep his distance for a few minutes or half an hour, that must be respected. Rushing the puppy or forcing the puppy to make contact with people or things which frighten it ("oh, don't be silly, sit on Uncle Roger's lap") simply exacerbates the existing fear. The puppy thought someone was a bit dangerous. Now you've proven him right by associating the strong fear response, brought about by coerced contact, with the person or thing you're trying to make seem benign.

Not a good move. Much better to keep the scary person or thing stationary and let the puppy approach at his own pace. Imagine yourself strapped to a chair and someone coming at you with a blowtorch. If they said, "there, there, it's okay, it's oooookaaay," would it feel okay? The only thing that would make it okay would be for you to have freedom of movement and access to the blowtorch. If someone kept putting cash right near it, you might, with great prudence, sneak in and collect the cash and get more comfortable about the presence of the fearful stimulus. You might even end up doing some welding.

Desensitizing timid puppies is no different. "Puppy's choice" must be respected. Every time the puppy, of his own accord, takes the risk to approach something scary and lives through it or, better still, has a positive experience, the puppy's confidence gets a boost. Adding tasty bait to the process is enormously helpful. For instance, the strange person must remain motionless but has sliced hot dogs sprinkled all over them while they read a magazine. Each time the puppy finally feels confident enough to approach, the approach is rewarded with a hot dog slice. The probability of future approaches starts to go up. You're off and running. Progress to moving people, approaching people, people who pat and demographic variations can gradually be added, with "puppy's choice" always respected. This approach is called "passive training" because, once you've set up the scary person or object and the sprinkled bait, your presence or intervention is no longer necessary. Go about your business while the puppy self-trains. Passive training is extremely valuable for socializing timid animals because of the time-frames involved. This is a slow process. Do not give up or switch to something counterproductive (such as pressuring the puppy) when working with shrinking violet types.

Puppy Temperament Testing

An extremely popular topic in the doggie crowd is puppy testing. Numerous formal tests purport to objectively measure fixed traits such as dominance, predatory drive, fearfulness and sociability. Unfortunately, some serious doubt has been cast upon both the reliability and predictive validity of puppy temperament tests. One fly in the ointment is that the presumed immutability of "temperament" has proven iffy, if not false. The temperament of dogs, right down to such seemingly basic traits as level of "dominance" and, more importantly, how outgoing the puppy is, is surprisingly plastic up until the socialization window closes. There is no compelling data yet correlating results from existing puppy temperament tests with measurable adult behavior. Temperament test results on any given puppy also vary wildly from one day to the next and from one tester to the next. Contact latency tests ("how long till the puppy goes right up to a person when he enters the room") are one such example: puppies who are slow or non-approachers can be turned into keen approachers in a couple of rewarded trials, so how solid is the underlying trait which the test allegedly measures?

Most of these tests fail to get at the underlying traits they are supposed to. For instance, a litter of six puppies will be individually tested on their reaction to a novel stimulus like an umbrella suddenly opening. Let's say puppies one and two are not spooked in the slightest; they wag and investigate the umbrella. Puppies three and four spook first and then investigate. Puppies five and six spook but don't come around to investigating by the end of the testing period. What have we learned about the temperaments of these puppies? The standard test interpretation would read that puppies one and two are very stable, puppies three and four are a bit spooky and puppies five and six are definitely spooky. The reality is that we haven't learned anything about puppies one and two, puppies three and four have demonstrated reactivity but excellent bounce-back and puppies five and six have demonstrated reactivity and some lack of bounce-back. Puppies one and two haven't been tested yet. Remember, the test is to determine the reaction of a dog to something which frightens it, not the puppy's attitude about wet-weather gear. Before it's possible to see how well numbers one and two respond to a fearful stimulus, you first have to supply one. All that can be concluded from the test is that pups one and two aren't afraid of umbrellas. We still don't know how they will react when they encounter something which scares them. They may react as did three and four, or they may be like five and six or worse. The jury is still out.

Even more interesting is that both the reactivity and bounce-back of all of these puppies could be modified through early experience. Take numbers five and six, and socialize them really well, and they'll end up more solid than three and four, if these go to incompetent homes. Owners of dogs like one and two are potentially also at risk because their puppies seem solid as rocks because they tend to be non-reactive. Non-reactive puppies or puppies who are very selectively reactive don't get as much of an opportunity to develop bounce-back and do not have as much attention paid to their socialization because they don't seem to need it. This is a big mistake. Remember the dual benefit of socialization: it's not just to reduce the number of items in the universe at which the puppy might spook but to repeatedly provide the experience of first feeling fearful and then getting over it. Bounce-back is one of the most valuable traits you can instill in a dog. Flaky or brittle temperaments are those which are unforgiving or acquire phobias more easily. The chances of a dog turning out this way are greatly reduced if bounce-back is developed early, regardless of whether the dog in question was highly reactive (spooks fairly easily) or non-reactive (spooks less often).

Dog-Dog Socialization

Dog to dog socialization is, if you think about it, a laughable problem. How far would dogs have gotten as a species if they routinely mutilated each other. An awful lot is wired into dogs to prevent this if we only provide an adequate crucible for the intraspecific social repertoire to develop. This is a big "if only" because many owners make such a mess. Dogs are, by nature, compulsive about making contact with one another so that they can engage in the important ritual of mutual rear-sniffing. They really want to know who the other dog is (familiar or unfamiliar, sex, reproductive status etc.), perform appeasement behaviors if necessary, jostle for rank if necessary or re-establish contact with a familiar animal. None of this can be established at a distance. Many owners find the urgency with which dogs pull on leash towards other dogs or otherwise "act up" (i.e., are motivated and animated) worrisome or irritating (another behavior "problem" requiring treatment). They punish the behavior or prohibit contact with other dogs. This leaves the dog with a corked up backlog of social juice which ends up actually contributing to unpolished social behavior when contact ever is made with another dog. The socially starved and inexperienced dog comes on too strong, and the owner's prophecy is fulfilled, so future contact with dogs is avoided, perpetuating the cycle. Bottom line: social skills develop with repeated exposure and deteriorate with isolation.

Things get even worse when the other dog is similarly handled, so that now two juiced up, socially naive animals are involved. Also, the owners often exacerbate dog-dog tension by choking up on leashes to hold the already frustrated dogs just out of reach. Dogs in general behave much more aggressively on leash than off. This is partly due to the leash providing a telegraph-wire transmission of tension back and forth between owner and dog. Even more importantly, I think, is that dogs are very aware when they are on leash that their options for manipulating social distance are very limited. They experience, in effect, either barrier-frustration or cornering. Barrier-frustration also contributes to the increased incidence of aggression observed by dogs who are tied out or in dogs who fence-fight. Dogs who are tied out repeatedly see things they would like to approach and investigate and repeatedly are prevented from doing so by hitting the end of the chain. If the dog has had traditional obedience training, leashes are intimately associated with increased probability of positive punishment in the form of leash corrections.

Many dog people have also suggested that tie-outs and fences provide too well-defined a territory, and this effect is responsible for the huge increase in aggression in these dogs. I don't personally buy this though I wouldn't rule it out as a factor. Dogs, who are timid or aggressive with people or dogs, usually need remedial socialization, not fuzzier territorial lines. A well-socialized dog will watch-dog bark and then go through all the normal motions: he will excitedly sniff and greet the newcomer, hopefully offer appeasement behaviors. An undersocialized dog will watch-dog bark and then stay back, growling, make tracks to somewhere else in the house and hide or oscillate between approaching and avoiding, probably barking the whole time.

We do know that fence-fighters are best treated by introducing them, off-leash, without barriers, provided the dogs in question don't have ultra-hard mouths. Owners typically expect a blood bath given the long history of blustering at each other through the fence, but these dogs almost always fizzle out after some minor jostling or scuffling provided they are not completely unsocialized or have zero bite-inhibition. Many become playmates. Needless to say, the ideal is for the dog to experience as little barrier frustration as possible in the first place. This is easily accomplished by not tying dogs out or leaving them interminably in yards. As well, you should allow regular contact and play between dogs who live on the opposite sides of a fence.

So, on leash, there is a barrier-frustration effect when a dog is held back from approaching at his own chosen speed. Worse, if a dog would choose to rapidly increase distance, this too is prevented by the leash. Flight options are cut off, so the dog switches to plan B, aggressive display. This brings out the worst in the other dog, and a vicious cycle is born. An accumulation of these experiences, even minor ones, results in a dog who knows that in any on-leash situation he's unable to move in and out at will; right off the bat he's more tense. The owner contributes by being generally edgy and possibly punitive. The discriminative stimulus for all this stupidity is the sight of another dog on the street. All this stress and punishment because a dog has caught sight of another member of his species. Pathetic.

Undersocialized dogs will not necessarily behave fearfully around dogs. They may still be interested in other dogs but socially extremely unrefined. There are two main social naiveté gaffes made by puppies and adolescent dogs: their greeting and appeasement behaviors are too big and sloppy and their rank establishment behaviors are too big and sloppy. They come on too strong from simple lack of experience. These social gaffes are best corrected by plenty of experience with well-socialized adult dogs, i.e., dogs who have regular contact with a variety of other dogs. They will not tolerate much crude behavior, but they will also do no harm when dissuading the puppy or enthusiastic, undersocialized adolescent. The tragedy is that naive dogs are usually kept away from other dogs by their owners who find their gross behavior and resulting scuffles too scary. Valuable social lessons are thus never learned, and the dog never improves. This is the vicious cycle described above. The solution is to bite the bullet, and let the goofy teenager take his lumps from established well-socialized adults. Gross appeasement and gross ranking will never be refined without practice. It's fascinating to watch experienced dogs interact: blasé, subtle, cool, virtually phoning in their greetings, rank manoeuvres and appeasement.

With chronic bullies and fighters, the most useful technique is to shape the absence of fighting. This means rewarding the dog for doing virtually anything but fighting in the presence of other dogs. It is a powerful technique because, for what may be the first time in his life, the dog is positively reinforced when around dogs instead of being punished. Dogs who fight usually do not do so every single moment they are in the presence of other dogs, so there are always rewardable responses, even initially. This regular rewarding rules out the presence of the other dog(s) as discriminative stimulus for punishment, if the owner also chooses to nail the dog for fighting. This isolates the fighting itself with the strong association to the punishment. The only valid role of the punishment in dog fights is, in fact, to buy rewardable responses by temporarily suppressing the fighting. This helps get the ball rolling on an alternative behavior around dogs. Remember that punishment on its own is a pretty useless and dangerous technique. At best, it buys you time to train an alternative behavior. Watch out for any increase in dog-dog object-guarding when you bring out a focus like a food reward. If you're skillful, you can troubleshoot the food-competition effect by teaching the dog that:

1) the close presence of the other dog improves his chances at reward
2) any aggression directed at the other dog scares the food away ("too bad!")
3) a treat for the other dog predicts a treat for him

If this is constantly exacerbating the fighting, you may be forced to switch to a less hot motivator, like praise.

The goal is for these dogs to make their first doggie friend. Good first choices to use to rehab fighters are extremely well-socialized, slick, friendly spayed or neutered adults who have good bounce back. They will be able to withstand the idiotic behavior of the fighter and stand a good chance of slowly seducing him into a playmate, if given adequate opportunity. Get the dogs together, off-leash, in a barren, boring environment, and watch from the sidelines. You can praise or reward neutral to positive interactions or stay passive, depending on what seems to be helping the most.

All of this presumes the dog is not a damaging fighter, i.e. that although he fights a lot with terrible noises and looks like he wants to kill, he does not inflict serious puncture wounds necessitating veterinary attention. If the dog routinely sends other dogs to the vet for suturing, his bite inhibition is poor, and the prognosis is less rosy. One interesting innovation is the advent of "growl classes," which are designed to help rehab dog-aggressive dogs. The dogs are all muzzled initially, to prevent damaging bites (to level the playing field, even those with soft-enough mouths are muzzled) and are given fun, simple, reward-oriented obedience exercises to do. These low-pressure obedience sessions alternate with free-interaction periods where the dogs, off leash, improve their social skills and sometimes even learn to play. With time and careful handling, many progress to being able to participate in class without a muzzle and even interact more normally and peacefully with other dogs.

In the case of inter-male aggression, neutering is often extremely helpful, not so much to turn off the dog's hormonal brain-bath but to make him smell less threatening to other males, thus helping to short-circuit the positive feedback loop two males often get into.

Food Bowl Exercises

Aside from socialization, there are other high-priority exercises for puppies. These are: food-bowl exercises, object exchanges, placement commands and handling exercises. Left to themselves, a huge proportion of dogs will become resource (food, objects, locations and owner) guarders, and many will be difficult to manipulate, even routinely. This is because they are normal animals, not because some particular individual is stubborn, touchy or vicious. Prophylactic exercises are therefore important for all puppies.

When you feed your puppy, hang around while he eats. Sit on the floor beside him, patting him and dangling your hands in the bowl. He needs to find out, through repeated experience, that your presence around his food and dish is not a threat. Feed him some meals in small installments to pound in the repeated association between your hand approaching the dish and good news: another helping. Practise taking the bowl away in mid-meal and sprucing it up by adding something tastier. This can be a spoonful of canned food, cottage cheese or a piece of freeze-dried liver. Also practise walking up to the dog while he's eating and dropping some nice morsel in. The goal is that your approach or removal of the bowl reliably predicts something good for the dog. This is to counteract his natural inclination to guard his food. In a natural environment, zealous guarding of scarce resources like food would be highly adaptive and thus selected for. It crops up all too frequently in domestic dogs in spite of hundreds of generations of artificial selection and an abundant kibble supply.

Have plenty of other people do food-bowl exercises to get a more generalized no-guarding response in the puppy. This type of exercise builds the dog's confidence. Any kind of resource guarding stems from insecurity and paranoia. The dog operates under the assumption that someone approaching his soggy raw-hide or bowlful of kibble is a major life-or-death deal. You are teaching him that it's no big deal - pleasant even. If you are working with an existing problem rather than doing prevention on a puppy or non-guarding adult, you must proceed more slowly and carefully. A prerequisite to working on an existing guarder is that the dog have a soft mouth; this may have to be installed first, if it is not present. Do plenty of bite-inhibition exercises like hand-feeding, ending tug-games with exaggerated squeals of pain whenever the dog makes accidental contact (however light), tooth-brushing and general hands in the mouth with lots of feedback on jaw pressure. (For food-bowl exercises on adult dogs who are already possessive, wear heavy gloves or put a groomer's muzzle on the dog until you're absolutely sure about his mouth.) A good starting point is to design a hierarchy of levels of difficulty. Here's one possible set of exercises for a hypothetical food-guarding dog:

1) approach empty bowl and dog, put a small handful of food in, retreat and repeat ten times
2) approach empty bowl and dog, remove bowl, put handful of food in, put bowl back down, retreat and repeat ten times
3) sit next to bowl and dog; keeping one hand on bowl, feed meal in handful installments using other hand
4) sit next to dog and bowl with one hand still on bowl, stroking and talking to dog while dog eats normal ration, occasionally adding a tasty bonus to bowl with other hand
5) sit next to bowl while dog eating kibble, remove hand from bowl to add tasty bonus to bowl
6) approach dog and bowl while dog eating, add bonus to bowl, retreat and repeat ten times
7) approach dog and bowl while dog eating, remove bowl, add bonus, replace bowl, retreat and repeat ten times
8) start at #1 with another person

If, at a given step, the dog demonstrates any guarding (including growling, stiffness, freezing up), back off to an easier exercise and proceed more gradually to the problem exercise. If the dog, for instance, is fine on exercises 1 - 5 but growls if you approach while he is actually eating (#6), insert the following steps:

5a) do a few more reps of #s 1 & 2 to prime the dog
5b) approach to a certain distance, say 3 feet, while the dog is eating and lob the chicken or liver at the dish, retreat and repeat, gradually closing the distance until you are able to touch the bowl
5c) wait until he's only just finished and is licking the bowl before approaching with "dessert."

Now try #6 again. The dog may also fall apart at #5 itself, where you first take your hand off the bowl. From the dog's perspective, this is very different from the previous exercises, where you kept one hand on the bowl at all times. That was sharing. By taking your hand off, you are relinquishing possession. You may need to gradually fade your hand off the bowl if the dog starts guarding when you try exercise #5. Do whatever it takes to get successful trials, so you can prove to the dog that you are not a threat and that he can relax. If you really get stumped at any point, lack confidence with this sort of thing, or if your dog is an explosive guarder or dangerous biter, get yourself into the hands of a qualified trainer or behaviorist.

Object Exchanges

Object guarders typically guard bones, valued chew toys and forbidden objects such as bones, plastic wrap, Kleenexes, stolen laundry items and garbage on the ground. With some of these dogs, there is a compulsive quality to their guarding; it resembles a wired-in reflex. Others seem triggered not just by the fact that they think the hamburger wrapper is so valuable but by the fact that you are treating it as though it is an extremely valuable artifact by demonstrating such heated interest in taking it away. This, I realize, is a catch-22 for the owner. Either ignore the dog and allow him to pick up and even ingest all manner of junk he finds on the ground or else increase the value of the item by showing great interest in taking it away from him. The ultimate solution for all object guarders lies in priming and rehearsing the problem scenarios in advance. The dog needs to have done zillions of object exchange exercises in preparation for the Big Day when he gets something truly dangerous which you have to remove from his mouth pronto. If he's relaxed and confident, he'll relinquish. If he's tense and insecure, he won't. You are one step ahead of the game if you start practising on your puppy. And, just like socialization, the younger you start the better.

The basic object exchange exercise goes like this:
1) give the dog an object (in early training this will be an object he is unlikely to guard, later you will progress to "hot" objects)
2) say "give" or "thank you"
3) take the object away
4) give a nice treat from your pocket
5) give the object back and repeat.

Do five or so in a row and then walk away. Try to do a few "sets" of five repetitions a day, varying the object each time so the trend emerges: when humans take things away, it is a Very Good Thing for

Dogs (VGTD). When some history of successful exchanges is in place (several days worth of a few sets per day), you may also start to practise taking away chew toys the puppy has spontaneously taken possession of. Do a set of five and then let him carry on chewing. Always be aware of the value of the item you are taking away. For "hot" (highly valued by the dog) objects, increase accordingly the value of the surprise treat he gets in exchange. You may reserve special treats, like a morsel of leftover turkey or chunk of old cheddar cheese, for exchanges with the trickiest objects. These rare rewards really make an impression. Here's a typical hierarchy:

1) set up exchanges with objects of no interest (several sets of five a day for 2 days)
2) set up exchanges with slightly more coveted objects (several sets of five a day for 2 days)
3) set up exchanges with hot objects, using extra special treats (several sets of five a day for 2-3 days)
4) exchanges with objects the dog spontaneously has taken possession of (do several in a row, then leave dog with it unless it is a forbidden object: then, give an extra special reward on the last trial and replace object with a chew-toy)
5) exchanges with hot objects the dog spontaneously has taken possession of (do several in a row for extra-special rewards, then return object to dog or replace with interesting chew-toy)
6) maintenance: occasional "cold trials" when dog has an object (one rewarded rep, then give toy back or replace forbidden object with chew-toy)

Proceed to the next exercise in the hierarchy only when the dog is good at the exercise you are currently working on. For the duration of working this hierarchy, it is helpful if the dog is never given access to anything which is above the level you are training. This sets you both up for a guaranteed failure. For example, if the dog is on step 4, keep "hot" objects out of reach until you are ready to start step 5. You can't run until you can crawl and walk. For exercise #5, you may have to deliberately leave around a hot object, so the dog will "spontaneously" take possession. It is much better to have rehearsed in advance the Kleenex or grease-covered plastic wrap-guarding drama than to have it sprung on you when you aren't ready.

Sufficient repetition of object exchange exercises results in a dog who is actually eager for you to take stuff away from him. Aside from the reinforcement of the food reward, the dog is getting a key bit of information: when humans take things away, they very often give them back. It is therefore No Big Deal. This is pretty unheard of in dog culture. When the dog is relaxed about exchanges, be sure to test the system with the occasional cold trial. Walk up to the dog while he's in mid-chew, take his toy away, pop him a surprise reward and then let him carry on. Like any behavior, relaxed relinquishing may drift if it's not maintained.

In dogs with existing guarding problems, proceed with great care, softening up the mouth if necessary ahead of time and using protective gear such as gloves, padding or muzzles. Under no circumstances should children do any of this. If there are kids in the house, they will need to practise with the dog but if and only if:

1) the dog likes the kids
2) the dog has a well-installed soft mouth or is muzzled for all exercises
3) all adult members of the household have successfully completed the entire hierarchy already
4) the exercises done by the kids are supervised by an adult every second.

This holds for all desensitization exercises (food bowl, location guarding and handleability), not just object guarding. Be aware that, if your dog is an object guarder and you get and keep it at bay with these exercises but don't have kids at home, your dog is still at very high risk to guard against kids. Dogs don't generalize very well. In fact, even if your dog has never guarded against you, there's a reasonable chance he will guard against strangers, especially kids, particularly if he is not beautifully socialized to kids. If you're a laissez-faire kind of dog owner, get your head out of the sand before your dog bites a visiting child. Owning a dog is a huge responsibility, both to the dog and to the public at large. Above all, start practising when the dog is young. With puppies, you can practise this exercise with all manner of objects, including the supper dish, bones, coveted chew toys and the ubiquitous Kleenex. Make it a game.

An extremely cunning move in the anti-object-guarding war is to teach your dog to retrieve. Aside from being an efficient exercise and predatory energy burner, using guarded objects as retrieve toys is a potent counterconditioning monkey wrench you can throw into the object guarding machinery. Simply playing with the dog with these "hot" items can be an enormous tension reducer for both dog and handler. Play your hand very carefully the first few times you try this. The dog should first of all have an enthusiastic, well-conditioned retrieve of non-guarded items. The first time you try using guarded objects in retrieve games, whatever you do, stay glued to your chair, so you don't slip into the usual rut of chasing the dog and demonstrating hot interest in the item itself. Play very casual and hard to get, just as you would for the dog's usual retrieval toy. Use safe items, so you can relax and train. Encourage the dog to come up with rewardable retrieves. Set lower standards if necessary. Be prepared, for instance, to click and reward evidence of turning towards you or any steps back in your direction once he's got hold of the object. Celebrate each step with enthusiastic cheering and extra large, extra nice food rewards. Then gradually crank up the standard as he gets better. It is perfectly reasonable to expect, with sufficient practice, your previously rabid object guarder to happily fetch and drop in your lap items which used to be hot. That's confidence.

Placement Commands

The classic location guarder is a dog who jumps on the bed and then won't let you in. Or, the dog who stakes out the sofa and growls or snaps when you order him off or ask him to move over. The antidote is to teach what are called placement commands. You condition the dog, with positive reinforcement, to move his body to or from wherever you indicate. Ideally, you do this before you have a problem. That's because it is predictable that a certain percentage of dogs will, one day, actively location guard. As well, it's handy to be able to easily move the dog around without a lot of pushing and pulling. Typical placement commands include: "into the crate," "off the bed," "into the car," "off the sofa," "out of the kitchen," "onto the grooming table" etc. You simply make it another clicker-training exercise, a game. First, give the command and then prompt the behavior. Any kind of coaching goes, including, if you bog down, food lures. When the dog performs smoothly, you fade the prompt as you would for any obedience exercise.

For example, practise "off the sofa" as follows. First, ask the dog onto the sofa. You need some fluency at getting him on so that you can have plenty of opportunities to practise getting him off. After you say, "onto the sofa," pat the cushion and make encouraging sounds ("c'mon, c'mon" + enticing kissy sounds is a nice prompt). When the dog jumps on, praise him and mess up his hair a bit ("clevvvvver boy!!" + pat-pat-pat-ruffle). Reserve the heavier artillery, the food rewards, for the hard part, getting him off. Now order him off and start prompting him down. ("Off the sofa," pat the floor, snap fingers, clap hands, make kissy noises to get him to move off.) If he moves off, give him a click and a treat, and order him back up for an encore. You also may want to order him on and tell him to lie down to better simulate the eventual real-life scenario. If he doesn't move off, crank up the prompt a bit: try backing away from the sofa, making the best lovey-dovey sounds you can. As a last resort you will manufacture the rewardable response with a food lure. If you had to go to a food lure to get him off, do this a couple more times, and then put the food into your pocket for the remainder of the session.

Do a couple of sessions and then practise cold trials. Cold trials are once-only repetitions of an exercise, preferably sprung on the dog when he is not expecting it, to test response to command in real life. You will get the best mileage out of cold trials if you vary the reward. This is quite a natural thing to do because a lot of the most potent rewards are not easily re-usable within formal training sessions. A good example of this is walks. Unlike food rewards and tug-retrieve games which can be repeated again and again within a training session, the potent, reinforcing event is the initiation of the "taking the dog for a walk" ritual. Because this happens, at most, a few times scattered throughout the day, try to exploit its value as a reinforcer by preceding it with an "off the couch" placement. It is the perfect cold-trial reward. Wait until the dog is dug in on the couch before doing your cold trial. The sequence is: 1) "off the couch" command, 2) dog complies, 3) click and "want to go for a walk?" and 4) initiate walk.

It is critically important that, if the dog does not comply with the command, that you do not bribe him off by using the promised walk as a prompt. Saying "want to go for a walk?" after he vacates the couch and then taking him for one is worlds away from offering the walk while he is still dug in, having not complied with the placement command. The offering of the walk is a reward for his compliance rather than an enticement. Unlike food rewards, one-trial style rewards like walks don't do well in the dual role of prompts the way food rewards do. Dogs tend to learn to hang tough for the bribe, in this case, the promised walk, before budging. So, once the dog is primed up in initial training sessions with command-prompt-response-reward trials and then command-response-reward trials with the recyclable rewards, don't use lures of any kind: he must keep his part of the bargain on faith, before you keep yours. Your eventual goal, remember, is a variable schedule of reinforcement. He won't always be getting a walk after his compliance. He may only get his hair messed up. He must become a gambler.

If the dog location-guards against one specific person, that person must do some of the placement command work. If it is a child or someone who lacks confidence around the dog, make sure the dog has a soft mouth and institute the standard precautions (gloves, padding, muzzles, supervision). If the problem is really severe, especially if there are kids in the picture, engage a competent behaviorist or trainer. I would also stress again the enormous value of doing placement-command exercises with puppies, before a problem develops. Teach on and off the bed sequences, in and out of the car and in and out of the crate. Dogs who are raised to be happily compliant are at far less risk for aggression directed at family members.

Handleability
In their lives, dogs will have to be handled for a multitude of reasons, including vet exams, being groomed, held down or otherwise physically restrained and being hugged, grabbed and patted by a wide

demographic sampling of humans. Good relaxed tolerance of handling does not come naturally for most dogs. One of the best favors you can do your dog is to teach him, while he's still a malleable little puppy, to happily accept all the handling he will have to put up with during his lifetime. You yourself, your friends, family and puppy classmates can all simulate the main handling situations and pair the puppy's relaxed acceptance with food and play rewards.

Start with grooming and basic physical exams. A good first exercise is to lay out all the grooming tools (brush, comb, tooth brush, toothpaste, nail clippers, scissors and any other equipment), let the dog come over and investigate these items and, as he does, click the clicker and give him an above average reward to make a good first impression. Then, practise holding the dog still and, with your hands, examining all his body parts, giving a small treat after each part. Look in one ear, treat. Look in the other ear, treat. Run fingers over gums, treat. Practise gently opening his mouth and putting a finger on his tongue. If he tolerates this, depress the tongue a little more firmly each time, then give a treat. If he struggles, back off and do something less intrusive. Keep the treats coming furiously so that his participation is voluntary. When he does not comply, simply say "too bad!" and withhold the reward. Feel his windpipe, treat. Go down each leg, between the toes and apply pressure to each nail. Treat after each nail. Many dogs dislike having their feet handled, but this is inevitably the result of having nail-clipping forced on them rather than being allowed to gradually tolerate and enjoy grooming by early association with rewards. Palpate the dog's belly and feel all the way down the tail. Each time you do a doctor session, do a little more examining for each treat. The final routine consists of an entire once-over for one treat or play reward. Dogs can learn to love being handled and massaged.

Play doctor with the dog often and also practise grooming. Early on in your dog's grooming career, the ratio of rewards to procedures will be high. One brush stroke, one treat. Then two brush strokes, one treat. Then four and so on. You will have, in a few short sessions, a dog who you can brush deeply from head to toe for one small treat at the end. When the dog is comfortable about having his feet and nails touched in the vet-exam simulations, start touching his nails with the nail clippers. One touch, one treat. Do this until he is very relaxed. Then, do two or more touches for one treat. Then hold the toe in one hand while you pretend to cut his nail with the nail clippers in the other hand. At this point, the nail clippers are not making contact with his nail, just with the air, but he is experiencing the restraint and sound of the clippers. Give one treat per nail until he is quite relaxed. If you own a high-energy dog, you may want to practise this initially when the dog is already in a relaxed mood. When the dog happily lets you "air-clip" all his nails for one treat, try a real clip. Take off very little so you don't risk hitting the quick, which is very sensitive. The goal is not to get the nails clipped but to set the dog up for a lifetime of easy nail clipping, so be patient. One tiny clip, one big treat. At the end of the session, have a short play period. In the early days, it's a good idea to have grooming sessions be a reliable predictor of things high up on the dog's reward hierarchy, like predatory game sessions, walks, command-training sessions or meals.

If, at any point in grooming and vet-exam training sessions the dog is reluctant or skittish, slow down and desensitize the anxiety-producing procedure more carefully. Dogs are often anxious about people looking in their ears, handling their feet and mouths, and pulling their coats (as when mats are removed). Invest time making the puppy comfortable about all these procedures. It's well worth it. When the puppy is highly groomable and easily examined, we call them "wet spaghetti" types because they are so relaxed and pliable.

Other things to practise are: grabbing the dog, patting, hugging and looming over him in scary ways. Make a game of these. Start off with slow, gentle grabs. One grab followed by one treat. Then grab faster, then faster and rougher, culminating in emergency grabs and wrestling holds, treating after each successful trial. Do things to the dog that you would expect a two-year old-child to do. Grab an ear and pull. Give a treat. Grab the tail and pull. Give a treat. Particularly challenging are skin grabs: do plenty with a high density of food rewards. Pat the dog the way children do: PAT PAT PAT. Loom over the dog like a monster and then give him a treat. Pretend he has a broken leg: lift him into the car. Your imagination is the limit. What might people do to your dog in his lifetime? When the dog is relaxed and enjoying every minute of these games, recruit strangers and kids to do them, under your close supervision. Let the kids give better rewards than you normally give the dog, so they can make a favorable impression.

It's worthwhile, if your dog will be regularly handled by a groomer, to visit the groomer a couple of times before the dog has to stay to be groomed. (Get the green light from your vet that your puppy is adequately immunized before taking him to dog-intensive areas, like groomers.) Bring him in, put him on the table and have the groomer feed him a bunch of treats or take a few minutes to play tug or fetch with the dog in the grooming room. Practise in and out of the cage placements. Let the dog explore a bit. Then go home. You can make similar visits to the vet's, just visits for fun to make a good, strong, positive imprint. Needless to say, it's a good idea to find vets and groomers who are gentle and willing to take a little time to hand-feed your puppy. And, last but not least, find a good puppy class and enroll.

If you have an existing problem with handleability, you will do the same exercises, focusing on the particular problem, but you will:

1) proceed more slowly and gradually
2) soften up the mouth if necessary
3) use protection like gloves, padding & muzzles
4) avoid presenting the problem situation at levels the dog hasn't yet achieved
5) if the problem is severe, get yourself into the hands of a qualified trainer or behaviorist

Rehab of Fearful and Aggressive Dogs

Aggression is like any other behavior: it can be elicited, and it is often driven by its consequences. Examples of likely aggression elicitors are: initiation of something painful, proximity of something the dog is afraid of, approach when the dog is in possession of some resource, any rapidly retreating object. A dog chasing and/or biting a squirrel, ball or squealing child you now know is predation (food acquisition behavior) which, although topographically resembling aggression in that it involves attacking and biting, is a whole other kettle of fish than the topic of this chapter: defensive aggression. If you think about it, there are only two kinds of aggressive behavior that would ever be selected for: food acquisition and personal survival issues. The rest would be a waste of any organism's valuable energy.

I include in the personal-survival category all conflict resolution. Inter-male battles over breeding rights and other resource-related conflicts (squabbles among lions at the carcass, territorial defense, Kleenex guarding in domestic dogs) are best seen, when thinking of integrating domestic dogs into human environments, as personal survival issues (or maximizing progeny issues, which is what personal survival is all about anyway) rather than through the lens of labels like "dominance," "territoriality" or some real or imagined breed or individual related predisposition.

It might be perfectly true that some dog or other is behaving in a manner that could be described as "territorial" when he bites the mailman, that some breeds or individual dogs seem trickier with kids than others and that a dog not letting you into the bed is exerting some imagined rank over you. It's just that these labels have not yielded particularly useful models or approaches to modifying behavior. And, if ever there was normal dog behavior which desperately needed modifying, it's this sort of stuff. Models need to be judged on how useful they are, not on how intuitive they are. Many existing models and classifications of aggression have turned out to be overly complicated labeling systems, seemingly based on the "if you can't dazzle them with brilliance, baffle them with B.S." philosophy. Any model of aggression in pet dogs is only useful insofar as it points to effective, do-able treatment and prevention measures.

Aggression is also heavily influenced by its consequences. If threatening and biting have proven successful at keeping scary people at a distance in the past, you can bet money that this strategy will be used again by the dog in the future. Let's say your dog finds the mailman spooky and, on a daily basis, barks, growls and carries on until the mailman is gone. Announcing that the dog is territorial doesn't yield any effective treatment, it invites a management-only approach: "oh, he's territorial, therefore make sure he doesn't get access to visitors." You now have the same problem with a label.

Announcing that the dog is uncomfortable with the mailman and succeeds in apparently making him flee every day by displaying ("BARKBARKBARKBARK!! Whew! See how good it works!?") opens up a lot of intervention doors. You can ask the mailman in for tea and cookies a couple of times so he can flip cheese cubes to the dog and hand-feed pieces of oatmeal cookie from his plate. You can get someone to dress up like a mailman and do a troubleshooting session or two, in which the "mailman," after each arrival, holds his ground until the dog quiets on command. This will take some time the first few trials. The dog's eventual silence gets a food reward as well as getting the "mailman" to flee. You can reward-train the dog to do some other behavior every day when the mailman comes. Make the mailman's arrival the cue for the dog to run into the kitchen and sit-pretty near the dog cookie jar. Teach the dog to hold a down-stay in the hall until you tell him to fetch the mail for a reward. Change what the scene predicts for the dog.

Similarly, if the dog is a location guarder, it's a little late to agonize about some genetic predisposition or second-guess your breed choice. Your dog is growling at you. The most fruitful course of action is to build up the dog's confidence about being approached when he's dug in and to practise placement commands. And, perhaps most tragically, a dog who is timid, growly or "reserved" around strangers is not "selective," "loyal" or "a good guard dog." He is undersocialized, period. Undersocialized dogs are not only dangerous but under chronic stress. They see innocuous things, like visitors to your home, as threatening. That's not a fun way to be. There are health implications for dogs that are under chronic stress.

Bite Threshold Model

One model of aggression in domestic dogs which opens up effective treatment and prevention strategies is the bite-threshold model. All dogs have a threshold at which they will bite. This kind of breaking point also exists for you and me. There is a level of provocation at which you or I will blow and behave aggressively, probably by way of an angry and abusive tirade of words. There is probably also the point at which you or I would get physical, even though we have been instructed otherwise all of our lives and are aware that it is against the law. There may be the odd person for whom nothing, including things like babies held at knife point or personal physical assault would ever make them use physical force, but these people are the extreme minority. There are definitely people who seem never to get angry and who often end up with problems like depression or psychosomatic illness instead. The point is, absolute passivity is not the yardstick we use to describe "normal" human behavior. There are no doubt dogs for whom no amount of abuse would make them defend themselves, but these are not normal animals. The Walt Disney ideal, however, would have us believe that absolute pacifism is the norm for dogs with the exception of extreme provocation or some "defence of master" scenario. Announcing that nice dogs don't bite and vicious dogs do is like saying that nice people never argue or get angry and vicious people do.

Real dogs have a bite threshold. They also have thresholds for other levels of threat, such as growling, snarling (displaying their teeth) and snapping (biting the air). Dogs also have things which bug them, which we can call risk factors. Typical risk factors include: categories of people to whom the dog is not socialized, hands and/or being touched, approach, presence of food-bowl or other guarded resources and any discriminative stimulus for positive punishment (such as a choke collar or a strap used to beat the dog). Presentation of any one of these risk factors by itself may elicit threat or biting depending on how heavy a stimulus it is and where that individual dog's particular thresholds lie. Combinations of more than one risk factor at the same time usually evoke a higher level of threat. This is the usual reason dogs bite "without provocation" or "for no reason" when they had never behaved aggressively before. Some novel combination of elements pushes the dog higher than the elements on their own have ever pushed him previously. For any dog, a tentative profile can be built using the existing history.

For instance, hypothetical dog Zaphod has always been uncomfortable around strange men. His other major risk factor is that he freezes up on approaches to his food bowl. The owner has also noticed that he seems just a little bit more sensitive at night than during the day and not perfectly relaxed with hands or when approached. These last two, by the way, are in the profiles, to some

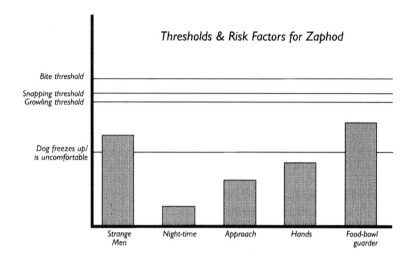

extent, of most dogs. One day, Zaphod bites a man who approaches to pat him. The owner is completely floored as Zaphod has never bitten or even growled at anyone before, and there was no provocation on this occasion, from the owner's perspective. As can be seen from his profile, however, Zaphod was a time-bomb which, unfortunately, went off. There is often a "suddenly and without warning" quality to dogs whose growl, snap and bite thresholds are

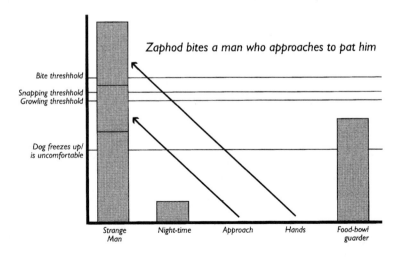

sandwiched close together like Zaphod's are. A stimulus which would evoke growling will also make it up to the bite threshold in these dogs. To say there were never any warnings is false, however. The warnings were always there in the form of his being uncomfortable about all those things. His owner simply bought into the "nice dogs don't bite" myth. Zaphod would probably also have bitten any strange man who went near him while he was eating. He is still, by the way, a nice dog.

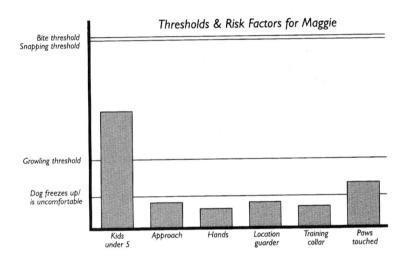

Another dog, Maggie, growls at children but has never, ever made contact. She is uncomfortable about having her nails clipped and has numerous other predictable minor bugs in her profile. What is insidious in this case is that her owner is convinced that Maggie would "never bite." After all, when a child approached her in her bed one day she still "only" growled. As you can see from her profile, it wouldn't take much more to push her into inflicting an actual bite. And, if she has a hard mouth, any bite would add to the child disfigurement statistics. But the owner was sure her dog would "never bite" unless severely provoked. For Maggie, the items in her profile are provocation. Note that she probably would never be observed to snap as her snap and bite thresholds are very tight. It

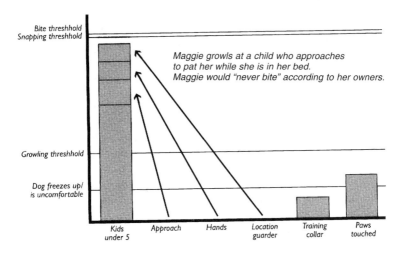

could very well be, by the way, that some individual dog has one or other of these thresholds omitted in his or her profile. Not all dogs give protracted warning before biting. The profile for Maggie would be as functionally useful if there were no line for snapping at all. It's a model, remember.

To treat dogs who behave aggressively, all the risk factors must be teased out and worked on separately and safely. Each bar in the graph of Zaphod and Maggie must be made as low as possible so that, even if many are stacked up, they don't get up to the bite threshold. This means remedial socialization, resource-guarding, approach and handling exercises. What the dog missed out on as a puppy has to be installed now. The dog must also learn to inhibit his bite, if a soft mouth is also missing. This is slow, painstaking work but definitely can be done in most cases. The moral of the story is to prevent all this by actively intervening with young puppies before these problems develop.

Prognosis

When dealing with adult biters there are three options. You can treat the problem, manage the problem or execute the dog. I say execute rather than euthanize because a biting dog is not suffering and does not need or want a merciful death. He is killed because of transgressions he has committed against humans. That's what an execution is for. The tragic part is that the dog, in most cases, is behaving normally, for a dog. Socialization and anti-aggression exercises were simply either omitted or insufficient.

Management refers to physically preventing the problem. If the dog is not socialized to kids, the dog is kept away from kids for the rest of his life. If the dog is a food-bowl guarder, the family stays away from the dog while he's eating. If the dog bites when his nails are clipped, he's muzzled and held down by two people whenever his nails are clipped. No attempt is made to get the dog over the problem. Sometimes, management is the best option. Some dogs, especially those with a narrow enough problem, can live a full, normal life and be successfully kept away from their triggers by astute, caring owners.

Treatment refers to efforts to change the dog's behavior, usually by tackling the underlying attitudes and insecurities. In any treatment program, for dogs who behave either aggressively or fearfully, management for the duration of treatment is always necessary. It wrecks any desensitization program to confront the dog with something he can't handle. The dog ends up with another rehearsal of his old, unwanted, insecure, paranoid, aggressive behavior rather than a chance to succeed. If, for instance, the dog is afraid of men with beards but has been desensitized to the point where he will approach and take a food treat if the man is sitting still, it is counterproductive for some bearded man to walk up and try to pat the dog. The dog will eventually get to that stage with careful training, but is not there yet. Better management would consist of the owner keeping bearded men from approaching until the dog is up to that point in the program. Prognosis is usually better the younger the dog and the softer the dog's mouth. Young dogs are more malleable, and dogs with softer mouths are, obviously, less risky to work with.

A lot of dog owners find they haven't the patience or inclination to put this amount of effort into a dog who bites. Hence the popularity of sending dogs to "the country" or "a farm," a popular management variation. This is the way out chosen by owners who don't know how or can't be bothered to treat but feel too guilty to execute their pet. This attitude really sours me towards people. The dog has been failed twice. Once by humans who didn't do any prevention exercises. And twice by humans who now won't clean up the mess they made by failing to do the prevention exercises. This is a pretty startling lack of empathy from the same people whose bond is so largely based on their conviction that dogs are "just like them."

4. It's All Chew Toys to Them

Empathy 101

Imagine you live on a planet where the dominant species is far more intellectually sophisticated than human beings but often keeps humans as companion animals. They are called the Gorns. They communicate with each other via a complex combination of telepathy, eye movements and high-pitched squeaks, all completely unintelligible and unlearnable by humans, whose brains are prepared for verbal language acquisition only. What humans sometimes learn is the meaning of individual sounds by repeated association with things of relevance to them. The Gorns and humans bond strongly, but there are many Gorn rules which humans must try to assimilate with limited information and usually high stakes.

You are one of the lucky humans who lives with the Gorns in their dwelling. Many other humans are chained to small cabanas in the yard. They have become so socially starved that they cannot control their emotions when a Gorn goes near them. Because of this behavior, the Gorns agree that they could never be House-Humans. They are too excitable.

The dwelling you share with your Gorn family is filled with numerous water-filled porcelain bowls, complete with flushers. Every time you try to urinate in one, though, any nearby Gorn attacks you. You learn to only use the toilet when there are no Gorns present. Sometimes they come home and stuff your head down the toilet for no apparent reason. You hate this and start sucking up to the Gorns when they come home to try and stave this off, but they view this as increasing evidence of your guilt of some unknown act.

You are also punished for watching videos, reading certain books, talking to other human beings, eating pizza or cheesecake, writing letters. These are all considered behavior problems by the Gorns. To avoid going crazy, once again you wait until they are not around to try doing anything you wish to do. While they are around, you sit quietly, staring straight ahead. Because they witness this good behavior you are so obviously capable of, they attribute to "spite" the video watching and other transgressions which occur when you are alone. Obviously you resent being left alone, they figure. You are walked several times a day and left crossword puzzle books to do (you have never used them because you hate crosswords; the Gorns think you're ignoring them out of revenge).

Worst of all, you like them. They are, after all, often nice to you. But when you smile at them, they punish you, likewise for shaking hands. If you apologize, they punish you again. You have not seen another human since you were a small child. When you see one on the street you are curious, excited and sometimes afraid. You really don't know how to act. So, the Gorn you live with keeps you away from other humans. Your social skills never develop.

Finally, you are brought to "training" school. A large part of the training consists of having your air briefly cut off by a metal chain around your neck. They are sure you understand every squeak and telepathic communication they make because you sometimes seem to get it right. You are guessing and hate the training. You feel pretty stressed out a lot of the time. One day, you see a Gorn approaching with the training collar in hand. You have PMS, a sore neck, and you just don't feel up to the baffling coercion about to ensue. You tell them in your sternest voice to please leave you alone and go away. The Gorns are shocked by this unprovoked aggressive behavior. They thought you had a good temperament.

They put you in one of their vehicles and take you for a drive. You watch the attractive planetary landscape going by and wonder where you are going. The vehicle stops, and you are led into a building filled with the smell of human sweat and excrement. Humans are everywhere in small cages. Some are nervous, some depressed, most watch the goings on from their prisons. Your Gorns, with whom you have lived with your entire life, hand you over to strangers who drag you to a small room. You are terrified and yell for your Gorn family to help you. They turn and walk out the door of the building. You are held down and given a lethal injection. It is, after all, the humane way to do it.

Top Ten Behavior Problems
of Pet Humans on Planet Gorn

1) Smiling

2) Watching TV

3) Use of porcelain bowls filled with water as elimination sites

4) Listening to music other than Country & Western

5) Talking to other humans

6) Smoking

7) Tooth brushing

8) Eating anything but (nutritionally balanced) human chow

9) Shaking hands to greet

10) Sitting on chairs ("How can I get him to stop sitting on CHAIRS?!")

This nightmarish world is the one inhabited by many domestic dogs all the time. Virtually all natural dog behaviors - chewing, barking, rough play, chasing moving objects, eating any available food item within reach, jumping up and pawing to greet, settling minor disputes with threat displays, establishing contact with strange dogs, guarding resources, leaning into steady pressure against their chests or necks, urinating on porous surfaces like carpets, defending themselves from perceived threat - are considered by humans to be behavior problems. The rules which seem so obvious to us make absolutely no sense to dogs. They are not humans in dog suits.

If someone tried to punish out behaviors you knew were necessary for maintaining your well-being or earning a living, would you cease doing them altogether or would you try to figure out when it was safe to do them and when it wasn't safe? How would you feel about the punisher? What kind of credibility would he have? It is as inherently obvious to dogs that furniture, clothing and car interiors are good for chewing as it is inherently obvious to you that TV sets are good for watching. If I reprimand you for watching the TV, your most likely course of action is to simply watch TV when I'm not around. And you're large-brained, conscience-laden human.

We smart, moral beings do this kind of discriminating all the time. Take speeding on highways. A lot of people have had tickets. What's the actual effect of this hefty, perfectly timed punishment? An immediate suppression of the behavior: you slow down right after you get the ticket: you're angry and upset. But what happens over the next few hours, days and weeks? Most people start speeding again. And they will tell you that they fully understand that speeding is against the law, that it is potentially very dangerous and that they understand the penalty if they are caught. Those last four words are the key: if they are caught. What you typically get with punishment is finer discrimination: you get better at smelling out speed traps, at knowing where and when you can speed. It's very important to understand that this is not a moral failing, just the result that is obtained with punishment. We are subject to the laws of learning. Dogs are even more so, because they don't have the understanding of the behavior being wrong or potentially harmful as we do; in other words they never self-punish the way we do with guilt and self-recrimination. This doesn't make them morally inferior. It's just how they are. We take far too personally phenomena which are simply products of animal learning laws.

Similarly, burning your mouth on pizza makes you check the temperature of the pizza next time before digging in but doesn't stop you from ordering it again. This is because pizza tastes good, and you know this. An organism will always look for a way around the punishment to get to the reward, if there is one. Rewards drive behavior ultimately. Punishments are just obstacles to overcome on the way to the reward. Likewise, a dog will rarely find it "wrong" or quit cold turkey his habit of digging in the azaleas although he may learn it's dangerous to do so when you're there. What else could a flower bed possibly be for, to a dog? Whenever you punish, you're the cop giving out the speeding ticket to a not very sophisticated and amoral being who really wants and maybe even needs to speed. Oh, he'll stop for a while if the fine is hefty, but he'll sooner or later be back to speeding, and he'll be better at avoiding speed traps.

Division Of Matter In The Universe

HUMAN	DOG
Furniture	Chew Toy
Footwear	Chew Toy
Car	Rapidly Retreating Object
Car Interior	Chew Toy
Carpet	Toilet
Dog Food	Food
Hors D'oeuvres For Guests	Food
Kleenexes	Food
Cello	Chew Toy
Book	Chew Toy
Cat	Rapidly Retreating Object
Squirrel	Rapidly Retreating Object
Plastic Wrap On Ground	Food
Hi Fi Speakers	Chew Toy
Hi Fi Speakers	Toilet (Intact Male)
Eyeglasses	Chew Toy
Rock	Food (Labrador)

Housetraining

Housetraining is another classic example. Remember the Gorns? If one of them leapt out of the bathroom cupboard and yelled at you every time you sat on the toilet to defecate, it would still feel pretty obvious that toilets were the "right" place to go to the bathroom. You may, however, start checking the cupboards before going to make sure the attacker wasn't there. You would also be pretty reluctant to defecate in any other location if you-know-who was standing around. This isn't spite. It's eminently sensible.

Owners see dogs who "refuse" to eliminate on walks and then go on the carpet when the owner leaves the room to answer the phone as "getting back at them." It's got to be the goofiest misreading of dogs going. The dog has simply learned to go to the bathroom on an obvious toilet when the attacker is not present. He behaves obsequiously on the owner's return to try and turn off the punishment which inevitably occurs when the magic context cues (owner plus poop on rug) are present. It is clear from his terrified, submissive posture that the dog would dearly love to avoid that punishment if only he knew how. If someone punished you in a certain circumstance, you would beg for mercy too, regardless of whether you had any clue as to why they were about to punish you. It's borderline Orwellian what we do to dogs.

The reason owners are stymied by the housetraining process is that it is too inherently obvious to them that the indoors/outdoors discrimination is the name of the game. Dogs, on the other hand, although capable of making this discrimination, don't necessarily leap to that conclusion based on the information provided by the owner. Owners also assume that the dog can learn right-wrong when what he really learns is safe-dangerous. When a dog is learning how the world works, there are many different pieces of the puzzle to assimilate. Let's look at a typical housetraining effort: the first 12 urination attempts of Max, a newly adopted dog:

MAX'S BEHAVIOR	CONTEXT CLUES	RESULT TO MAX
Urinates in hall	Braided rug, owner absent	Bladder Relief
Urinates in living room	Thick carpet, owner present	Yelling, scruff-shake
Urinates in yard	Grass, owner present	Relief, praise, cookie
Urinates in living room	Thick carpet, owner present	Yelling, scruff-shake
Urinates in hall	Braided rug, owner present	Yelling, scruff-shake
Trip to yard, no urination	Grass, owner present	Taken back in
Urinates in yard	Grass, owner absent	Relief
Urinates in bedroom	Thick carpet, owner present	Yelling, scruff shake
Urinates in dining room	Under table, owner absent	Relief
Urinates in dining room	Rug in corner, owner present	Yelling, scruff-shake
Trip to yard, no urination	Grass, owner present	Taken back in
Urinates in basement	Sofa, owner absent	Relief

From the owner's perspective, there were only 3 mistakes: the first one in the hall, the one under the dining room table and the one in the basement. All the other attempts were caught and punished or occurred in the desired location, the yard. But what has the dog learned? It's possible that the dog is learning that all indoor locations are dangerous and that the grass is safe. It's equally possible that the dog is learning that bedrooms and living rooms are dangerous, dining rooms are dangerous if you're not under a table, and grass, sofas and basements are, so far, safe. *The one sure thing is that it is never dangerous when the owner is absent and dangerous almost half the time when the owner is present.* If you were the dog and had to play the odds, you might start holding on when the owner was with you, including in the yard, and then nipping down to the basement to pee in order to play it safe. Your hypothesis would be proven correct. It is always safe to go when you're alone.

What's missing from this housetraining example is *a solid history of rewarded trials in the desired location,* the yard. This not only removes ambiguity from early attempts, but also establishes both the owner's presence and the location as rewarding. Subsequent punishments will therefore have a narrower possible interpretation: the location must be unsafe. This solid foundation is usually missing. Owners start to assume learning after two or three correct trials, which is only a drop in the bucket.

To guarantee success in housetraining all that is required is for each and every performance by the dog be caught and given feedback. That's rule one. Rule two is that the owner needs and wants to be the good guy most of the time. To give feedback every time and be the good guy, you must arrange for elimination to occur outside. You must be present when the dog performs outside so you can supply the well-timed reward (praise and treat from pocket). You also need a way to prevent any mistakes indoors. Each and every instance of elimination which is prevented inside the house is one saved up for the right place - outside - another opportunity to condition outside elimination through reward and be the good guy at the same time. This is the major thrust of the housetraining. The minor addendum in housetraining is to catch mistakes indoors with well-timed interruptions.

Crate Training

To get an uninterrupted reward history, the dog has to be prevented from even attempting urinating in the house. This can be achieved using a dog crate and frequent trips outdoors at likely times. Most dogs will do their utmost to hold on and not eliminate if closely confined. This makes the crate a valuable tool. Reams of material exists on the subject of crate training. It's astounding that the concept is still resisted in the name of being humane. The alternative to crate training is a possible early punishment history that will not only stress the dog but may derail the whole process. People get the job done in other ways, but the wear and tear on the dog is considerable.

Before using a crate as a training tool, take the time to make a good first impression. Make it comfy with a nice crate pad or pillow and blanket, situate it in a high traffic area like the kitchen and whenever the dog isn't looking, drop a couple of treats at the back. Let the dog discover the Wonders at the Back of the Crate on his own. Feed him meals in there, always with the door open. Using heavy string, tie an attractive stuffed chew-toy to the rear inside so that the dog must lie in the crate in order to chew on it.

After a few days of this, start teaching the dog to enter and exit on command. Say "into bed" or "into the crate," throw in a treat, praise as the dog goes in and eats the treat and then order him out with the command of your choice. Encourage him to come out and when he does, praise him (no food treat for exiting). Repeat this a few times, and then change the order of events slightly: instead of throwing the treat into the crate after you say "into bed," wait for him to go in on his own before dropping in the treat. If the dog doesn't enter on command, simply wait. Do not command him a second time, and do not crack and throw the treat in. You can encourage him in with hand gestures, but even this is riskier than simply waiting. If he doesn't go in, end the training session without comment. Try another session in a little while, still withholding the reward until the dog goes in on his own. When he does (and they all do eventually so hang in there), give him a double or triple reward, do a few more rewarded reps and then end the session. Always leave the dog wanting more.

When the dog is going in and out on command, you are ready to try the first lock-in. Rent yourself a favorite video and stuff a couple of chew-toys with something extra-special. Set the crate up right next to your comfy movie chair, and just before you sit down to enjoy the movie, order the dog into the crate. When he goes in, give him the chew toys, close the crate door and start the movie. Leave a few times to get popcorn, a drink, but always come back within a minute or so. The first experience being locked in the crate must be an overwhelmingly easy and good one. Any noise, agitation or tantrum from the dog can either be ignored or reprimanded. At the end of the movie, if the dog is quiet and settled in the crate, simply open the door and order him out. Under no circumstances will you open the door to the crate if the dog is misbehaving, otherwise you are conditioning that behavior. If you do not like it, do not reward it. When you do open the door, don't gush and hug the dog. Make the exit an anticlimax. Behave very neutrally. All the good stuff should happen while he's IN the crate, behaving nicely. Once he's out, order him right back in for a food treat or two without closing the door before you finish your training/movie session. If he refuses to go in, do whatever it takes to get him in, reward him and get your in/out exercise polished up again.

Now spend a few days locking the dog in the crate when you're at home, going about your usual business. Ignore or reprimand any noise and provide interesting crate puzzles (i.e., chew toys) each time. When the dog is going in without fuss and no longer distress vocalizing, you may start leaving the house. Voila. Crate training.

There are dogs who are not inhibited by crates. They merrily urinate and defecate. They may have early histories of being caged for long periods, forcing them to eventually eliminate. They lose their cleanliness instinct. Sometimes it can be nursed back by keeping the crate and dog immaculate and getting them out often enough so they never get close to being full, and thus eliminating, in the crate. For dogs who continue to eliminate without reserve when closely confined, the crate is less valuable. The principles of housetraining are the same, however: arrange for a lot of right responses and reward each one. Interrupt wrong responses. For crate-impervious dogs, this means close supervision.

Develop the ability to distinguish and keep track of empty vs. full dog. Freedom in limited dog-proofed areas of the house can be granted at empty periods: in other words, you have just witnessed and rewarded the dog for doing both functions outdoors so you know you're safe for a short while. Full dog has two choices: 1) in his crate or 2) outside at the elimination area with his owner who has liver in pocket in case the dog guesses right and performs. You must time the reward perfectly.

Housetraining Procedure

1) *Establish a reward history* by taking the dog out to the same place at frequent intervals and rewarding with both praise and a food treat all elimination in that spot. The reward must be in your pocket so that you can give it within one second of his performance. Praise as he's going and reward immediately after. Use a reward the dog really, really likes. In order to reward immediately, you must be present: sending the dog into the yard through the back door while you watch from the window may result in a dog peeing or pooping in the yard, but there is no training effect without the immediate reward. You are setting the dog up to prefer going out of your presence: remember, you will later be reprimanding the dog for going inside, and you don't want him to associate that with you. The dozens of times he has been rewarded for going in front of you while outside will make your subsequent reprimand easier to interpret.

You may also reward the dog by taking him for a walk after he has eliminated in the toilet area. When he learns that the walk starts after he eliminates, he will tend to eliminate more quickly. Most people train this backwards: they walk the dog in hopes of getting him to eliminate and then end the walk, taking the dog directly home as soon as he's empty. The dog learns that eliminating ends walks and starts to delay going to the bathroom in order to extend the walk. This is not a plot by the dog, simply the laws of learning in action again. In my house, the rule is: empty dogs play Frisbee. The dogs like Frisbee and know the game doesn't start till they are empty, so they empty themselves with a fair amount of urgency. Most dog owners should learn to focus more on providing consequences than on trying to manipulate behavior with elicitors. More on consequences and elicitors later. Much more.

2) When the dog is empty (he has just done both outdoors in front of you and been rewarded), he may then and only then be loose in the house for 30 minutes or so in a dog-proofed area. If he is perfectly chew-trained, you may choose to give him the whole house. This is an academic point as most dogs who require housetraining are probably untrained in other areas like chewing as well. If it's a new dog or puppy, don't presume he's okay because he has not yet taken out the dining room set. Presume he will chew virtually anything at any time, so don't let him discover his love of oak or oriental rugs. If he occasionally produces an addendum (pees or poops again within half an hour of being completely emptied), don't take the chance of this happening: crate him for a couple of hours to get him to stretch and to prevent any accidents. Every accident inside is 1) one you weren't able to reward outside and 2) one you failed to catch inside which gets that habit rolling or 3) one you caught inside, but which might set you up as the bad guy, before your reward history has provided sufficient cushion for you to punish without screwing things up. Avoid mistakes indoors in early training at all costs.

3) Crate the dog except during supervised empty/free periods. Make the crate comfy and give him plenty to do in there in the form of chew-toy puzzles. If you must leave the dog alone for more than a few hours on a regular basis, you cannot in all conscience crate him. It's hard to advise here, given that someone with so little availability has gone and acquired an unhousetrained dog, a world-class stupid act, but here are the damage control measures, for what it's worth. The dog will have to be left in a dog-proofed room with a toilet area at the opposite end from the sleeping and eating area. The room should have a hard floor, like a kitchen floor and the toilet area should be something porous like a good thickness of newspaper or, even better, turf. All this will maximize the likelihood of the dog choosing the right place when he needs to go. It in no way guarantees this, with no feedback happening every time.

When you are home, you will do the rewarding as usual at the selected outdoor toilet location. Crating overnight is fine. I do recommend putting overnight crates in your bedroom. Sleeping en masse is very much a dog thing. If the dog wakes up early and whines, simply do not respond until two conditions have been met: 1) it's your rising time or later and 2) dog is quiet in the crate. Dogs learn quickly that there will be no action before a certain time (they estimate time very well) and that noise doesn't work. You may also reprimand noise-making although this will likely only stun the behavior temporarily: the extinction is what kills the whining. Be advised: a small reprimand functions as an attention reward. "Now, Fluffy, Mommy doesn't appreciate..." or worse, "shhh, re-laaaaaax" is a reward.

4) When a reward history is well established in the outdoor toilet area, you may now set the dog up to make mistakes indoors. Deciding whether you have sufficient reward history to risk some punishments is a judgment call. Usually an adequate reward history will be indicated by the fact that the dog will almost reflexively start eliminating as soon as he reaches the chosen site. Think in terms of a few days to a week or two, provided you have not been allowing mistakes to occur indoors during the same period. Sometimes, if you have been diligent with the reward part, the dog never even makes a boo-boo, and you're off Scott free. In many cases, though, although the dog now has a preference for the toilet area, alternative toilets, like the rugs, have not necessarily been ruled out yet. To rule them out cleanly and efficiently, you must catch the initiation of the act. If the dog has completely emptied his bladder or bowels by the time you interrupt him, it is far less clear. If you are two behaviors late, i.e. the dog pees on the carpet, walks away and sighs and then you reprimand, you have, you guessed it, reprimanded sighing. It is not inherently obvious to dogs that there is anything emotionally charged about urinating on carpets as opposed to sighing, so stop thinking it's obvious what you're mad about. If you wish to modify behavior, keep up with the flow of behavior change.

If the reward history was well executed, it will take between one and three reprimands indoors to finish the job. That is, if those are two or three in a row. If the dog sneaks one in which is not reprimanded, count on a more protracted struggle. This whole thing has nothing to do with dog stubbornness or other emotional content; it's a raw, unadulterated conditioning procedure. That goes for leg-lifting males, unhousetrainable breeds and any other classification you feel exempts your dog from the laws of learning. To condition an animal, all you need is a spinal cord and brain stem. Most dogs qualify. In leg-lifting males, the complicating factor is that there will be things which will likely elicit urination, like novelty, the scent of other dogs, any vertical surface etc. The procedure is the same, though: establish a reward history, prevent mistakes and finally, rule out wrong options. Once the dog has it down, reward outdoors occasionally. At this point, you may now consider sending the dog out rather than taking him out, as well as gradually extending his free periods in the house. Note: gradually.

Training Regressions

People are terribly mystified by any change in their dog's behavior and go on a lot with the "why? WHY?" as though there should never be any variability whatsoever in this living organism's behavior. Training regressions are a frequent occurrence and no big deal. It is so important to remember that behavior is always in flux, constantly subjected to whatever contingencies there are in the environment. In the case of behavior problems, there are three main reasons for behavior which seemed to be "fixed" to break down again:

1) Undertraining: the behavior was never that strong in the first place

2) Contingency change: the behavior extinguished or another one was trained by the owner or environment

3) Failure to generalize: this is Karen Pryor's "New Tank Syndrome"

These three reasons are really variations on the same theme, undertraining. It is extremely difficult in a real-life setting to reward enough trials to get the response strength most people expect. It is also hard to keep on top of changing circumstances to maintain training and get responses generalized across new contexts.

Remember the first 12 urination attempts of Max? He was headed for chronic inverse-housetraining. Let's say Max's next couple of dozen trials continue in similar fashion. Also, the door to the basement and bedrooms have been kept closed and Max is crated when the owners aren't home. This arrangement ends up with Max appearing to understand that he may only go in the yard. But how trained is Max? His safe options are now limited to the yard, which he has been consistently using. After a few weeks, the owners successfully leave Max alone for brief periods uncrated. One day, Max's owner happens to go out to water a plant in the garden when Max goes out in the morning. The owner's presence nearby inhibits Max from going in the yard, so he comes back in with a full bladder. The owner wasn't paying attention and goes about his business. When he leaves the room, Max urinates on the baby blanket, the only porous surface available. No one says otherwise, so Max assumes this is okay. A new habit is born.

This simple case of undertraining may have been interpreted by the owner as jealousy of the baby or any number of silly interpretations. This case, in fact, wouldn't qualify as a training regression at all because the dog was never trained. This phenomenon of a masked problem is at the root of a lot of punishment directed at dogs who supposedly "know" what they should do. People have a strong tendency to assume a very thorough knowledge on the part of the dog based on observations of some desired responses. The dog's understanding of contingencies is usually quite different from the owner's. What's the solution for Max then? 1) A solid history of rewarded trials in the desired location, 2) prevent mistakes until #1 is accomplished, 3) rule out mistakes with set-ups when #1 is accomplished and 4) maintain behavior with occasional reward. Be ever ready for regression if contingencies or contexts change. No magic potion. Housetrain the dog.

Contingency Change: Inadvertent New Rules

A contingency change might look like the following. The dog has learned that it's safe and often rewarding to urinate in the yard and dangerous in most places he has tried in the house, and so a fairly solid yard habit is in place. The owner has become upset about the yellowing of grass from dog urine and has decided to limit the dog to eliminating in one corner of the yard. The owner takes the dog on leash at elimination times for a couple of weeks, always going to one corner and praising the dog for urinating. The first couple of times the dog goes out off leash, she urinates in the wrong area. The owner punishes the dog. On the third day, the dog will not urinate in the yard. The owner sees this and takes the dog for a walk. The dog has a very full bladder and finally urinates and is praised by the owner. The owner likes the idea of the dog urinating on the walk rather than in the yard and starts taking the dog around the block to eliminate, which is successful and keeps the yard urine-free.

A few months later, the owner is in a rush to prepare for guests arriving so lets the dog into the yard to pee while finishing the cooking. The dog does not urinate in the yard and comes back in full. When the guests arrive, the owner puts the dog on leash to calm one of the visitors who is afraid of dogs. The dog urinates on the Persian rug. The owner thinks the dog sensed that one of the guests didn't like her and urinated to demonstrate her resentment. In fact, the dog has learned to urinate when on leash only, based on the new contingencies inadvertently set up by the owner. Dogs aren't into big agendas. They just need to know where and when it's safe to pee.

Elimination on Command

Dogs fail to generalize across every facet of dog training. In the case of housetraining, lapses will occur on visits to other people's houses simply because the dog has learned not to eliminate in the owner's house but has not generalized to all indoor locations. Location, surface and whoever is around are the cues dogs attend to the most when it comes to housetraining. Some dogs are sensitive to weather as well. The best way around this is to put elimination on cue. People who frequent dog shows have learned this trick because they must get dogs to eliminate in new locations and on odd surfaces on a daily basis. To teach this, first observe the dog for a few days to get a precise idea of when he does which function and, specifically, the intention behaviors which immediately precede elimination. Then start training as follows.

Just before the dog urinates, give a urination command, wait while the dog urinates and reward afterwards as usual. Do the same for defecation, using a different command. If the dog is thrown for a loop by your speaking just as he's about to pee, don't sweat it. Work to a nice sequence of command-behavior-reward. This is classical conditioning and will result, after enough trials, in a dog who will urinate or defecate on command. In early training, don't risk giving the cue unless you're sure he's about to go, because this results in a missed association. You need a sufficient number of trials under your belt before the cue will actually trigger any action. The key to this technique is recognizing the early signs of the dog's intention to eliminate, so that you can give the cue before the behavior. This technique also works without rewards. The best method is to selectively reward any eliminating that was preceded by the cue. When he goes without a command up front, simply thank him without giving a reward. This will strengthen on-cue elimination in preference to off-cue. Taken to the extreme, this could produce a dog who has a hard time eliminating without the cue, so watch out.

Dogs' underdeveloped ability to generalize can come in handy. For instance, dogs can be easily taught that it is okay to lie on this sofa and that chair but not the other sofa and the other chair. This makes "consistent" no-furniture-at-all rules unnecessary. I don't mean this as a value judgment in any way: if you don't want dogs on any furniture, that's fine too, provided you've provided a decent alternative, comfort-wise for a dog who demonstrates a preference for furniture (otherwise the dog will likely earn when it's safe to lie on the sofa: when you, the radar-trap, are gone). What I am saying is that it's not unfair or difficult for the dog to assimilate that some furniture is okay and some is not. Dogs discriminate tiny differences with great ease. In fact, they discriminate so well that it greatly complicates training in those instances where you want generalization. In all this, it's important to remember that the dog is not learning that he "should" or "shouldn't" do something or anything to do with right and wrong. He's learning about contingencies, i.e., what are the immediate results to him of doing this, that or the other thing. Repeat to yourself, as a mantra: dogs don't learn right vs. wrong; they learn safe vs. dangerous. This doesn't make dogs less sophisticated or valuable than if they moralized about it, either. It's simply how they are.

Non-static Nature of Behavior

People get very shirty about training regressions. Once the dog has demonstrated understanding of a rule or gotten into habit A, many people presume some deeply personal motivation must be at the root of a breakdown. The truth is that behavior falls apart all the time. Often you will never know why. This goes for carefully trained in behavior or behavior which seems under pretty tight environmental control. Professional figure skaters quite regularly fall on their butts without an inquisition into "why?!" being set up. Agonizing about whywhywhy a dog makes a boo-boo is interesting over coffee but doesn't solve the problem. Behavior is in constant flux. There is never a finished product. Retraining or touch-up training is part of the process. Experienced trainers understand this and take dips in stride. A useful tip is to not take long-established behavior for granted. Even nine-year-old dogs need to hear at least an occasional congratulatory mumble when they make wee-wee in exactly the right place yet again. My dog Lassie is becoming more of a world-class expert at wee-wee with each passing year.

Barking
Dogs bark for a variety of reasons.

1) Watchdog Barking serves the dual purpose of alerting other pack members that there is an intruder or change in the environment and warning the intruder that they have been noticed. Dogs bark much more than their ancestors, wolves, who hardly ever bark. In domesticating them, we have selected for more barking. The predisposition to watch-dog bark, or bark-threshold, varies among breeds and individuals. The modifying principles are the same, though, whether you're trying to coax a little more barking out of a couch-potato Newfoundland or tone down barking in a hair-trigger German Shepherd or Miniature Schnauzer.

2) Request Barking is the dog's way of communicating to the owner that he would like something NOW. It's a behavioral experiment by the dog, kind of a "let's see what this produces..." Typical requests include door-opening or yard-access services, attention, hand-outs from your plate, the owner's return from an absence, being let out of a crate or confinement area, invitations to play and access to the dog across the street. This behavior is a problem not because the dog tries out the experiment but because the experiment usually succeeds: the owner rewards the barking by granting the request, and a habit is born.

3) Spooky Barking occurs when the dog is fearful or uncomfortable about something in the environment and barks to help increase social distance. It's the dog's way of saying: "don't come any closer." This is much more serious than garden-variety watchdog barking because the dog in question is advertising that he is undersocialized and therefore, potentially dangerous if approached.

4) Boredom Barking can result when the dog's daily needs for exercise and social and mental stimulation aren't met. The dog barks compulsively because of boredom. This is very much like pacing back and forth, tail-chasing or self-mutilation. Dogs left outdoors in yards get into this one a lot.

Controlling Excessive Barking

The goal of any bark training is usually to limit the number of barks per sequence and sometimes to limit the number of contexts in which the dog erupts. Addressing the underlying issues of undersocialization and insufficient exercise and stimulation are also crucial. So, first identify what kind of barking you've got and refer to the instructions which follow.

Watchdog Barking The goal is to limit the number of barks per sequence by teaching the dog the meaning of the words "bark" and "quiet" (or any word you want to use as an "off" switch). First, you have to teach the dog to both bark and stop on command as a trick for a reward, like a treat. To elicit the barking so that you can practise, you must use something you know makes the dog bark, like the doorbell or a weird noise outside. You may require a helper for this. Arrange the following sequence of events:

1) your command "bark!"
2) the doorbell or other prompt (bark elicitor)
3) barking from the dog
4) praise from you: "good! wonderful!" after a few barks
5) your command "quiet"
6) show the dog the treat
7) the dog's (eventual) distraction from barking by the treat
8) 3 - 5 seconds of quiet during which you praise: "goooooooooood quiet!"
9) give him the treat after the 3 - 5 seconds of perfect quiet

10) do it again from (1) and gradually extend the length of
time of the "quiet" up to a minute or two

Do it over and over till the dog knows the game. It may take a few sessions, so hang in there. How do you judge whether he knows the game? He knows the game when he barks on the command and doesn't need the doorbell anymore, and he quiets on the first quiet command but without having to be shown the treat. You still give him one from your pocket or from the cupboard if he quiets on command, you just don't show it up front anymore. If he ever interrupts a quiet time with even a muffled bark or two, give him a no-reward mark such as "oh! too bad" and start counting the quiet time from the beginning again. He has to know that barking during the quiet time was a mistake that cost him his treat.

You have to acquire the ability to yo-yo the dog back and forth reliably between bark and quiet in training sessions before you try out your quiet command in real situations. Barking is deeply compulsive for many dogs, and you've got to build them up to actual visitor trials. The most common mistake is trying to use the quiet command before it's well enough conditioned in training sessions. Think of quiet on command as a muscle you're making stronger. The more practice, the stronger the muscle.

When you can turn barking on and off anytime, anyplace as a trick (you've conditioned a strong muscle in other words), you may now start practising the quiet command when the dog barks on his own in real-life situations. The first couple of times, the dog will respond poorly to the command, so you have to be ready. Have really good treats handy and go back to showing him the treat up front if necessary. Another option, although a tricky one, is to reprimand the failure to quiet. The best way to do this is, when the dog ignores your nicely conditioned quiet command, to flatten him with the growliest, loudest "I said, QUIET" you can muster. Even better, get every human present to simultaneously do this. When he quiets, become sweet again as though nothing untoward had happened: "goooo-ooood quiet." Practice makes perfect. Remember, quiet on command is a muscle that will get flabby if you don't train.

A good adjunct for fuel-injected, turbo-charged barkers is to teach them down-stay as well as quiet. To earn their treat, they must hold a

115

stay on a mat near the door and keep their mouths buttoned for the full duration of the quiet period. The hardest thing about bark training is how futile it seems the first couple of times you try, either in a training session or during your first real-life dry run. It's also the most interesting thing about this training because, no matter how bad it seems to go the first time or two, it gets better rapidly if you persevere. Many people never get over the hump. The best thing to do is thoroughly understand the instructions and simply practise with a Zen-like resolve, because this procedure works if you give it the critical mass of training.

If your dog has a very low threshold, "going off" for the smallest sounds and changes in the environment, it would help the cause to get him better habituated. Take him out more and invite the world in to visit more often. Expose him to a wider range of sights and sounds. It's not particularly fun to be on chronic yellow or red alert the way these dogs are. Examine your own behavior and make sure you are not inadvertently reinforcing the little tike by soothing (i.e., rewarding) him or giving him attention whenever he explodes into a barking frenzy.

Request Barking When they want something, dogs will experiment with various behaviors to see if any of them work. They quickly figure out that barking works with humans. If you don't like barking, stop rewarding it with attention, door-opening services, releasing from crates etc. Period. No buts.

Rather than the dog telling you when to take him out, take him out at regular intervals, always making sure that none of them are preceded by barking. Never let a barking dog out of a crate or confinement area. Always wait for a lull of 30 seconds or so. Ignore dogs who bark at you. Keep in mind that if you have been rewarding it for a while, the barking will get worse before it goes away. You're changing the rules, and the dog will be frustrated at first. The behavior going away is called "extinction," and the intensifying of the behavior before it goes away is called an "extinction burst."

We have extinction bursts all the time, too. When your demagnetized credit card doesn't function when the store clerk runs it through the machine, she doesn't give up immediately and start manually punching the number in. She runs the card through a few more times, usually each time more vigorously than the last, or else runs the card through at different speeds or even varies the pressure against different parts of the machine. The radical shift in behavioral strategy, in this case to tedious manual dialing and number punching, occurs after the card-running behavior extinguishes, with a typical extinction burst. All that vigorous swishing of your card and its variations was the extinction burst. Likewise, your dog will not immediately abandon barking as a strategy, not without a fight anyway. Like the store clerk who has a strong history of being rewarded with completed transactions by running cards through scanners, your dog has had a history of being rewarded by barking. He will lean a little harder before he switches behavioral strategies.

The quintessential extinction burst is found in the elevator vs. stairs analogy. When you step into an elevator and push the button for your floor, the button should light up, the door should close and the elevator should start moving. Your button-pushing behavior gets a nice, boring reward history. What happens, then, if the light doesn't go on, the door stays open and the elevator remains grounded? Do you immediately leap out and take the stairs? No. You push the button again. Harder. With rapid-fire bursts. With a battering ram if you have one on you. Then you take the stairs. So, when dogs escalate their crate whining or barking when you stop rewarding it, say to yourself "he's pushing the button harder before he switches to the stairs."

What makes this a bit more wrinkly is that, very often in real life, variations in intensity or delivery offered during the extinction burst are rewarded either deliberately or by chance and end up getting trained in. This is a tragedy of large proportions for dog owners. Rather than just having crate barking now, you might have crate screaming or crate barking with digging-in-corner. When you use extinction as a tool, be fully conscious and prepared to make Rover go cold turkey: wait for a strategy shift that you like, such as lying quietly, before rewarding with the approach and crate-door opening.

Above all, start noticing and paying attention to the dog when he's quiet, something we all forget to do. Failing to do so is using extinction, one of the most powerful tools in training, to get rid of our favorite behavior: dog lying quietly providing doggie ambiance. Dogs find out that a strategy shift to laundry-stealing or pawing guests - or barking - gets attention much more reliably. Teach your dog that there are pay-offs for lying quietly, chewing his own chew-toys and refraining from barking. Everyone could stand to cultivate a knee-jerk "gooooo-ooood quiet" reflex for those instances where the dog might have barked and didn't.

Barking when alone was discussed in alone-training. It can be thought of as a common form of request barking: the dog is requesting that you come back. To summarize how to get rid of it: Don't let the dog shadow you around so much when you're at home. Lock him in various rooms away from you to practise "semi-absences." Reprimand or ignore any barking which ensues (ignoring is actually the more powerful tool). If you try for the quick, temporary fix by reprimanding it, burst through the door, scold the dog and then immediately disappear again, closing the door behind you. Remember that he's barking to get you back: with some dogs, a reprimand is better than nothing, so you may be rewarding him.

Practice zillions of brief absences every day. Go out and come back in after a few seconds over and over to get the dog desensitized to your departures. Do it in a matter of fact way, ignoring the dog whatever he does. Then do outings of 10 seconds, 30, a minute, 10 minutes etc. Mix it up. Dogs need abundant proof that your departure doesn't predict a traumatically long period of isolation. Keep all your departures and arrivals low key. Never make an entrance when the dog is barking. Wait for a 30-second lull. Increase mental stimulation in the form of training and predatory games. Make him work for his food. Hide it around the house before you leave or stuff it into Kongs and hide those. Tire him out physically before long absences. Make him bring a toy to you when you come home to provide a focus for the nervous energy.

Another type of request barking which needs to be mentioned is talking back, i.e. the dog barking at you when you attempt to reprimand him. This barking is a combination of displacement of low-grade anxiety - you've interrupted something he really, really wants to be doing right now with your mildish punishment - and a "you and which army" experiment. It's vital that you make your point at this cusp. Remember that game where you and your buddy put your hands above each others' on the way up a baseball bat as a kind of oneupsmanship thing? When you reprimand the dog and he talks back, it is a similar minor escalation. You must not escalate only one more notch. You must escalate so suddenly and so far up into orbit that the dog will think twice about ever playing this game again. You're going to use punishment here, and of course, it will buy you what punishment always buys: a temporary suppression of the behavior. Into this temporary void opened by the punishment, you will actively install another, more likable behavior. Remember that the dog isn't learning that it was "wrong" to do what he was doing. He is learning that it is dangerous. So, make it clearly dangerous by really going into orbit. This means throwing an extremely intense, scary-looking tantrum in front of the dog. Go as berserk as you can, stopping short of touching the dog. Then, soon after you psychologically flatten the dog for talking back, set up the original scenario and reward an alternative behavior choice.

For example, if the dog was excavating a plant and starts barking at you when you try to reprimand him, go utterly ballistic, growling and screaming at the heavens, sending a book flying into the wall. Don't worry if you scare the dog: that is the point. He should seem very impressed, slinking around and/or sucking up. Wait a couple of minutes, then make up by asking him to come over and sit. After making up, allow him near the plant again and thank him for ignoring it. Or, better yet, direct him to one of his own toys or dissection objects. All this, of course, begs the question: what was the untrained dog doing in an area that's not dog-proofed. It will, of course, occasionally happen that a dog who seemed trained makes a boo-boo like that. If this is happening "all the time" however, basic chew-training needs to be addressed, whatever the age, breed or previous history of the dog is. This dog hasn't a clue and is behaving like, guess what, a dog. If you will remember from chapter 4, plants are chew toys.

Spooky Barking In this case, it is always important to get at the underlying undersocialization. Prevention is the easiest: socialize puppies extensively to as wide a variety of people and dogs as possible. You cannot overdo it. Expose them to plenty of places, experiences, sights and sounds, and make it all fun with praise, games and treats galore. Find and attend a reward-oriented puppy class. Socialization is covered in detail in chapter three.

If you missed the boat socializing the puppy, you'll have to do remedial work with the adolescent or adult. Whatever your dog is spooky about must now become associated with lunch. This is how undersocialized dogs work for their food. If he doesn't like strangers, meals need to be flipped to him and eventually hand-fed to him by strangers until he improves. If he's spooky about traffic, hand feed him his meals on the sidewalk, one handful each time a car passes. It takes a while to resocialize adults, so be patient. Above all, prevent problems by blitzing it with puppies.

Boredom Barking If you don't have time for a dog, don't get a dog. If you have an outside dog, do whatever housetraining, chewtraining and obedience training it takes to make him an inside dog. There are very few guarantees in behavior, but one is surely this: dogs chained out in yards self-condition to bark, dig and lunge. Boredom barking is just a symptom of gross understimulation. What's needed is a radical increase in interesting stuff in the dog's life. Increase training, walks, socialization and predatory games. Only when that is accomplished would you do a bark and quiet protocol as is described under watchdog barking.

Jumping Up

A classic culture clash example is greeting rituals: in most human cultures, we shake hands or bow. In dog culture, they buzz around excitedly, lick and sniff each other. The origin of jumping up is in infancy. Puppies will jump up to lick the corners of adult dogs' mouths which triggers the latter to regurgitate food that the puppies can eat. This jumping up and licking behavior is retained in adulthood as a submissive greeting. It's exaggerated when dogs live with humans because the social group is continually being fractured, then re-united: we leave and come back a lot, necessitating constant broad rituals. We're also vertical: the dog wants to get at our face. We also tend to let tiny puppies get away with it and then change the rules when they commit the crime of growing.

Jumping up isn't inevitable. The main reason dogs jump is that no one has taught them to do otherwise. I'm not talking about punishments like kneeing dogs, pinching their feet or cutting off their air with a strangle collar. This sort of abuse has been the prevailing "treatment" but is inefficient, laden with side-effects and inhumane. Imagine yourself being kneed in the diaphragm or pushed over backwards for smiling or extending your hand in friendship. It's not the fault of dogs that their cultural norm is at odds with our greeting preferences.

The key in training dogs not to jump up is to strongly reward train an alternative behavior which is mutually exclusive to jumping. It's called counterconditioning. The dog cannot jump up and sit at the same time. (Nor can he dig through walls while working on a chew toy, lie on a mat and food-solicit from dinner guests simultaneously, or chase cars while maintaining eye contact. The applications of this technique are limitless.) Counterconditioning can be used on its own or in conjunction with other techniques. Its use is virtually mandatory if you plan to use punishment. Punishment used on its own will get you that temporary suppression, if it works at all. Without an alternative behavior trained in to fill the void, you will sooner or later be back to square one. Think of the punishment as buying you time to get a more desired behavior trained in. That said, counterconditioning works marvelously without any punishment whatsoever, and you get to avoid all those nasty side-effects. I personally much prefer to be the good guy.

Counterconditioning comes up in child rearing, too. Rather than simply punishing toddlers for throwing Wedgwood off the coffee table and again for writing on the walls with magic markers and then once more for putting a pencil in the dog's ear, we give them things to occupy them and keep the Wedgwood out of reach till they're trustworthy. The message is "please color in your coloring book," "watch Sesame Street," or "play Nintendo" rather than a never-ending series of "don'ts." It is a given that children need something to pass their time or else they're going to get into trouble, and it's exactly the same with dogs. Dogs are also much more likely than kids to guess wrong about what are appropriate pastimes and ways to behave around humans because they are an even more foreign species than 2-year-old kids are. Which is saying something.

The behavior you choose as your competing behavior must be one that physically cannot occur at the same time. Do not, for instance, teach barking to countercondition food-soliciting; it will probably result in a dog who now food solicits with barks rather than drools and stares (teach down-stay on a mat away from the table instead). You often have to practise the new behavior up to a pretty reliable level in a couple of training sessions before trying to bring it into real-life context. In the case of jumping up, the dog should have at least a rudimentary sit and stay before attempting to use this as a countercondition to a strong compulsion like jumping up. So, first practise sit-stay for food-rewards in a variety of locations, especially those places where the jump-ups take place, such as the front door area and on the street. Details on how to teach commands are in chapter six. When the dog is an ace at sit-stay in low distraction, you will now teach him to not jump on you (and other family members) at high-risk times.

You will start by setting him up: open your arms wide, pat your thighs and do everything you can to make it look as though you want him to jump on you. Really ask for it. As soon as you get it, reject him totally with a No-Reward-Mark. This is simply a signal that tells the dog he guessed wrong and has zero chance of getting a reward for that behavior. ("AH!AH!" or "OH!TOO BAD!" and their other uses will be covered in detail in chapter five.) Quick timing helps. If you initiate your mark as soon as the front feet rise off the ground, it is infinitely clearer to the dog than if you start saying "AH!AH!" when he's taken his feet off the ground, lifted them one meter high and landed them on the front of your body. That's sluggish training. You may teach him eventually but it'll take you a lot more repetitions, and I mean a LOT. So, pay attention. After you quickly "mark" a couple of jump attempts, he will probably try something else on your invitation. A lot of dogs will simply sit. If he doesn't, you may suggest it. As soon as he does, praise very enthusiastically, pat him and give him a treat from your pocket. Then, do it again.

Practice until you can't get the dog to jump on you no matter what you do. At this point, your jump-up invitation is becoming an alternative command for sit. Neat, eh? Not only does this drive the point home to control the impulse to jump, but it prepares the dog for those unavoidable idiots who will sabotage your training by asking for or allowing your dog to jump up on them ("it's okay! I loooo-oooove dogs!") If one person in 10 allows or encourages your dog to jump, the behavior will remain alive, so prepare your dog for this actively with the anti-jump exercise.

Dogs learn remarkably quickly to not jump on you in the first training session. What they don't necessarily learn is to not jump on you tomorrow either, or when you're upstairs or when it's another person. This poor generalizing is characteristic of dog learning. Get used to it. Luckily the session is quick and each subsequent re-train even quicker so just buckle down and proceed to cover all the bases. The best way to do this is by using troubleshooting sessions.

Troubleshooting

Once the dog has had that bit of priming, arrange a simulated guest-greeting session with a few friends. Each one will ring the doorbell, come in and do the anti-jump exercise on the dog. As soon as they get a refusal to jump (sit), they reward the dog with a warm greeting and food from their pocket. If the dog lunges back up to "help" with the greeting or treat collection, they will give a no-reward mark ("AH!AH!") and cancel the reward till he's sitting again. All rewards of warmth and food must be collected in the sit position. Then the same person goes out the door and comes in again to repeat the exercise. Do 10 re-entries. With each successive trial, the dog's performance improves because of a) practice and b) decreased level of excitement ("oh, you again"). After a few trials, the dog sits without jumping and usually without being told to sit. Carry on through to re-entry number 10 anyway. Think of the new behavior as a muscle and the training as having a weight-lifting effect. The more repetitions, the stronger and more toned the muscle. Behaviorist extraordinaire Ian Dunbar suggests an actual party as a troubleshooting set-up, with repeated entries by guests made necessary by storing the beer outside. This provides a bonus in the form of socialization to humans at various degrees of intoxication!

After person #1 has done their 10 reps, the next person does the same thing. What you will find is that it is as though the dog had never experienced training and is off the wall jumping all over the novel person. Failure to generalize again. However, it will take fewer repetitions this time to achieve the final product of a sit-to-greet without any preliminary jumping. Go to 10 reps anyway. You're playing the same game the dog has perfected once. Then, do another 10 with the third person. By the time half a dozen people have done the exercise, the dog will probably be sitting without jumping and without command for novel people. You can't make it fall apart now. Or can you? Wait 24 or 48 hours and try again and you'll have another regression. This is an example of spontaneous recovery. The dog, throughout an individual troubleshooting session, habituates to the visitors' arrivals until sit-to-greet is achievable due to his lowered excitement level. The excitement and jumping up recovers in the interval between sessions. But that's part of the process. The learning rate in your second session will be accelerated. Now the dog takes one or two trials for person number one and by person three has "remembered" the game. You're seeing light at the end of the tunnel. The ideal way to do this is to train with three or four people to the level of a non-jumping instant sit, wait 48 hours and do another training session with fresh people. You may need a third or fourth session, but a lot of dogs become sit maniacs after only two blitzes. Then you can reward occasionally and schedule a brief refresher session if you get a regression. End of problem.

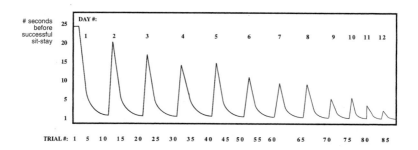

Counterconditioning Jumping Up On Visitors
by Rewarding Sit-Stay at Front Door

People may be overwhelmed at the thought of all that "work." Training is such an inherently fascinating endeavor that I have trouble relating to this. It's like saying it's so much work to eat a 12-course gourmet meal. I'm constantly puzzled by people who like dogs enough to buy one yet find it a chore to interact with one in the most interesting way: training. A troubleshooting session is fun and takes no time at all. Part of the problem with this, or any technique which does not bear instant fruit, is that the trainer fizzles out before the critical mass of trials is completed and says "oh, I tried that, and it didn't work." If you didn't get to critical mass, you didn't do troubleshooting. This technique works every time if you don't quit too soon. Then you can have a lifetime of coasting if you wish.

If you still find yourself underendowed with the energy to train, i.e. you don't care what this dog does as long as behaviors X, Y or Z are eliminated right now, you are probably stretched way too thin to do a decent job educating a dog. It is my overwhelming experience that owners who absolutely demand fast fixes to undesired behavior need to downgrade from organic to plush animals. Dogs are time-intensive and not for everybody. It is a huge privilege to own one, and we've got to start feeling some obligation to do right by them.

It's a turn-around experience for the trainer to get a success with a technique like troubleshooting. No matter how good it looks on paper (and this one looks very good on paper), the owner must experience for himself the initial bout of effort, some "this isn't working..." feelings and the final success at the end. It makes one a believer and a much keener trainer. Experienced trainers forget what it feels like to not know where a process is headed. Green trainers must train very much on faith.

Food Stealing

Dogs are programmed to be opportunistic: if it's edible and within reach, hell, eat it as fast as possible. This is tricky to live with in most households. Counterconditioning is again the technique of choice. Let's look at jumping on the kitchen counter when food is being prepared. In this case, the only priming necessary would be a fast session or two of down-stay on a designated mat in the kitchen. Then, I would wade right in and train during actual meal-preparation times for subsequent sessions. These would be extended preparation times - because you're training - but worth it. The dog learns that the best way to score a tid-bit is to hold position on the mat. Reward him every 10 seconds for the first couple of rewards, then every 20, then 30 and so on. You can use his own dinner. It sure beats giving it to him for free in a bowl. Every time he leaves the mat you pin a no-reward mark ("AH!AH!") on it and then escort him back to the mat. As in anti-jump training, the trainer's timing makes a big difference in how quickly progress is made. Catching him after he has risen, left the mat and walked several steps is light-years behind catching the first muscle contraction or intention to break the stay. An experienced trainer can do this and do a reasonable job preparing the meal at the same time. A green trainer will need to budget a fair amount of attention on the dog. This is why, for a few days, meal-preparation times will be extended to allow for the concurrent training session. The dog learns that if he breaks the stay, he's going to be put back anyway, but if he holds the stay on his own, he has a fair chance for rewards. When the dog has it down, he will stay the entire meal-preparation time for his one reward at the end.

You may need, after this initial bout of training, to add a sting-style set-up to this, if the dog makes a go for the counter when you leave the room. Bear in mind that there is no big agenda on the part of the dog: he's simply learning the safe-dangerous discrimination again, just as we learn the safe-dangerous speed-trap discrimination when driving on the highway. You will only make yourself miserable if you agonize about him "knowing" that it's "wrong" etc. etc. Teach the dog that it is ALWAYS dangerous to try going up on the counter. To achieve this, you really must catch the first trial: his first experiment at sneaking his behavior in when you're absent. So, rather than having him spontaneously spring the behavior on you when you're not ready with your very best timing, spring it on him by setting him up. This is the classic sting operation. Once your down-stay on the mat is nicely conditioned, deliberately leave something tempting on the counter and exit the room nonchalantly. But you're spying, you're ready, you're Clint Eastwood saying "make my day." As soon as the dog contracts a muscle to leave the mat, burst back in and enforce your down-stay. If you do this a couple of times, the dog simply incorporates the clause that Big Brother is always watching, so his best chance of scoring rewards is by staying on the mat whether you're in the room or not.

The problem occurs when people do not initiate training until the dog has already succeeded a few times in stealing food. Now you have a dog with a reward history for counter jumping. You're swimming upstream because no matter what you do, the behavior has been reinforced. This results in efforts by your dog to figure out when it's safe to do this behavior. It's obviously safe and rewarding sometimes; his successful attempts have told him that. In other words, you've made him motivated by letting him get away with one, or worse, two or more. Your solution sting operations will have to be repeated many more times in the case of a previously successful dog.

The smart thing to do is to plan ahead and set up your sting for the first trial. You can safely assume that because you own a dog and dogs are opportunistic, your dog will try to counter jump if there is food there, so be good and ready for this. It's no tragedy that he tried. It is a huge tragedy if he succeeds once, and then you start training. Do your counterconditioning, and then set up your sting operations prophylactically. We know he's going to try, so catch the first experiment. This way you get the imprint (first trial) rather than food-stealing getting the imprint. Above all, don't shackle yourself with useless laments about right and wrong.

The dog will not generalize your kitchen counter regime to hors d'oeuvres on the coffee table, ice-cream cones in kids' hands etc. so be prepared to set these up before you have a problem. It's perplexing to trainers the way many dog owners wait until they have an entrenched problem before doing anything. The reason is the misguided expectation that "good" dogs don't do things like steal food or jump up. This is the thinking that has to go. It is a cultural norm for dogs to engage in many of our most despised behavior "problems," and therefore the onus is on us to educate dogs.

TOP TEN PREDICTABLE BEHAVIORS WHICH OWNERS CONSIDER PROBLEMS YET RARELY DO ANY PREVENTIVE TRAINING FOR

1) Reflexively pulling on leash

2) Jumping up as greeting

3) Indiscriminate chewing of all matter

4) Eating any food within reach ("food stealing")

5) Distress vocalization when socially isolated or confined

6) Interest in members of own species

7) Cannot be handled or groomed easily

8) Fear of strangers/biting strangers

9) Resource guarding

10) Chasing & biting moving objects/rough play with children

5. Lemon Brains But We Still Love Them

How Dogs Learn

Everything you would ever want to know about how dogs learn has been available for decades in the countless papers and books on the topics of operant and classical conditioning in animals. It is astounding how little use has been made of this information in an arena of such obvious direct application: dog training. It's not simply an example of the predictable lag between theoretical understanding and application of theory either; dog trainers are at least 50 years behind. Partly, it's that the enmeshment between dog owners and Walt Disney has been too tight to allow behaviorism in. We've been clinging to the wish that dogs might just have big, convoluted, melon brains like humans and have a natural desire to please. The fact of the matter is dogs have little, smoothish lemon brains and are looking out for number one. I personally still like them.

The resistance to adopting flat out behaviorism in obedience methods is also partly due to the reality that existing training models have, with all their weaknesses, enabled a sufficiency of dog owners to muddle through with a species that is relatively easy to train. Marine mammal trainers, by contrast, have had no choice but to adopt sophisticated training methods because their subjects won't tolerate the abuse dogs do. Yet another reason behind the reticence of most dog trainers to bone up on behaviorism is that it is not necessarily easy to translate all that theory and knowledge about rats and pigeons in perfectly controlled environments to Basset Hounds coming and sitting reliably on command. Every obedience school has tales of psychiatrists and people with PhD's in psychology who are unable to get their Labrador to down-stay in class. Exerting "dominance" is, apparently, a lot simpler.

Operant conditioning is, quite literally, the conditioning of operants. Conditioning just means training by providing reinforcement (I use the words "reinforcement" and "reward" interchangeably to mean providing a consequence which results in an increased probability of responding, although I realize "reward" is often defined differently). An operant is a class or category of behavior, like "sitting" or "grabbing laundry" or "biting 5-year-olds." Operants get stronger through conditioning the same way muscles get stronger through physical conditioning. When the dog sits at any given instant, it's called a "response," an individual example of the operant "sitting." An individual response in weight training is usually called a "rep" or repetition. Get it?

So, if you're conditioning an operant, you're making it stronger, raising its probability or frequency of occurrence by reinforcing responses. If, whenever the dog sits, he gets a cookie, the operant "sitting" gets some conditioning and becomes more probable. There isn't a magical moment where the dog has a flash of insight and "knows" sit. This is where people need to start revising their thinking. The dog either has a strong sit, weak sit or perhaps nonexistent sit. Training changes probabilities; it doesn't transmit "knowledge." Your quadricep doesn't "know" or understand that the weight lifting has the goal of making it stronger; it gets conditioned through training. And, remember, this doesn't make the dog an input-output machine or any less an important member of your family. It is simply the best model to explain how he learns. It's also one of the principle ways we learn too. Operant conditioning is like a window of communication between species.

Classical conditioning is the pairing of something which has no meaning with something which has intrinsic meaning, so that they become associated. The result of the association is that the animal reacts to the previously meaningless thing in a similar way as it did to the thing that always had meaning. For example, food has intrinsic meaning to dogs, as it does to all animals. Cookie jars have no meaning on their own. Dogs quickly learn to associate the sight and sound of cookie jars with cookies because the sight and sound of the cookie jar reliably predicts cookies. The same phenomenon explains why dogs get excited when you put your coat on and take the leash out of the cupboard or get depressed when you grab your car keys and ask them to go into their crates. It's what the picture has come to mean, through repeated association with things of intrinsic relevance to the dog.

Dog training always incorporates elements of both kinds of conditioning. Because behavior is under the control of its consequences, we deliberately manipulate consequences to control the dog's behavior. Operant conditioning. Because we want dogs to understand commands and behave appropriately in varying contexts, we want them to learn to associate words and signals with behavior and its consequences. Classical conditioning. If all of the preceding seems too tricky, don't worry. You don't need a perfect understanding of learning and motivation to train dogs, although the more you know, the easier it is to train. You do need to drop some of your baggage like "he knows, he's just stubborn/mad/too excited/the wrong breed etc." and start thinking like a trainer. You also don't need to be a forceful, dominant personality the dog will "respect." You just need to know a few of the basic rules.

Important Rules to Know

1) Dogs do whatever works (behavior is under the control of its consequences: law of effect)

2) There are four kinds of consequences:
    1 - good thing starts   (positive reinforcement)
    2 - good thing ends   (negative punishment)
    3 - bad thing starts   (positive punishment)
    4 - bad thing ends   (negative reinforcement)

3) All these consequences must be immediate

4) The good and bad consequences will end up being associated with other things present at the moment of the consequence as well as affecting the probability of the behavior

5) Dogs are experts at reading the environment to know which consequences are likely for which behaviors in any given situation. Let's look at these rules as they apply to dog training.

Obedience Training

Because behavior is under the control of its consequences, obedience training is about providing consequences to the dog. Life is a never-ending series of "if you do this, this happens; if you do that, another thing happens." There are two kinds of things that happen in life, good things and bad things, so there are four kinds of consequences: good stuff can 1) start and 2) end. Bad stuff can 1) start and 2) end. Your dog is constantly trying to start the good stuff, end the bad stuff, avoid ending the good stuff and avoid starting the bad stuff. He's playing his entire environment, including you, his owner, this way. If you, the owner, can recognize this and exploit it, voila! Control of the dog.

As it happens, you have tremendous control of the starting and stopping of all the good and bad stuff in your dog's life. You simply have not been making much use of it. You're not aware of what the "good stuff" and "bad stuff" are on a conscious enough level and may be inadvertently installing through conditioning exactly what you don't want as well as missing valuable opportunities. You might even feel that your dog is controlling you. This is because your behavior is governed by the same principles. You want to start good stuff, end bad stuff, avoid ending good stuff and avoid starting bad stuff. Every living organism with a brain stem is doing this. And, because the dog provides consequences too, you may come under doggie control. Brings new meaning to the term "dog trainer." Luckily, you have the bigger brain and can get one step ahead of this game by boning up on operant conditioning and he can't, so read on.

You have control of your dog's access to everything he wants in life: food, the outside world, attention, other dogs, smells on the ground, play opportunities. You can make toys come to life by throwing them or initiating tug games; you have opposable thumbs which can open doors and cans. A lot of people don't make any use of this. A lot of people recognize this but expect the dog's obedience out of some sort of gratitude. Because they are providing all these things, they then expect obedience in return. The symbiosis only works, however, if you make the dog do his part of the bargain first in virtually each and every exchange. This means that feeding him faithfully for a week, taking him for walks, rain or shine, providing exercise and games every day has little bearing on whether he will return the favor by walking through doors nicely or coming when called in the park. You must arrange it so that it appears to the dog that, whenever he wants park privileges to continue or the front door to open, he must do obedience first. Always make the dog do his part of the bargain first, then provide your end. The dog will see obedience as way to get things he wants rather than as something that is interfering with him getting what he wants.

Take control of the goodies the dog wants in life - stop handing them out for free. Nothing is "free" anyway: you are always rewarding something when you open doors, put din-din down, initiate walkies or play sessions, or let him out of his crate. This is because the dog is always doing something, and that something gets a reward jolt whenever one of the goodies is initiated. All you're going to do now is become aware of this process and select the behavior to reward rather than simply rewarding whatever the dog happens to be doing at that second. You must also be prepared to withhold the reward if the dog doesn't comply. Put your money where your mouth is.

Rewards tend to become more potent after a period of deprivation: hungry dogs work harder for food than satiated dogs, dogs who haven't been out for a while are more eager for the walk to begin etc. The most common example is the urgency with which dogs seek to make social contact with other dogs on the street. The majority of domestic dogs live relatively socially-deprived lives, especially when it comes to their own species. When trainers deliberately use deprivation to increase motivation, it is an example of what's known as an "establishing operation." Food is established as a reinforcer through deprivation. This applies to us as well. For most people, a huge gourmet meal is an enticing reward. Think, now for a minute, about how you feel about a huge gourmet meal presented within minutes of over-eating at Thanksgiving, or when you have the stomach flu. Food in this context is an aversive. And, just as food must be established as a primary reinforcer, signals like clickers and praise must be established as secondary reinforcers. Establishing operations are like pre-training measures to make sure training will be effective.

Dogs and humans learn to recognize when one or another of any given consequence, good or bad, is likely because naturally, different situations call for different behavioral strategies: environmental clues let you know when any given behavior is likely to be successful. Putting money into drink machines will get you a soft drink. Putting money into garbage cans doesn't. Putting money into slot machines usually gets you nothing but occasionally gets you something and, rarely, gets you something really, really good. So, humans put money into soft drink machines, never put money into garbage cans and get addicted to slot machines, sometimes putting in their life savings. Your ability to discriminate between a soft-drink machine and a garbage can enables you to be successful with your coin-inserting behavior. "Successful," in animal learning terms, means that the behavior was reinforced. It got something good or turned off something bad. In other words, it worked. Behavior which works gets stronger. This is a law which applies to all living things. It's a law like gravity: apples fall down, behavior which is reinforced increases in frequency. This is the essence of dog training, so memorize it. All that has to be accomplished is to let the dog know "if you do this, this happens; if you do that, that happens" and how he can recognize which flow-chart is operative at any given time.

Behavior as Experiment

The environment is training the dog all the time, expertly. Sofas reward dogs for lying on them by being warmer and more comfortable than the floor. Sofa-jumping goes up in probability. Squirrels reward dogs by fleeing (dogs are predators and thus find fleeing objects intrinsically rewarding). He's more likely to do it again tomorrow if he comes upon a squirrel. For the squirrel, bee-lining for a tree works better than heading for an open field: escape is rewarding for the squirrel. The behavior works. He'll head for a tree next time a dog shows interest. If the dog moves towards a mailbox, it doesn't flee, so that behavior never gets rolling. If the dog stares at the fridge, it never opens, so he doesn't do it for long, even though it's where all the good food is kept. The behavior dies; it doesn't work. Neither does scratching on the fridge. It may be done as an experiment, but it probably will die quickly unless it works. Staring at the owner when he's eating sometimes works, so that behavior lives. If he scratches at the back door, a human opens it. That behavior works, so it will live to occur again tomorrow or the next day. If it keeps working, it gets stronger and stronger until it plateaus out at some elevated frequency. This is not simply anybody's opinion: this is a law.

An important thing to understand is that the dog is not working this out logically in his head: "hey, maybe he'll give me some sandwich if I look hungry enough" any more than he thinks "hey, maybe the sofa will give me some warm and comfy if I jump on it and lie down." The dog will do whatever works. If putting one paw over the other and sighing while lying in the bathtub got him bits of sandwich, he'd do that instead of staring. Dog behavior is like a never-ending experiment. Zillions of hypotheses are thrown out every day, such as rushing mailboxes, staring at fridge doors, scratching fridge doors, coming when called. When behavior dies from lack of reinforcement, it's called extinction. Extinctions like mailbox-chasing, fridge door food soliciting and coming when called happen so fast, the owner is usually not aware that the dog is ever even trying anything out. It's all extremely efficient and highly organized. No animal would have evolved who wasted time in dead-end behaviors, behaviors that didn't somehow contribute to keeping him alive to reproduce and pass on his learning ability.

This is usually where "what about desire to please..." crops up. We really need to put this one to bed once and for all. Praise is a weakish reinforcement for most dogs unless there is absolutely nothing else around to do, so it ends up being of only partial use in dog training. It is useful in those zero-distraction situations, and it is also of value in more normal levels of distraction as an encouraging signal to the dog that he is getting warmer, i.e. on the right track to winning reinforcement. Desire to please is a product of human desire to be worshipped as a demigod. It's not an empirical entity. It's a myth we have never tested to see if it really exists. My guess is that it doesn't. It does get heavily in the way of training the dog. Normal, trainable dogs have been marginalized and needlessly punished as a result of human weakness for the DTP thing. It's going to bog down your brain when you need every brain cell you've got to train correctly, so get over it. Your dog is a magnificent example of his species without this.

Hard-Wired vs. Installed Behavior

A few behaviors are hard-wired, requiring almost no learning to be carried out to their fullest: dogs chase moving objects, distress vocalize when alone, go for any available food, compulsively greet all novel people and dogs, pee away from their sleeping area etc. without conditioning histories. The rest of their behavior is the product of contingencies in the environment. Owners have nearly total control of their dogs' environments: where they live and sleep, if and when they may go outside and if so, which limited pockets of the galaxy they may visit, when, where and what they eat, if and when they will ever see a member of their own species, the nature of their toys and activities, even whether they live or die. Owners who feel like slaves to their dogs need to understand this. You have total control; you've just never demonstrated it to your dog. It's we humans who have the opposable thumbs, the big, convoluted melon brains and the roomfuls of information on animal learning and motivation. Lemon-brain can't help but get trained.

As it happens, most of the behaviors that we want to tone down come hard-wired. We must countercondition, finesse or redirect chasing, rough play, distress vocalizing, eating whatever is in reach etc. And, most of the behaviors we want to install don't come with the package: sit, down, stay, come, heel (all on command) are, from the perspective of these social predators, useless, silly, irrelevant behaviors. That is, unless you make it worth their while. The way you do this is to get the little lemon brain motivated. Compile a list of all the things he wants in life - it's a finite list for any dog - and start using these as prizes the dog wins by providing you with correct responses, by being obedient. This means no more free food, attention, walkies, dog-dog play etc. This is an attitude shift for the owner: rather than relying on a built-in desire to please, you are now proceeding to build a desire to please by exploiting your control of the dog's environment. So, there is such thing as desire to please, if you install it in your dog. Once he's a believer, once you have proven to him that he must play his cards right with you in order to get all the Important Stuff For Dogs, he will have desire to please. Not because you're wonderful, although you may very well be, or because he worships you, but because it's in his own interest to please you. It's how he gets what he wants. Everybody wins.

Once this attitude shift is done, all you need is two things, in this order: 1) a way to communicate to the dog how he's doing on winning the prizes and 2) names for all the different things he has to do. This process is done absolutely backwards by hack-trainers. They start trying to name behaviors (i.e., give commands) that they haven't yet conditioned and in an animal who's not even playing the game yet, i.e. no motivation.

The dog, when presented with a signal like the word "sit," first must identify if the signal means anything (classical conditioning) and then, very important, work out the odds of the suggested behavior winning a prize (operant conditioning). Has this behavior worked in the past? What's the cost benefit analysis in terms of effort expended performing the action and likelihood of prize? Dogs are, of course, not asking themselves these questions and performing statistical analyses in their heads. But, and this is very important, they behave exactly as though they were (So, maybe they are...). There is most certainly some behavioral efficiency mechanism in dogs which ensures that they will, most of the time, engage in behaviors which work to their net benefit.

The difference between someone who knows about training and someone who doesn't can be summarized most easily as follows: answer the following question: "what makes a trained dog sit?" Someone who doesn't know about training thinks "the command" makes the dog sit whereas someone who knows about training would answer that the prior history of reinforcement for sitting makes the dog sit. The command is merely a signal.

So, how does it all work? First, let's identify some of the rewards we've been wasting on a daily basis.

Things Which Are Likely Reinforcers for Dogs

1. Food
2. Access to other dogs
3. Access to outdoors and interesting smells on ground
4. Attention from people and access to people, especially after isolation periods
5. Initiation of play or other enjoyed activity: fetch, cuddling, tug-of-war, keep-away

Those are the big five, although individual dogs will have other quirks which you can use. Like most reinforcers, these are always more potent after periods of deprivation. All you need to train a dog is to get control of his favorites and start doling them out only when he does what you want. If the dog is keen on all these things or extremely keen on a couple in particular, he's an easier dog to train than one who is extremely laid back and not very into any of them. Yet, most pet owners would love to have such a dog, who doesn't food steal, is never excited around other dogs, doesn't sniff the ground on a walk or pull on leash towards the park or dog run, doesn't jump on people, never distress vocalizes when alone, doesn't steal laundry or bug you to pat him all the time. Very hard dog to train though. He doesn't want any of the prizes you're offering, so why should he play your game.

Contrast this dog with the 6-month-old prototypical Golden Retriever: immediately consumes any organic matter it comes across on the coffee table, ground or gutter as though it had never eaten, gives you a rotator cuff injury when it sees another dog across the street, knocks you over when you come home from work, urinates on guests from sheer excitement, chronically leans against you and paws you until you wear the fur thin on its head from stroking and grabs your kid's stuffed animals, so you'll chase it all over the house. This is the dream dog for trainers. You've got its number. Explain to this dog, through training, that there are now new ways to obtain all that stuff and watch the dog fall into line. Trainers love reward-junkie dogs.

In most practical training, we do the bulk of the reps with one or two easily dispensed rewards, notably food and tug-toys and use the rest as consolidators when their use is available through normal day to day living. This is because the opportunity to initiate dog-access, attention after absences and many of the other motivators is so limited to make them impractical as principle motivators. But be aware of them, and use them when the opportunity does arise because 1) they are potent, 2) varying motivation gives a stronger response, 3) what a waste not to, 4) it will make you train under a wider range of circumstances and 5) it will ensure you're not inadvertently rewarding some other, goofy behavior with these things. You will become conscious. For example, you can food train sit all you want, but if jumping up WORKS when there are novel guests arriving, your sit will not kick in in that situation. You must add the attention/greeting itself as a sit reinforcement.

Feedback: Formal Conditioned Reinforcer

To train well, you need a communication system, ways of telling the dog the exact instant when he has gained something good, ended something good, gained something bad and avoided something bad. The first and foremost of these is the gaining of something good, positive reinforcement. We need a signal to tell the dog that positive reinforcement has just been won, rather than just handing him the cookie or toy or dog-sniffing moment of bliss because 1) the timing has to be so precise and 2) sometimes we want to signal the dog at a distance. This signal is called a conditioned reinforcer or bridging stimulus. The conditioned reinforcer is so named because it becomes associated with the real ("unconditioned") reinforcement by repeated pairing; it's classically conditioned. It's sometimes called a bridging stimulus because it bridges the time gap between the behavior you liked and the actual reinforcement. It's like saying to a child: "this report card has earned you a fudge sundae!" The link between the sundae and the report card and even the hard work for the grades that got the good report card is made hours later. Dogs are nowhere near the league of kids when it comes to making these links, largely because they have no language. With dogs, you have to provide the real reinforcement, the piece of liver, as soon as physically possible after the signal "that sit earned you a treat." Otherwise, other intervening behaviors will end up being reinforced by the liver, and your signal will start to lose its charge.

In dog training, we try to avoid pinhead words like "conditioned reinforcer" and say, instead, "reward mark." The signal you choose marks the behavior you wish to reward. More and more trainers are using clickers as reward markers rather than words or phrases like "good!" or "yes!" because the clicker is a very brief, crisp, consistent and distinctive sound whereas a word or phrase will always have small variations in intonation and volume, not to mention all kinds of prior-existing associated baggage. It also may come up in regular conversation and thus lose some of its charge. A clicker is basically a children's toy which fits easily into the palm of your hand and makes a cricket noise when you press the mobile part. The occasional dog will be initially spooked by the sound of the clicker, but this is far from a prohibitive obstacle. The trainer can gradually desensitize the dog by muffling the sound with either layers of fabric or distance and reducing these as the dog gets used to the sound. The clicker itself is not supposed to be inherently reinforcing, remember; it's what it will come to mean that counts. It is certainly worth persevering with spooky dogs because of the timing advantage clickers give to your training.

Charge your reward mark by giving the dog a series of rewards always preceded by the click. Click-treat, click-treat, click-treat. The click becomes a PREDICTOR for the dog of the treat. For this reason, make sure the click always comes before the treat, and make sure the click is always followed by the treat. Otherwise, it is not a reliable predictor. The way to do this is to hand-feed the dog a couple of meals, one kibble at a time, or use tiny dog treats like sliced hot dogs or freeze-dried liver. If you want a powerful charge on the clicker, vary the reward which follows it: sometimes it's kibble, sometimes it's cheese, sometimes it's a walk, sometimes it's a tummy-rub, sometimes it's liver. Make this association dozens of times.

At this stage of the game, you're not training any behaviors yet. In fact, you're deliberately refraining from training any behaviors, and this may take some care. The reason is that, as soon as the click gets any charge at all, you will be rewarding something every time you click. There's a real risk that the dog will auto-shape. This just means that he might self-train to do some odd thing like take a step backwards because this got rewarded by chance a couple of times by the click-treat, and then he started doing it more and more, so a few more got rewarded, and the next thing you know, the dog thinks the backwards step is necessary to get the click to happen. It's called superstitious learning and happens frequently in day-to-day dog training. It's not the end of the world because you can always kill the backwards step later, either deliberately (fail to reward whenever you see it) or by simply letting it die a natural death as you train other things.

The efficiency of behavior will work for you in the long run. If you want to minimize the risk of getting anything too trained in while you charge up your reward mark, make a conscious attempt to randomly vary the behavior occurring at the time of the click in those early charge-up sessions. This isn't easy because "looking at the trainer" behavior will quickly get conditioned. This is not such a bad bit of baggage though, so you may want to let it get rolling. The dog will easily get unhooked from it if ever you train something requiring him to stop looking at you.

You will also want to vary the time interval between click-treat instances as well as between the click and treat. Varying the time between click-treat trials is insurance that you're not being too predictable. It is easy to fall into a rut of doing click-treat trials every 5.8 seconds, and the dog will tune in to this. If he does, the clicker is no longer the sole predictor of the treat -the time interval is - and so is not very well charged up. You want the click to be the only thing the dog has to go on that he's about to get the treat. Varying the lag between the click and the treat in an individual trial helps the dog better tolerate lags later when you're employing the clicker as a feedback tool. It's like saying to the dog "Don't worry, even if you don't get it in half a second, it's still on the way." Do this within limits, especially early on, because you are trying to make the click a reliable predictor of food. Other things to vary include your body posture, orientation vis à vis the dog and the distance between you and the dog. This is easily accomplished by wandering around as you randomly click and give or throw treats to the dog.

The most efficient way to get the dog clicker conditioned is to do a couple of sessions of 10 minutes each, perhaps in different locations and separated in time by 24 hours. Usually by then the dog will visibly startle to the click and charge you to collect his prize. Now you can start using it as a tool. When you use the clicker as a tool, you still provide a reward whenever you click. To not do so teaches the dog that the click is not a good predictor anymore. This is like a battery losing its charge. Remember, there is nothing inherently rewarding about the click or about a praise word: it must remain associated with the real reward. This is why real rewards are called unconditioned reinforcers (as opposed to conditioned reinforcers like clickers and praise words): they work without any conditioning. The animal doesn't learn to like and work for food: that comes with the package. He learns to like and work for the click which has come to mean food.

Feedback: Low-grade Reinforcers

In formal animal training such as conditioning exotics in zoos to facilitate their handling for medical or maintenance purposes and in marine mammal training, the use of conditioned reinforcer and primary reward is pretty well all that is used. In dog training, this is the most important feedback tool, but there are others as well. This is where general praise comes in. Praise, for many dogs, is a moderate or perhaps weak primary or unconditioned reinforcer and so, has value. It also can acquire or increase its value if used in conjunction with a well-trained formalized system like click-treat. Praise, in this case, is a signal to the dog that he is on the right track towards getting a click and primary. It can "prop up" a long duration behavior in order to increase tolerance of duration between primaries as well as allowing faster gains in parameters like distance, distraction-proofing and multiple-choice behaviors. Dogs do learn that praise means they are "getting warmer."

Shaping

Shaping was discussed in the section on retrieving, so I will just reiterate the main points here. Every animal and person has a repertoire of behaviors which they have performed at least once. If any of the behaviors in this repertoire are reinforced, they will start increasing in probability. This is the foundation of training. However, some behaviors we would like to have our dogs do are never offered. These behaviors are described as not occurring "at the operant level." There are never any responses to reinforce. In cases like this, it becomes necessary to build the behavior from scratch by using shaping. Here's an example.

Lying down is a behavior which occurs at the operant level in dogs. To train it, simply click and treat every time the dog lies down, and the dog will start doing this more and more often. When it is occurring with great and predictable frequency, you may add a command to the process, so you control when the dog does and does not perform a "down." As it happens, we can speed up the process by luring and rewarding instances of down rather than simply waiting for and clicking spontaneous occurrences. But, if you wanted to, you could train formally, without luring or prompting, by simply waiting.

Spinning in a tight left circle is a behavior which tends to not occur at the operant level in dogs. There is no use waiting for it to occur so that you can click and reward it when you see it. The dog never gives you one. To train this, it is necessary to first reward some approximation of this behavior which occurs at the operant level. In other words, what's the closest thing the dog is already doing at least occasionally? This may be a left head or body turn. Select such a behavior and click and reward it whenever you see it. When it goes way up in frequency there will inevitably be variations that the dog does which are an even better approximation of a tight left circle. So, start selecting those for reinforcement. It is like going up rungs on a ladder. This gradual raising of the standard until, sooner or later, you are reinforcing your original target behavior is called shaping. Shaping is an art which takes a great deal of practise.

Reinforcement Schedules

Up to now, we've been talking as though every correct response is rewarded with a click and a treat. This is because, if you're a good trainer, in the early history of any behavior, you will and should reward every instance of the behavior you're trying to install. Each reward, in early training, is a valuable piece of information to the dog on what it is you are after. Failure to select an example of the behavior (i.e. not rewarding it) goes toward creating doubt in the dog: is that what you want or not? Rewarding the behavior over and over makes the trend emerge more readily. Each and every time he, for instance, lies down, he is reinforced. Lying down must be the target behavior.

Later on, however, things are different. When the behavior plateaus out in its frequency, you will stop rewarding the behavior each and every time it occurs. You will reward most, then half, then sometimes, then occasionally. The dog is absolutely sure now that this is the target behavior, so withholding reinforcement does not make him change strategies immediately. It is, therefore, now safe to start withholding. This intermittent reinforcing of an operant is called putting the behavior on a "reinforcement schedule." The reasons for doing this are:

1) the behavior is more resilient to extinction
2) it facilitates the shaping process
3) you get more for your money

Resilience to extinction goes like this: If an animal is too used to getting rewarded every time, there will be an abrupt, behavior-crushing contrast when rewards cease coming. The behavior goes into extinction: it stops happening because reinforcement has stopped. By contrast, if the animal gets rewarded only occasionally, it will take a lot longer for him to "notice" that rewards have ceased. The best analogy is soft-drink machines vs. slot machines. You yourself expect reinforcement in the form of a drink every time you put money into the soft-drink machine. If the machine stops producing drinks, you will not put money in more than a couple of times before your money inserting behavior extinguishes, and you try another strategy, such as calling some authority or body-slamming the machine (arguably an extinction burst rather than a "strategy"). When you play a slot machine, however, the rules are different. You expect to not be rewarded every time and so put money in again and again in the hopes that the next one will be the one that is reinforced with a winning combination. The programming of slot machines has been done with the laws governing reinforcement in mind: schedules of reinforcement designed to maximize your money inserting behavior per reinforcing payoff are always used. You can't help but get hooked on them because you are subject to the laws of learning. And, so is your dog. This means that, once a behavior is acquired, you should put it on a schedule if, for no other reason, to obtain this compulsive resilience to extinction.

Reinforcement schedules facilitate the shaping process by providing you with more variations on the behavior to select from at each step in shaping. Let's say you're shaping the dog to open the refrigerator door. One of your goals may be to get the dog to grasp the handle of the fridge in its jaws. This isn't happening at the operant level, so you decide to shape it. You click and treat every time the dog approaches the fridge, to the point where he's walking directly to the fridge over and over again. You put this behavior on a schedule so that it will be resilient to extinction. You especially need this behavior to be resilient to extinction because you are going to be getting choosier about these approaches: now you want an approach and nose-prod or some other physical contact with the door-handle rather than simply an approach. Once you put the approach on a schedule, you will get a greater variety of approaches. The dog now is trying to discover what you like about the reinforced approaches and experiments to find out. The frustration of not being reinforced every time will often lead to faster and more vigorous responses. There is a maxim in training: variable schedule = variable behavior. One of those approaches to the fridge might include something like a nose-prod or some sort of contact with the door handle, and so you're off and running with your new criterion for reinforcement.

The third reason to employ reinforcement schedules is obvious: you get more for your behavioral buck. Rather than getting one sit for one treat, why not have an obedience routine lasting several minutes for one treat? There is a breaking point at which the schedule of reinforcement gets too "thin," and behavior tends to fall apart. Sometimes this has to do with the type of reinforcement schedule used, and sometimes it is simply biological mathematics.

Schedules in Dog Training

There are four main kinds of reinforcement schedules. These are Fixed Interval (FI), Fixed Ratio (FR), Variable Interval (VI) and Variable Ratio (VR). An example of a fixed interval schedule would be to reward the dog every 10 seconds if is he's still doing the behavior at that time. An example of a variable interval schedule would be to reward the dog on average every ten seconds if he's still doing the behavior at that time. For example, this could mean that the dog is first rewarded at the 8 second mark, then the 13 second mark, then after 9 seconds, then after 11, then after 15, then after 10, then after 6 and so on. The mean interval is 10, although 10 doesn't necessarily come up very often itself. A real-life example of a fixed interval schedule would be a salary which you draw every two weeks from your employer. This schedule is not used much in dog training. Variable interval schedules are good for installing duration into behaviors like stays, heeling and attention. The problem with fixed interval schedules, and fixed ratio schedules for that matter, is that if the value of the schedule gets high, there tends to be a pause in responding after each reward. It is as though the dog knows that once he gets rewarded, there's always a long road ahead before the next one. This is called an FI scallop in the case of interval schedules and a post-reinforcement pause in the case of ratio schedules.

A fixed ratio reinforcement schedule means that the dog is rewarded every X number of instances he performs the behavior regardless of how long this takes. In real life, this is called piece-work. You get X amount of money for every 50 widgets you produce. A variable ratio reinforcement schedule provides reinforcement for every X number of correct responses on average. This means, when training paw raises, on a VR5 schedule, that the dog gets a click and treat after 6 paw raises, then after 2, then after 4, then after 8, then after 3 and so on. A variable ratio schedule produces a steadier rate of responding than a fixed ratio schedule. In dog training, we frequently use differential schedules. As soon as a behavior is put on a schedule, the trainer selects the best examples of the behavior for reinforcement. Many of the things we train dogs to do are not all-or-nothing type behaviors. Sits, recalls and retrieves can be faster, straighter, cuter, better. These many shades of gray permit the trainer to reward differentially and thus perpetually crank up the quality of performance. How stringent the criteria are on a differential schedule is a trainer's judgment call. The ideal is to obtain an optimal rate of improvement without ever losing the dog's interest.

Good trainers have good internal senses of these schedules as well as a good eye for reading how thin a schedule is appropriate for any given dog in any given training situation. This is part of the art of training. Before you can develop the art, however, be sure you are crystal clear on the science. This is exactly what has been lacking in traditional dog training.

Prompts

In dog training we have the luxury of being able to work up close to the subject, and this opens the door to a variety of short-cuts to obtaining the actions we wish to reward rather than simply waiting for them to happen. These short-cuts typically take the form of luring movements with our hands, food or toys, vocal enticement and physical placement with hands or leashes. The technical term for this is, with the exception of the physical manipulations, elicitation. Rather than simply waiting for the animal to do or emit the behavior you wish to reinforce, you try to get him to do it . In dog training, we usually don't call them elicitors: we talk about prompts. A prompt is anything which helps manufacture the behavior you are looking to reward. Clapping and crouching, for instance, tend to make dogs approach so are often used to prompt recalls.

Perhaps the most valuable type of prompt in dog training is luring. Getting the dog to target a food treat with his nose is an example of luring. Once control of his head movement is thus obtained, an amazing amount of behavior can be manufactured. If the treat is moved up slightly and backwards the dog will probably sit in order to continue comfortably targeting. If the treat is drawn under your leg as you sit on the floor, the dog will probably lie down to continue targeting the treat through the tunnel created. If the treat is held at your hip, the dog will probably walk at your side.

Luring is infinitely preferable to old-style prompting which consisted of manipulation and leash tugs. Not only is it aversive to squish dogs into sits and downs, strangle them into heeling and jerk them towards you with leashes to obtain approaches, the dog is made a passive victim of the training rather than an active participant, and so learning is slower. It is furthermore more difficult to wean off these kinds of prompts when the dog is performing smoothly. Tugging on leashes is notorious for overshadowing commands. If you simultaneously tug and say "sit," the dog is attending to the physical prompt, and the command goes virtually unheard. We have Dr. Ian Dunbar to thank for spearheading a revolution in dog training in the last 15 years, away from pushing and pulling to these efficient lure-reward methods.

Early training sequences of any behavior will be one of three patterns:

        1) command
        2) prompt
        3) response
        4) reward

        1) prompt
        2) response
        3) reward

        1) response
        2) reward

Which one you will use depends a lot on what you are trying to train. When you are employing behavior shaping as your technique, you will always use the last sequence because you cannot add the command until you have shaped the behavior to its final incarnation. Although shaping is usually described in strict response-reward terms, you may use prompts to initially elicit various rungs on your shaping ladder.

It is somewhat risky to use the first sequence, the one with the command in it, because you are gambling that your prompt is going to work to produce the response. If it doesn't, you have a missed association. You have uttered the command word, but it failed to be associated with the behavior because your prompt didn't work. This whole area is very difficult for beginner trainers to understand. They are obsessed with commands: with what tone of voice should the command be given, should it be a one-word command, should it be a hand-signal or verbal command etc. etc. This command fetish is a gigantic red herring. In early training, you should have one obsession: the response-reward part of the sequence. Obtain and reward the behavior as many times as possible. The command can and should be added later on. For simple behaviors like sit or down, which we feel very confident prompting reliably, we often make an exception and add the name of the behavior (i.e., the command) at the front of the sequence early on.

The eventual goal with any of these is to get the following sequence:

        1) command
        2) response
        3) intermittent reward

In order to get to CRI (command-response-intermittent reward) using the first early-training sequence, all that must happen is for the prompt to be gradually reduced until the dog responds to the command only and for the final version to be put on a reinforcement schedule. To get to CRI when you have started training using the second sequence, you must, when the behavior is reliable enough, add the command at the front, fade the prompt and put it on a schedule. With the third sequence, CRI is achieved by adding the command and the schedule.

Prompts vs. Rewards

The most important thing to understand about prompts of any sort is that they are not an end in themselves: they are valuable because they manufacture rewardable responses which you must then reward. Missing this point is a very common and suicidal mistake. The trainer claps and backs away, the dog approaches, and the trainer thinks the recall is being trained. There is a very real possibility that the recall is actually being extinguished by this procedure. If the response is not rewarded, it will start to die. A good prompt will buy you a few responses, but in the long run, the behavior is conditioned by its consequence: did it get rewarded, yes or no? Owners constantly muddle the manufacturing of a response with the rewarding of that response. The most important act is the rewarding of the response, whether it occurred spontaneously or was obtained by prompting.

Sometimes rewards get lost in the shuffle because prompting is so rewarding for owners: it seems to work all by itself in that prompts get the dog to do the action. But it is not training: training is the manipulation of the consequence of the dog's actions. You must reward the individual response you create if you want to condition the operant. If you don't, your prompt will sooner or later become meaningless and cease to work. At that point, you will probably switch prompts and maybe buy yourself a few more responses. But it is all for naught if you fail to reward those responses when you get them. I've seen countless people kill their recalls by exhausting every prompt in the universe and then announce that their dog is stubborn because he clearly "knows" how to come (after all, they witnessed those correct recalls the first time they used one of the prompts). This is an example of a technical problem being mistaken for evidence that some particular individual dog is a lemon. This sort of thinking is rampant and really must stop. I'm personally very tired of dogs being saddled with the blame for poor training technique. Remember: behavior is an experiment: the prompt is a suggestion to the dog ("this might work..."). You are only helping the cause if you reward the response you manufacture. Some dogs will even stop targeting food lures if it is proven to them that the behavior seldom works. Dogs are not obedient to commands; they are obedient to the laws of learning.

Prompts are phased out when the response is reliable and smoothly executed. Think of this as a transition from the behavior being under control of the prompt to the behavior being under control of the command. Many trainers, in anticipation of going to a more stylized command, use as their choice of hand signals gestures which have some resemblance to the original prompt used to help install the behavior. This prompt can then be gradually modified until the dog is performing for the command only. This usually involves making the original gesture less and less broad and apparent and is an example of what's called "prompt fading." Verbal commands are much harder to train in because they have no relationship to the original manufacturing prompt and are usually less attended to by dogs than are hand signals and gestures.

In the case where the command was always given before the prompt in early training, all that has to happen is for a sufficient number of trials to go by: the dog will start anticipating. Once he perceives the command, he expects the prompt and performs the behavior before the prompt is given. Once this starts happening, you may start selectively rewarding him for this type of performance and withholding reward when you also have to prompt. The dog will tune in to this new contingency and become extremely attentive to the command.

This process is not always cut and dried. Variations in training context will usually cause regressions. If the dog repeatedly fails to make the new standard (i.e., rewarded only for unprompted performances), you must drop the standard and prompt a few responses to get him back on track. If you don't drop the standard and let him win some rewards, he will lose interest or become frustrated. This willingness on your part to relax criteria goes for all training endeavors, by the way, not just prompt removal. Whenever the dog seems to fall apart, don't agonize about whywhywhy, simply drop the standards temporarily so that the dog has a reasonable chance at succeeding at being rewarded again. This keeps him in the game. You will be able to get up to your previous standard and beyond in no time. If you don't drop the standard, sooner or later you will end up with a dog who dislikes training and would rather do anything else. Remember, the environment is competing with you for your dog's behavioral dollar: he will play the best game in town.

Phasing Out Lures
Food, used as both lure and reward, has the invaluable fringe benefit of a strong association between the reward and the rewarder, i.e. you. Because food lures are so seductively effective, owners sometimes run into difficulties weaning the dog off them. Firstly, a distinction has to be made between food as a lure, the prompt or target used to elicit the behavior, and food as a reward, the thing which comes after the behavior but is often the same piece of food. If you hold a piece of food in your hand, allow the dog to sniff it and then back away, you have prompted/lured his approach. When you give the food for approaching, you have employed it as a reward. This little treat has two distinct roles. Problems arise when the dog learns that the food in its role of reward is only likely when food is present in its role as lure. The way around this is very simple. As soon as the dog is performing reliably and on a reinforcement schedule, reverse the contingency.

For example, say you are practising basic position changes, like sit, down and stand. The dog now reliably follows the lure and will perform a dozen changes enthusiastically for one reward. At this point, do the following exercise. Warm the dog up by doing several changes in a row with the lure in your hand but fail to give any reward. Then, remove the lure, put it in your other hand which is behind your back. Show the dog your empty command hand and ask for one position change with your usual hand signal and verbal command. Usually the dog will perform the behavior, even if somewhat tentatively. Remember: you have radically changed the picture. The dog is doubtful that this is going to work. As soon as he adopts the right position, immediately give him the hidden reward from your other hand. Now, put another piece of food back in your command hand and lure a few more changes which you again fail to reward. Then, once again, hide the food and ask for one change for an empty-handed signal. Immediately reward it. Keep repeating this procedure. You are teaching the dog that not only does it not matter whether there is food in your hand or not, it is even better, from the perspective of reward density, for there to be no food in your hand when you give the command. This is the first step in making the dog a believer.

People drone on continually about how their dogs only obey when they have food in their hands. What they don't realize is that they have actively trained this in over the dog's lifetime by constantly supplying a reward when the reward was visible and almost never supplying one when the reward was not visible. Why not simply teach the dog that that is not necessarily how the universe operates? Remember: he is obedient to the laws of learning which specify that he will do whatever works. Dogs learn early in life that performing when no reward is visible means there will not be a reward. It only requires some artful hiding of rewards and some understanding of reinforcement schedules to teach them otherwise.

The same can be used for heeling. Initially, to get the behavior at all, the dog is targeting the food lure which you hold against your pant leg. When the dog is good at following and will follow for long intervals between rewards, start selectively removing the lure for a brief instant just before giving him the reward. By doing this, you are teaching the dog that the removal of the visible lure predicts the reward. With practice, he will be able to tolerate longer and longer stretches of lure-removal because he knows that this is very good news: the reward is on the way. He will, in fact, come to prefer following you without a visible lure because this behavior now works better than following lures. Sometimes in this specific exercise, it is necessary to substitute another prompt such as a stream of enthusiastic praise or verbal coaching the first couple of times, to ease the transition from lured to unlured heeling.

This technique also works for training the dog to watch your face while heeling, or simply to look at you on command. You can even use the first training sequence, the one with the command at the beginning, because watching is such an easy behavior to prompt. First, say "watch," then prompt the dog to watch your face while he sits in heel position by slowly moving a tasty morsel from his nose up to your face. Reward him as soon as his head is up and his eyes make contact with yours. Repeat this over and over for several days. Once again, the dog starts anticipating eventually and watches before you have to supply the prompt. This now becomes the new standard. If he watches on command, he is rewarded. If he does not, you prompt the behavior but withhold the reward. You can then proceed to gradually add features like duration, movement and distractions.

Training Parameters Separately

When you do things like adding duration, movement, distractions etc. to an exercise, you are adding parameters. Sit-stay, for example, has the parameters of

1) distance: how far is the handler from the dog
2) duration: for how long must the dog hold the stay between reinforcements or even visits from the handler
3) distraction: how distracting is the environment in which the dog is performing

When training sit-stay, these features must be trained separately before attempting to combine them. Failure to do so is extremely poor training and produces incredible wear and tear on the dog. Both trainer and trainee must agree on what the criteria for reward are, and this is unclear when there are multiple parameters being trained at the same time.

For instance, if you are in a distracting environment and you ask a beginner dog to sit stay at 30 feet for 2 minutes, he will probably break the stay. Somewhere in there, however, is a single parameter to train, such as "holding the stay at all amid this amount of distraction": try a 2 second sit-stay from 3 feet away and reward a few of those. Or, if you're in an undistracting environment, you may choose to play around with distance by leaving the dog at gradually increasing distances for 1 second at a time, bouncing back in to reward him as soon as you reach the target distance. And, on a separate occasion, gradually increase the length of time of the stay (from 2 seconds to 5 to 10 to 15 etc.) never going more than a few feet away, rewarding after each newly successful interval. When the dog has mastered each of these things separately, you may begin combining them, first two at a time at moderate levels, then three, only increasing difficulty if the dog is successful.

Training several variables at the same time is the hallmark of an inexperienced or "hack" trainer. They appear to be getting away with it at times, but this is usually at very great cost. Training this way will, sooner or later, blenderize the dog's brain. It may seem tedious and hypersystematic to break down exercises into individual parameters, but interestingly, training progresses much more quickly this way because you remain at each level only briefly before moving on, and you seldom lose the dog's interest. Because it is clear to the dog what standard he must make to achieve a reward, he complies more readily.

Feedback: No Reward Marks

In our communication system so far, a click means the dog has won a reward and praise means the dog is on the way to winning a reward. Another signal, called a No-Reward-Mark (NRM or "mark") functions as a conditioned negative punisher: a signal that the dog has just lost a reward or that his chances for reward dipped to zero with the behavior he just offered. When dogs learn what a mark means, this signal can stop a behavior dead in its tracks. Dogs are very good at abandoning dead-end strategies. This is why dogs often fail to come when called: it has proven to be a dead-end strategy.

Approaching the owner in the park when he calls leads either to nothing in particular, maybe a bit of praise or worse, the leash being put on and an enjoyable run ended. It is not surprising dogs do not come when called. Ending fun should be paired with a no-reward signal rather than the command "come" when you think about it.

The no-reward mark acquires its meaning through repeated pairing with a clear-cut and dramatic removal of an expected reward. This is efficiently accomplished by training a simple behavior such as sit-stay or "don't touch." If you hold a tasty treat at dog nose level a foot or two in front of a sitting dog, the dog will immediately move towards the treat. This is Plan A, targeting. The instant he does, simply say "Too Bad!" or "AH!AH!" and snatch the treat away into oblivion. Then re-command the sit and repeat the same thing. If your timing is good, the average dog will make the same mistake two or three times before changing strategies, i.e. not moving, lying down, barking or some other behavior besides targeting the treat. This next strategy would represent Plan B. If the dog opts to simply freeze and stare at the treat, you will click and reward. Repeat the exercise several times. You are now on the way to conditioning the behavior sit-stay as well as installing an NRM signal.

As soon as the dog gets two or three right in a row, change something so that he will make another mistake. Usually a simple change in your position in relation to the dog is enough to make the freezing behavior fall apart. Remember, when you hold a treat at nose level, Plan A is almost always to target the treat: this is how we were able to lure sit, down and heel position after all. It is extremely obvious to dogs to target food, so the switch to Plan B, i.e. not moving, will fall apart frequently. For some dogs, freezing may be Plan C or D. This is okay: you want a lot of mistakes, so that you have more opportunities to pair your mark signal with the snatching away of the lure. Changing the picture accomplishes this end beautifully. If you were standing to the left of the dog, now stand to the right and dangle the treat again, always ready to give your mark signal and snatch away the treat when he breaks the stay, which will almost inevitably happen. The reason the dog falls apart when you change sides is that dogs do not generalize very well. New picture, new exercise is the maxim. The dog will also fall apart for a trial or two if you drop the treat on the floor, change the type of treat, try the exercise in a new room or change trainers. Cover all these variations to make this fledgling sit-stay more solid but more importantly, to give you grist to charge up your NRM by repeated pairings with reward removal.

The choice of NRM depends on the dog and the context. You may choose to have more than one installed in a given dog. "AH!AH!," for instance, when said with some intensity and harshness, tends to be inherently aversive and so is not, strictly speaking, only a conditioned negative punisher. It functions in this case as a mild primary positive punisher as well. But this is hair splitting because the goal is to inhibit or reduce the likelihood of a behavior, and a positive punisher will only help the cause. It simply means that it may work a bit even without "charging." "Too bad" or "wrong" would be more neutral. Either may be preferable for extremely soft dogs or in those instances where you do not wish to inhibit behavior generally but merely wish to signal to the dog the fruitlessness of whatever he is doing. The more tools you have available, the better. Choose marks that roll easily and comfortably off your tongue because you will have to use them with precise timing in the heat of training.

Feedback: Positive Punishment

The tools we have discussed so far are reward (positive reinforcement), reward mark (conditioned reinforcement), low-grade reward (praise), reward removal (negative punishment) and no-reward mark (conditioned negative punishment). One tool we have not discussed yet is positive punishment. This is the initiation of an aversive (something unpleasant). We usually just call it punishment. It is by far the favorite technique of human society. Our formal system of conduct control, the law, is centered around its use. You obey the law to avoid going to prison, not to gain anything or turn anything off. Its use in criminal justice is controversial, not just on moral grounds but because there are efficacy questions: recidivism is extremely high. A huge proportion of those punished with fines and jail terms go out and re-offend. In other words, it doesn't seem to work very well. We tend to view this as a problem with the species being trained, i.e. humans or "criminal types" rather than a problem with the technique itself, i.e. punishment. Our response is usually to escalate the punishment: if fines don't work, throw them in jail for a while. If a while doesn't work, throw them in for a longer while. If that doesn't work, kill them. We have never fully faced the question that the technique, punishment, may not be a very effective one in the first place. Punishment is too woven into society to disappear easily. I think it's the compulsive observational learning legacy thing: we do it because it has been done to us. We've been raised with punishment and have been saturated with examples of it throughout our lives. Even most religions have strong punishment themes in their attempt to keep behavior in line. Yet in spite of this, we seem to keep sinning a fair amount, especially considering the size of the consequence: eternity in hell, the ultimate late punishment.

Given this context then, it is impressive indeed how the revolution in dog training over the last 15 years has resulted in methods based on positive reinforcement. Some training styles have abandoned aversives altogether, often with great success. So what, if any, role is there for aversives in dog training? My personal feeling is that negative reinforcement is a tricky technique to use correctly and is, furthermore, not irreplaceable. A negative reinforcer is anything which, when it ends, increases the likelihood of the behavior which ended it. Negative reinforcement is the termination of an aversive, as opposed to positive punishment which is the initiation of an aversive, an event which reduces the likelihood of the behavior which initiated it. Although in the right hands negative reinforcement is extremely potent, in the wrong hands it is a dog brain mutilator. I also feel very strongly that, even done correctly, its use is completely unjustified for the training of stylized behaviors like retrieving (remember the ear pinch?), for which it is a popular technique. I would therefore argue against its widespread use. So, what about punishment?

Examples of punishment in dog training are verbal reprimands, swatting, spanking, hitting with rolled up newspapers, spraying with water or citronella, shaking by the scruff of the neck and the ubiquitous leash jerk. These interventions typically have to be used over and over - in the case of leash corrections probably thousands of times in the course of the dog's lifetime - to have much impact on behavior. This is because most behavior is already strongly under the control of its reward history. If a certain behavior is occurring in the first place, it is, by definition, being reinforced somewhere, somehow. Failure to address this reinforcement dooms any other technique, in this case a punishment, to failure over the long haul. We tend to think that if rewards install or bring behavior to life, then punishments disinstall or kill behavior. But this is a major fallacy. Punishment does not kill behavior. Extinction, or the removal of reward, kills behavior. Punishment merely stuns behavior. It interrupts the flow temporarily by creating emotional upset. This effect is temporary. The animal, sooner or later, figures out ways, if any, around the punishment to get at that still existing reward. Sometimes the animal doesn't even need to look for ways around the punishment because the punishment wasn't experienced as such by the animal. In other words, it was too mild. To better understand all this, let's take a look at what makes a punishment work.

Our preconception is that if you do anything nasty at all to the dog, you have punished him. But this is not necessarily so. Punishment is formally defined as the initiation of any stimulus whose termination will reinforce behavior. Sound complicated? All this means is that if it works as a negative reinforcer, it is also, technically, a punisher when it first starts. You will recall that an unpleasant ongoing thing is reinforcing when turned off: If I'm twisting the skin of your arm until you say "uncle" and then I stop, your saying "uncle" was negatively reinforced. You are now more likely to say it again under similar circumstances. If, however, I keep doing it when you say "uncle," you will switch behavioral strategies until one works. Whichever one works is reinforced, in this case negatively, because it turns off the discomfort. So, a punishment in this case would be defined as the instant I initiated the twisting on your arm. Whatever you were doing at that instant would be punished. But what does that mean vis a vis the future likelihood of you doing whatever it was you were doing when I started hurting you? The answer is, as it happens, not a heck of a lot in most cases.

To make a punishment work, i.e. to have it reduce the likelihood of behavior even temporarily (remember, it hardly ever kills behavior), the punishment has to meet a lot of conditions.

Years ago, the rules for administering effective punishment were laid out in an excellent book by Dr. Daniel Tortora called "Help! This Animal is Driving Me Crazy." In order for a punishment to have even a temporary effect on the future probability of the punished behavior, several conditions must be met:

1) The punishment must be immediate

2) The punishment must be sufficiently aversive. If you start small in an effort to be kind and then scale it up, you will build a "punishment callous." You are performing systematic desensitization: by gradually increasing the punishment you are toughening the dog up. Never start small and get bigger; start big right off the bat.

3) The punishment must follow each and every attempt at the behavior and be associated only with the behavior; there should be nothing else to tip off the dog that he's about to get punished. When the dog is punished for behavior which has been unpunished up to now (and also has been reinforced otherwise it wouldn't exist in the first place), he immediately asks himself "what's different this time?" If it is the fact that you're in the room, his question is answered. He learns to avoid doing the behavior when you're there. You still have a behavior with a reward history. It's a matter of time until the dog figures out when the punishment happens. He is obedient, remember, to the laws of learning, not to you. A behavior which has been reinforced in the past will continue to occur as soon as he discriminates when it is safe to do so.

If you get all this right, the punishment may buy you a temporary suppression of the behavior. Remember, you have not killed it but merely brought about an emotional state which is incompatible with the behavior you want to get rid of (the animal is too upset by the punishment to do it for the time being). He is also, incidentally, too upset to do much of anything right after a punishment. Punishment is like carpet bombing. The behavior you wanted to target gets hit but so does a huge portion of the dog's whole repertoire. Dogs who are punished a lot behave a lot less in general. What's particularly scary is that is what a lot of dog owners actually want. They want a general toning down of the dog. It is a sad comment on human-dog relations when we claim to love dogs and then attempt to behaviorally lobotomize them with thousands of leash jerks in the name of "obedience." The bland, behaviorless animal many people bond to so strongly can scarcely be called a dog. It is the ghost of what once might have been a dog. The target behavior, for its part, still has that annoying reward history which keeps it alive and kicking.

Here's another example. The dog has been jumping on and mouthing the kids. This is fun and reinforcing to the dog because it burns his predatory gasoline and gets nice shrieks from the prey objects. Mom first tries saying "no" in a firm tone of voice, but the dog quickly habituates to this sound, and there is no impact on the behavior. She may as well be saying "harder! rougher!" in a firm tone of voice. Dad, the first time he sees the dog do this, picks the dog's entire front end up off the ground by the scruff of the dog's neck, growls into the dog's face "NO!" and gives the dog a nasty backfist under the chin. The dog slinks off to mull this over. He doesn't mouth the kids for several days, but then the behavior, like a phoenix, rises from the ashes. It had only been stunned by Dad's well-timed, highly aversive punishment. What is the dog's likely course of action now? Has he learned what "no" means? Does he care? So what has he learned? Right. Never mouth the kids when Dad's around. The dog now mouths the kids during the day when it's safe and refrains in the evening when it's dangerous. No substitute behavior has been trained in to fill the gap, so the original one, kid-mouthing, emerges, whenever it's safe. Again, the dog is obedient to the laws of learning.

If you plan to ever use punishment, you must have a second nature sense of these conditions. Remember, the punishment must be:

1) immediate
2) big
3) doled out every time he misbehaves, without exception
4) associated only to the behavior

These conditions, right off the top, make success difficult using punishment. And, even if it's successful or partially successful, there are side-effects to contend with: a strong association with the punisher, a global inhibition of behavior - that narrowing of behavioral repertoire which comes with chronic use of punishment - and the possibility of pain elicited aggression. Stories about dogs "turning on" their "masters" are pathetic attempts to turn into high drama a dog defending itself, after a history of punishment, from its owner. Any dog, or human for that matter, has a breaking point. The most placid among us might resort to violence to save one's self or one's offspring from perceived threat. In dog culture, as we shall see, there are no words, litigation lawyers or letters to the editor: fleeing or threat display are their only tools when angry, arguing or afraid.

Punishment is so prevalent that, in many peoples' minds, it is a virtual synonym for "training," in spite of the fact that it doesn't work very well. If you walked into an obedience class 10 years ago you would see dogs marching around in a circle receiving leash jerks scores of times in the course of the lesson. Even today, when many people ask how to stop the dog from doing something, they expect to be told what particular flavor of punishment is "best": yelling, hitting, throw-chains, booby-traps, electric shock. What helps drive this fascination with punishment, aside from our compulsive observational learning tendency, is that there are often two immediate gratifications for the punisher. One is release of anger and frustration. It's maddening trying to control dogs for most people. The other is even more insidious: the temporary suppression you get with punishment works as a well-timed reinforcer for the punisher. At the moment it's doled out, it looks like the punishment worked. When the behavior comes back later, this is too late to impact the earlier punishment administration. And to make matters worse, it usually only appears to work some of the time, so your punishing behavior is kept alive and resilient to extinction by being on an intermittent reinforcement schedule.

A further problem with punishment as a technique is that of the association with other elements in the picture at the time of the punishment. We tend to punish our dogs interactively so, even if it's well-timed, i.e. the dog is "caught in the act," and big, you risk a good part of the association being with you, the punisher, rather than strictly with any aspect of the behavior itself. This side effect leads to innumerable problems in other areas, most notably getting the dog to come when called. No sane animal would approach someone so intimately associated with punishment. Another problem is late punishments. If well-timed punishments are feeble training, punishments delivered more than a second or two after the intended act are basically abuse.

Punishments (and, rewards for that matter) mark an instant in time: whatever the punishee was doing the instant that the punishment was initiated. They also mark a punisher (or rewarder) as the most salient discriminative stimulus. That simply means that, of all the things you could remember about a punishment - the design on nearby wallpaper, time of day, what you were doing - the most accurate predictor of the punishment is whoever did it to you. The submissive behavior of dogs who have experienced lots of punishments - incorrectly interpreted by owners as "guilt" - which are predicted by the owner's arrival or approach, begins to make sense.

There are three ways to make punishments work even a little bit in dog training:

1) One is to catch the very first trial with a well-timed, large punishment. Often there will never be a second trial. This way there is no reward history to contend with, and when the animal poses the question "what's different?" (i.e., what predicted this punishment), the answer will inevitably be the behavior itself. That was the new part. So, in this case, the question works for you rather than against you.

2) Another way to make punishment more effective is to employ a warning cue which goes in front of each and every instance of large, perfectly timed punishments. Before giving a leash correction, say "don't pull..." and give the dog the option of avoiding the correction: if he slackens off, he avoids it; if he continues to pull, he gets the correction. The warning cue serves as a kind of "magnet" which takes the association with the punishment, when the animal asks "what was different?" ("oh yeah, right before I got nailed, I heard 'don't pull...'").

3) The third way to make punishment a more valid tool is to use it (still and always with a warning cue) in close conjunction with

other techniques, such as counterconditioning and rewarding the absence of a behavior. After warning and giving a leash jerk, prompt and reward another behavior, such as walking on a loose leash.

This last niche for punishment could very well be its main role in practical dog training. Think of it as another way of manufacturing reinforceable responses. Right after a punishment, there is that temporary suppression. It is as though a behavioral void has opened for a short while. If you reward another behavior in that interim, the void will start to be filled. If the void gets filled, the original, punished behavior will have no behavioral "space" to come back to. The punishment buys you time to install a "replacement behavior." Dogs can't do two things at once. So, if you plan to punish the dog for attacking the kids, also reward him for quietly watching the kids or for attacking appropriate dog toys. After you punish door-dashing, reward some sit-stays at the front door. Whenever you punish a dog in a certain situation, you must come up with and reward some other behavior to fill the void you opened with the punishment. The punishment functions as a prompt. Its value lies in what other behaviors follow it and whether those behaviors are rewarded or not.

Needless to say, we want to administer as few punishments as possible. The key is to install behavior in advance using positive reinforcement rather than waiting for the (inevitable) offenses and then punishing and counterconditioning. Too much of the latter could even result in a dog who misbehaves in order to be punished because the only time he is ever positively reinforced is after a punishment. A masochist has been created. We know in advance how dogs naturally behave: they jump up to greet, chase and bite anything which moves, urinate and defecate when they get the urge, distress vocalize when alone, pull on leash etc. We must start planning ahead.

Chops

All these techniques - positive reinforcement, counterconditioning, negative reinforcement, negative punishment and positive punishment - work perfectly in theory and in behavioral science labs. It's much stickier in the real world. How good someone is at applying all this in real-life human-dog interactions is called their training "chops." A lot of people have chops with little acquired knowledge; they are just good natural animal trainers. Most of us have to build our skills, but luckily for us and for dogs, chops are acquirable. So what exactly are "chops"? A few years ago, I videotaped young dogs from beginner level obedience classes being trained by two groups of people. The first group consisted of the dogs' owners and the second group consisted of professional or highly skilled amateur trainers. My aim was to get a handle on exactly what the difference was between a good, experienced trainer and a rank novice. All the participants were told the study was to do with learning styles across dog breeds, so that they wouldn't change their training styles. What I was most interested in was counting instances of attempted feedback from the handler to the dog. These included all examples of verbal praise, food reward, pat, offering a toy, reward removal and no-reward marks, grab, strike, verbal reprimand and leash correction. The person who did the counting from the videotaped record did not know which people were the trainers and which were the non-trainers.

The impetus for this study came from years of observations in obedience classes. Dogs who behaved badly for their owners became "different dogs" when one of the class instructors borrowed them for demonstration purposes. This was all without any training history or priming. Once the dogs were given back to their owners, they immediately reverted back to misbehaving. What goes on, in the moment-to-moment interaction between dog and trainer, that makes the difference? My hunch was that trainers give a lot more information per unit time to a dog they are handling. The difference in the amount turned out to be even greater than I would have ever imagined.

The owner-handlers delivered some kind of feedback to the dog every 20 seconds on average for a rate of attempted feedback quotient (RAF) of 2.8 per minute. The trainers gave feedback about every six seconds for a RAF of 10 per minute. The feedback was of both kinds, positive and negative. Trainers praised and gave out food rewards three times as often as non-trainers, but they also doled out more punishments, mainly in the form of leash corrections or no-reward marks ("AH!AH!"). It was as though the trainers used the punishments to "slam doors" on behavioral strategies they wanted the dog to abandon, so that the dog would be more likely to offer something they might be able to reinforce. They were opening those temporary voids. So, right off the bat, behaviors like lunging, pulling on leash and jumping on the trainer were temporarily removed from the repertoire or stunned. The trainers would then capitalize on the void thus created by adeptly prompting and then rewarding what they wanted. They also timed their rewards better. These rewards came so fast and furiously because it appeared the trainers had a mental image of what they were after ahead of time and never hesitated to reward it when they got it. This got a roll going. In short, the trainers defined a tighter envelope or narrower range of behavior by marking or punishing deviations, so the dog, with a narrower range of options, offered rewardable responses which the trainers unfailingly rewarded. They ended up getting many more rewardable responses than the non-trainers because:

1) they prompted for them relentlessly
2) they punished lunging and pulling very quickly and cleanly
3) they set reasonable criteria for rewards
4) their timing was excellent: they never missed a chance to reward
5) their training delivery was fast: they took no coffee breaks

These qualitative differences were even more striking than the RAF difference between the two groups. Trainers were good "slot-machines" for the dogs to play, much better than the other available things, such as the floor, doorway, other people or dogs in the room. When one views the videotape, the fastest way to tell whether you are observing a trainer or a non-trainer is to simply look at what the dog is "playing." If the dog is playing the handler, it is likely a trainer. If the dog is playing the floor or something else in the room, it is likely a non-trainer at the helm.

The non-trainer group could be characterized as "trees." They supplied little in the way of feedback to the dog for either good or poor responses; from the dog's perspective, it must have felt like being tied to a tree. Dogs tend not to interact much with trees when they are tied to them. The non-trainer feedback is best characterized as:

1) stereotyped: regardless of whether the dog did something utterly brilliant or only slightly better than average, the same reward was dispensed. For instance, one owner would say "good dog" and give a scritch behind the ears each and every time he wished to reward the dog. Trainers were much more varied in their feedback: they used a huge range of feedback "tools."

2) Non-contingent or slow: slow feedback was just that: slow, often two or three behaviors late. In other words, when the dog would sit, by the time the handler had perceived the sit and dispensed any kind of reward, the dog had stood, lunged and sneezed. Sneezing ended up being rewarded.

Non-contingent feedback was an interesting non-trainer phenomenon. Quite often when the dog was absolutely gone, either lunging or playing the floor or watching the doorway, the handler would offer praise in an apparent effort to get the dog's attention. This kind of prompting, incidentally, was counted as attempted feedback, for the purposes of the study, which inflated the RAF for non-trainers. The feedback density situation is, therefore, probably even worse than the numbers would suggest. Interestingly, a couple of dogs used in the study were "ringers"(trained dogs with obedience titles), and these, too, ended up tuning out the non-trainers by halfway through the allotted time, in spite of a lifetime of training. Although they offered great responses, these were quick to extinguish, and these dogs ended up playing the floor as well.

When you think about it, it's not surprising that there is such a gulf between people who make dog training their passion and people who like dogs and buy them as pets. Just because someone loves dogs doesn't mean they have any training skills. And, there is a lot of great latent animal training talent out there who probably will never own a dog because they don't particularly like dogs, at least not enough to own one. Those who become good at training usually love training on top of the fact that they love dogs. They may or may not start out with any natural gifts. Their love of training, however, will make them better at it over the long haul because they will end up logging a lot of training time and pursuing knowledge. But most owners are not in this group. They love dogs, not animal training. And it is pretty astounding the way we develop dog training skills in these well-meaning people. We take them and what do we do? They have, quite naturally, no conception of how to set criteria (i.e. they don't know what a rewardable response looks like much less how to reward it), no timing and almost no experience at prompting. What tools do we give them to commence learning these very basic skills? We give them their own completely out of control adolescent pet and a strangle collar. It's like teaching 16-year-old kids to drive by giving them a formula one car and putting them on the autobahn.

Think, for a minute, about the implications of this. The fundamental skills of training are: the ability to recognize a rewardable response (criteria setting), the ability to obtain that rewardable response (prompting, shaping and, arguably, punishment) and the ability to immediately reward it when you get it (timing). Later on, skill at raising criteria and reward schedules come greatly into play. These are not easy tasks. The animal we want trained is a dog, typically a young dog, a dynamic animal with a relatively high rate of behavior change who may be actually trying to maul (playfully) his owner during the session. If a dog owner, with virtually zero development of any of these skills, is issued an aversive tool, like a choker, what happens? The answer is random punishments with the owner as the principle discriminative stimulus. The dog learns slowly, necessitating more and more leash jerks and the result is often a zombie-like dog who has had huge amounts of behavior veritably wiped out. We would never condone this anywhere else but in a dog obedience class.

Let's say you are a novice violin player or a novice pole-vaulter. You are going to start learning your new skill. Every time you make an error, a 6-month-old dog gets a small electric shock. How many errors do you estimate you will make in your first week of learning to pole-vault or play a musical instrument? How many in the first month, the first year? What is the effect on that dog of all those shocks? Is that okay? Now, how many timing or criteria setting errors is a novice dog trainer going to make in his first month of training? If the main training tool is a strangle collar, that makes for quite a lot of poorly timed punishments. What has been making us think that this is okay? If someone can't deliver a food reward with any timing or skill, should we be arming them with devices that dispense pain?

A new way of developing basic training skills in dog owners is needed. It must identify the deficits that dog owners bring to class. These are:

1) they don't give enough feedback
2) the range of their feedback is too narrow
3) their feedback is non-contingent or slow
4) they have a hard time switching gears from positive to negative feedback
5) they don't know how to set criteria
6) they don't know how to prompt
7) they don't know when in the sequence to prompt

The first breakthrough for many dog owners is recognizing that their principle role in obedience training is to give feedback, as opposed to giving commands. This speaks to a huge and widespread fallacy in the dog owning public: that commands or antecedents drive behavior. The evidence for this is the endless quest people have for the right "tone of voice," the right number of words in the command, the correct word to use, the correct hand signal. By now, of course, you know that commands don't drive behavior, consequences do. The main focus in early obedience training is manufacturing, recognizing and rewarding those rewardable responses at every possible opportunity. They are like gold. The command is merely a signal to the dog that an opportunity for reinforcement just came up and suggests which behavior he ought to try. You can't command a behavior that you have not yet trained.

Your own skill at training will start improving the instant you start installing your basic training tools, the conditioned reinforcer (the clicker) and your no-reward mark ("AH!AH!" or "AW!Too Bad!"). Then you need to get yourself as rapidly as possible into the hands of someone who knows what they are doing. You need to find a good instructor for three reasons: 1) to coach you, 2) to provide a model or example of good training skills and 3) to provide sequences for the basic commands you want to install in your dog. The progression you can find in a book like this one. The modeling you can get from hanging around and watching good trainers and from watching videos of good trainers in action. The coaching, however, can only be accomplished in vivo by an experienced trainer-instructor. The skills of training and instructing are separate, by the way. A good trainer is not always a good instructor and vice versa. Ideally, in an obedience class, there will be one of each, sometimes in the same person but sometimes not. Try to find a school which has both an ace trainer and someone who can impart knowledge to others. Teaching people is an art form that few truly master. All that said, here are a few suggestions to improve your own basic skills.

1) First of all, never miss an opportunity to watch good trainers in action. Whenever I am in the presence of a good trainer, I shamelessly stare and soak in as much as I can. You may also want to consciously and deliberately avoid looking at poor trainers, even if you're aware that their example is a poor one. Humans are such compulsive observational learners, you could be "infected" by their bad habits. So, avert your gaze and only put the right pictures into your brain.

2) Stop giving the dog so much free food and start using it as rewards in training. Exploit the most potent motivator in animal training. If you have puritanical misgivings about rewards, get over them and fast. I'm continually assaulted with the line "yeah, but if I give him food, won't he always expect something?" Firstly, no, not if he's on a reinforcement schedule. But, secondly, and I think this really addresses the root problem here, this is like saying, "yeah, but if your employer gives you a pay check for working, won't you always expect one?" I often want to ask people who make that remark what exactly they thought this endeavor was about. I don't ask because I know the underlying assumption has to do with commands driving behavior and with DTP (desire to please). Suffice to say that you're shooting yourself in the foot if you deprive yourself of food training and expect to compete with the rest of the environment using your personal charm only. People must understand that food training in no way cheapens or ruins the bond you have with your dog. It enhances that bond by associating you with one of the most potent unconditioned reinforcers on the planet. The alternative to training with positive reinforcement is training with aversives. Choose and stop agonizing.

3) Use vocal intonation more. High-pitched or enthusiastic sounds - baby talk - are mild to moderate reinforcers for a lot of dogs and can be established as "getting warmer" signals for all dogs. Reservations about behavior in public shackle many people when it comes to praising their dogs. This is yet another reason to get yourself into the hands of a good trainer. A good trainer will have very broad vocal tools which will serve as an invaluable model for you. Support for this compulsive observational learning theory can be found in groups of trainers who train around each other a lot. They pick up each others' idiosyncrasies right down to individual words and phrases.

4) Become aware of your timing of rewards, NRM's and punishments. Were there any intervening behaviors between the one you wanted to give feedback to and your actual feedback? If so, tighten that up. If your timing is pretty good and you want to make it better, train fast-moving, "hyper" dogs, young, impetuous puppies and rodents.

5) Improve your delivery. Delivery is inter-trial latency (as opposed to timing which is response-reward latency). Good trainers are very efficient: as soon as a trial has ended with either a reward, praise, release, NRM or punishment, they immediately commence another trial. They have great "flow." The pay-off in terms of efficiency is obvious: more trials per unit time means more progress. In 10 minutes, a good trainer can accomplish more than someone with poor delivery can in an hour, even if their skills match up otherwise. But delivery has another fringe benefit. Trainers with good delivery lose the dog a lot less. Post-trial loss of the dog's attention is a common problem, necessitating time and energy to get the dog refocussed before the next trial. Rapid-fire delivery solves this. Train intensely, having as your goal keeping the dog's attention on you for the entire session. Keep training bursts brief if necessary.

6) Be very cool-headed when you train. This will enable you to shift gears easily between NRM's and rewards. If you take everything very personally, you will be inclined towards what I call "low-grade, chronic punishments." This is something we humans do to each other all the time. We seethe, mope and brood and give dirty looks for hours or days to family members and colleagues who have wronged

us. We elicit guilt. This kind of punishment may work on people. It absolutely does not work on dogs. It may make them behave very carefully if a crabby mood has come to predict a higher probability of reprimands and Yucky Stuff for Dogs, but as a specific feedback tool, it's shooting yourself in the foot.

Take, for example, a dog who lunges at another dog in an obedience class. The owner gets angry and starts glaring and seething at the dog. The dog sits and looks up at the owner and is met with what? You got it: glaring and seething. The owner is now applying this mild punishment to ongoing behavior, including those beautiful sitting-and-looking-up responses. You must be able to shift gears with ever-changing behavior. For this reason, it will feel rather artificial for a while. Your rewards, NRM's and reprimands have nothing to do with how you feel about the dog's performance. You are employing them as feedback tools to influence the future probabilities of the behaviors. If you do this based on your real feelings, you will be slow and inaccurate. Get into a Zen-like frame of mind when you train. You will never be able to oscillate quickly back and forth between a no-reward-mark and reward-mark if you get upset at mistakes the dog makes. Emotions will slow you down. Remember that your job when you are training is to condition behaviors, not moral goodness in the dog.

7) Get over any obsession you have with commands and start focusing on providing consequences. Commands are just signals which inform the dog which behavior might earn him reinforcement right now. You have to have a behavior first. If the behavior is weak, there is no point trying to signal for it. Same thing with elicitors or prompts. Like commands, these are antecedents of behavior, the thing that comes before. Elicitors are like discriminative stimuli for behaviors that have been genetically selected for rather than selected for by training histories. They are subject, however, to learning laws and can become useless if the consequences of responding are not attended to. What all this means is that your primary goal, as dog trainer, especially in the early stages, is to strengthen behavior by providing positive reinforcement as a consequence whenever you see the behavior you like. The manufacturing of the behavior, by eliciting, commands, narrowing of options with punishment of other

behaviors or simply waiting for the dog to do it (to "emit" the response) is not the point. The point is reinforcing it when you get it.

8) Think about the criteria you are setting. Be aware of the standard, at any given moment in training, that the dog must achieve to get rewarded. This standard can and should constantly change. Its fluidity is dictated by the rate of progress of the dog. It is never arbitrary. This is a common flaw in beginner trainers. Because the goal in mind is a dog who will hold a five-minute sit-stay as dinner guests arrive at the front door, the owner is frustrated because, although the dog can do a 30-second sit-stay alone with the owner in the living room, he still jumps all over people and is oblivious to all commands when guests arrive. The frustrated owner needs to train with more gradual increases in the level of difficulty, culminating in the guest-at-the-door scene. Every command is like a wall you are building. The first row of bricks, representing the first level of difficulty (sit-stay alone with the owner in the living room for a few seconds from two feet away) may be already laid down, but there are many rows to be laid down before you have your ultimate goal. Each row must be laid down solidly before laying down the next.

6. Nuts & Bolts of Obedience Training

Another way to think about criteria setting is to think about what "grade" the dog is in in a given subject. If your dog is in kindergarten or grade 1 on sit-stay, he will flunk a test at the grade 12 or PhD level. This is not malice, revenge, spite or stubbornness: it is how dogs learn. The following sequences for teaching sit-stay, down-stay, stand, come, heel, don't jump and don't pull are organized by increasing level of difficulty from kindergarten through to the college and PhD level. Before training any of these, charge up your clicker (conditioned reinforcer) as described above.

Kindergarten Sit

Put a treat in the palm of your hand, and cover it with your thumb, so it stays in. Allow the dog to sniff this goodie. Ascertain if he is targeting the treat by moving your hand around. Does he try to follow the hand? If yes, he is targeting, and you may now proceed to lure a sit. Move the treat slowly over the dog's head, high enough that he must crane his neck up to continue targeting but not so high that he jumps to target. Move the treat backwards over the dog slightly, maintaining the same height. Then just wait. If the dog jumps or backs up, remove the target for an instant and start over. Most dogs will eventually sit to make it more comfortable to continue targeting the treat. As soon as the dog sits, click and give him the treat. Imagine that the dog is training you to open your hand by sitting. Repeat this over and over until the dog sits instantly with less and less effort from you with the target. Your hand gesture can now be executed quickly with your palm facing up. This paves the way for the hand signal you're about to train.

Now, put the food reward in your pocket or in your other hand behind your back. You will now use your empty hand as a target by giving a broad, clean, confident hand signal to sit. The hand signal is an upwards scoop with palm open. Always conceptualize 'sit' as an attempt to get the dog's head up rather than getting the rear end down.

If you get the head up and back, the rear takes care of itself. When the dog sits, immediately click and give him an extra large food reward from your other hand or pocket. The bonus food reward is because the dog sat without a visible lure. This is much harder than sitting for the food lure. It also reinforces in the dog's mind the notion that his behavior produces the reward and that this does not have anything to do with whether the reward was visible or not. The reward, in fact, is a better one when it is invisible.

This is a critical juncture in training. Failure to get reliable response with the reward invisible sets you up for a possible lifetime of a dog who "only does it when I have food in my hand." Practise until the dog sits as reliably for the hand signal as he did for the original lure. If the dog balks at any stage for the blank hand, don't crack and put food back into it. Simply wait and reward the sit when you finally get it. It is vitally important that the dog learn that the blank hand is just as worth responding to as the one with the food in it. For the dog, this is like a leap into the unknown. Many dogs initially sit for blank handed signals in a manner that looks as though they think "well, this couldn't possibly work, but I'll try anyway." You have to make them believers by reliably rewarding responses to empty handed signals.

When the response for the blank hand is very snappy, put it on a reinforcement schedule by rewarding at first about three out of every four sits and then reduce further to about half the time. You may tighten the quality control during this process. Given that you are only going to be rewarding about half the sits, why not select the better ones for reward? This may mean faster, cuter or neater sits. It's up to you. When the dog is still sitting enthusiastically for a reward 50% of the time, go on to the next step.

The next step is to associate the word "sit" to the behavior by saying "sit" before you give the hand signal. The word "sit" is the new part, so it always goes first in the sequence. Work on the sequence:

1) verbal command "sit"
2) hand signal
3) dog sits
4) click
5) hand opens and dog gets reward

Be careful to say the verbal "sit" before you give the hand signal (as opposed to simultaneously as is most peoples' inclination), otherwise the known command will block the new command you are trying to establish. The new command needs to stand in isolation for a full second before you define its meaning to the dog with the known signal.

After rewarding several in a row this way, try the following. Command "sit" verbally and simply wait, with the food treat behind your back or in your pocket. At first the dog may simply stand and stare at you, whine, bark, paw at you or try to target the treat in your pocket or behind your back. Simply ignore all this and wait for 20 or 30 seconds. If the dog sits at any point, click immediately and then give him a treat from your pocket or hand. Then do it again. If the dog does not sit after 20-30 seconds, review the initial process of giving verbal command, hand-signal and rewarding a couple of sits to remind him of what works. Then give the verbal sit command, and try the waiting game again. With this stalemate, you are teaching the dog to attend to the verbal command. Commands are opportunities the dog will eventually learn to not miss.

Remain at this stage of training, rewarding every response to the verbal command, until the dog sits immediately after every verbal command to sit. Then go down to 50% reward again. This simply means you reward about every second time the dog sits on command. When you do this, by the way, don't do one reward, one no-reward in a fixed pattern. Randomize it more. Pick the nicer ones. The rule of thumb is that, whenever you make it harder (such as by demanding the behavior for a verbal cue only), you go back up to 100% reward, and as soon as the dog is perfect, you go down to 50% before making it harder with yet some other variation on how you want it done. When all the criteria have been added, you may wish to go for a lower maintenance schedule than 50%. For now, a thin reinforcement schedule is not necessary.

The Kindergarten sit is harder than you might imagine because although staying is not expected yet, the goal is reasonable stimulus control over sit. In theory, this means that the dog always sits immediately whenever the command or hand signal is given, the dog does not sit in the absence of the command, the dog does not sit when any other command is given and the dog does not do any other behavior after the sit command. In real life, what you're after at this stage is that the dog sits immediately whenever the command or signal is given. Achieving stimulus control is a formidable task which is never truly perfected in any practical animal training endeavor. What we do in dog training is train and proof our training throughout the dog's life to get as close to that elusive perfection as possible. As you shall see, there are a lot of pieces to the puzzle, especially when there are a lot of different commands and behaviors to be learned and the context is constantly changing: dog trainers are like jugglers who have a lot of balls to keep in the air. The best place to start this entire process is by teaching a good, solid sit.

At this point you have a dog who sits on both a hand signal and verbal command. Now you start proofing. Proofing means you will continue to strengthen the response to the sit command while you:

1) vary the level of ambient distraction
2) vary locations
3) vary your orientation to and distance from the dog
4) vary command elements such as faded commands & different handlers
5) practise inter-command discrimination

When you proof, you increase reliability. You are teaching the dog that the only ingredient necessary to set up the contingency for sit is the command or hand signal for sit. You do this by deliberately and systematically varying everything else to prove its irrelevancy. A certain location is not necessary. Nor is a certain trainer, tone of voice, particularly low level of distraction, time of day, dog mood, full moon or other non-essential element. All that's needed is the word or signal for "sit." This is called generalizing a response. The dog does it anytime, anywhere, no special conditions necessary. The first four proofing areas concern this generalization as well as pure strengthening of response. The fifth area involves the opposite of generalization, discrimination. Can the dog tell the sit command apart from all the others he knows to the point where he never guesses wrong? This is a discrimination proofing drill. No matter what order you throw commands at him in, he always gets the sit right immediately on the first try. For now you won't need to practise #5, inter-command discrimination because sit is the only command your dog knows. Later on, inter-command discrimination will be one of the balls you must keep in the air.

Before we get heavily into proofing, however, let's get a few other commands up and rolling, so that we can discuss proofing in a more general context.

Kindergarten Down

The first order of business, as it was for sit, is to repeatedly obtain and reward the behavior of the dog lying down. The fastest way to do this is to sit on the floor with a treat and bend one of your knees so that your leg makes a tunnel. Once the dog is targeting the treat, you will slowly lure him through the tunnel. He will have to lie down to keep his nose/mouth on the treat. As soon as he is in the down position, click and open your hand so that he wins the treat. Repeat this half a dozen times. If the dog does not readily target the treat as you move it under your leg, you may be pulling it through too fast. Go slowly, especially for dogs who seem suspicious about crawling under your leg. Perhaps let him win a couple of treats for putting his head under before raising the standard to head and shoulders and finally an actual down. If the dog jumps over your leg to continue targeting on the other side, simply say "too bad!" and start over again. This behavior will fade if it never works.

When the dog is diving readily under your leg to make your hand open, see if he will offer you a down without the tunnel. Sit on the floor (no tunnel now) with a treat in your hand. As soon as he's targeting the treat, move it slowly straight down between his front paws with your fingers covering the treat so that it is between your hand and the floor. Then, just wait. He will probably worry at it, licking, gnawing, pawing at your hand. You are simply waiting for him to lie down. Ignore all the other behaviors. They will die if they do not work. Eventually the dog will lie down. Click right away and open your hand. Then repeat. The second and third time may still be fairly protracted, but most dogs catch on in very few trials thereafter. The dog is simply becoming more efficient: worrying at your hand with mouth and paws has never worked, so he more rapidly cuts to the chase and lies down. Lying down, after all, keeps proving to be the best strategy to get that hand to open. Other strategies get ruled out through trial and error.

When the dog is instantly lying down as you place your target hand with the treat in it on the floor, you now have the task of removing the food target again. Before doing this, with a treat in your hand, practise several "push-ups" using hand signals. Push-ups are sequences of sit-down-sit-down. If the dog has difficulty moving upwards to a sit from the down position, simply move your target hand with the treat in it up and back slightly and then freeze. The dog will pop into a sit sooner or later in order to continue targeting. When he does, you simply click and open your hand again.

Through all of this, the dog is not only learning sit and down, he is learning how to learn. Inexperienced dogs must not only learn which behaviors you want and what the signals for these behaviors are, they must learn the concept that there is something quite specific that you want at all. Experienced dogs, who have great responses to dozens of commands, learn much more rapidly because they know how the game is played. They try out and abandon behavioral strategies in a fast, efficient manner and pick up what the right option is often after the first click. This flies in the face of popular mythology about young dogs learning more rapidly than older dogs. Naive animals of any age learn more slowly than experienced animals of any age. It is prior education that counts. So, be patient when working on neophyte dogs.

Once the dog is warmed up by doing brisk push-ups over and over with the target in your hand, remove the target and show the dog your empty hand. Have a treat ready in your other hand or in your pocket. With your empty hand, give your down signal, palm to the floor, the same way as you have been doing during the push-ups with the treat. Now, wait. If the dog stands, mark the mistake ("too bad!"), get him back into a sit and replace your palm on the ground. Eventually, perhaps reluctantly ("this couldn't possibly work..." the dog seems to say) the dog lies down. Immediately you click and treat. Repeat several times, so that the trend emerges. Your goal is for the dog to go down as easily for the blank hand as he did for the food lure. When that is happening, you may start to reward less often, demanding two, then three or more complete push-ups per reward.

By now, you are more than ready to add the word "down" to these proceedings. Before giving the hand signal, say "down" and then give the signal as usual. Your verbal command will become a reliable predictor of the known signal and will become associated with the behavior of lying down. After plenty of sequences of 1) verbal command, 2) hand signal, 3) correct response and 4) intermittent reward, try giving the verbal command and simply waiting. As soon as he lies down, immediately click and give the reward. Again, the first few trials might be painfully slow, but you must live through this to get to the other side: a dog who reliably lies down for a verbal command only. Give the reward every time for a while until he is an ace at this. Then you can put your verbal-command down on a reinforcement schedule as well.

Elementary School Sit & Down:

Inter-command Discrimination becomes an issue the minute the dog has two choices of response: sit and down. What do you, the trainer, do if you command down and the dog sits? You have four main options: one is to mark the behavior ("oh! too bad!")and then bail the dog out by commanding down again and rewarding it when you get it. The second option is to simply mark the behavior: "oh! too bad!" and pause in the training by looking away for a few moments or even walking away briefly before starting the next trial. Only a correct response on the first try gets rewarded. The third option is to mark the boo-boo, prompt the correct response but withhold the reward since the correct response required this extra help. Again, only a correct response on the first command gets rewarded. The fourth option is to simply wait, no click, no reward, no praise, no mark, nothing and then start another trial after a pause.

So, which option should you choose? Knowing what to do in any given circumstance with any given dog is part of the fine art of training. These judgment calls are what separate the adequate from the gifted. Don't agonize about it too much. You'll get better with experience.

If you bail the dog out by first marking and then re-commanding the behavior, the dog is likely to guess right on the second or third trial, especially if the discrimination is between only two commands.

This is an okay option for beginner dogs because it gives them another chance with little pressure on them. The game is kept easy to win. The disadvantage is that the incentive to not guess wrong in future is low. This comes into play when the discrimination task is harder, i.e. when your dog has many responses to choose from rather than just two. With this training style, if the dog gets it wrong, the worst thing that happens is the chance for reward is delayed slightly by having to be re-commanded after the mark.

The second option is a little tougher. The mistake is identified as such by the mark ("too bad!"), but the dog is not given a second chance. The disruption in training delivery is a small time-out. The idea is to motivate the dog to guess more carefully in the future. The stakes are higher. Only correct first guesses are rewarded and thus keep the flow of training going. Use this option if no improvement is gained using option one or if the dog is very keen but guesses a lot. Keen dogs give up less easily, and this allows you to minimize impulsive guessing.

The third option, to mark the mistake and prompt the right response but withhold the reward, is even tougher. The dog is effectively made to comply every time, one way or another, but rewards are only given for those responses that the dog makes on his own by guessing right the first time, as in option 2. If the dog is not keen enough, you will lose him fairly often by training this way.

The fourth option, to simply do nothing if the dog guesses wrong works marvelously with very motivated dogs but has one drawback. When the animal is on a reinforcement schedule, not every correct response is rewarded anyway. Ignoring wrong responses will feel the same to the dog as those unreinforced correct responses. In early training, this is hard on the learner. For this reason, it is necessary to praise the dog for the correct responses that go unreinforced so he can tell the difference. Praise helps the dog discriminate between a right response that is unreinforced because of the schedule and a response which is unreinforced because it is wrong. The praise is a signal that the dog is on the right track with that response whereas the silence means "dead end: no way that will ever be reinforced." The same effect can be achieved by marking wrong responses ("too bad!") and ignoring correct responses that are part of the schedule. My advice is to experiment with all these tools and discover what works best for you and the particular dog you are training at your particular stage. It is good to have a grasp of all these options so that you can switch strategies if necessary during training.

All this talk about the dog "guessing" may have you wondering at this point how the dog could possibly need to "guess" between two easy commands like sit and down. The answer is that, although dogs learn the behaviors relatively quickly, getting perfect stimulus control, i.e. getting dogs to the level where they never guess wrong, is much, much harder than dog owners imagine. Dogs, when given a command, typically guess sit first or whatever the most prevalent command is. By "prevalent," I mean whichever command has received the most reinforcement in the training history to date or was blitzed most recently (the "latest trick" syndrome). Dogs also seem to learn patterns of responses more easily than they learn commands. A classic example of this is a dog who, regardless of what command is given, performs sit-give-a-paw-down-roll-over in a stereotyped sequence. It is as though order-of-events learning overshadows the learning of the cues. If you want your dog to learn the actual commands, you must always vary the sequence.

It seems to be the policy of many dogs to notice that they have been given a command, not tune in to what the command was specifically and proceed to guess their way through their repertoire until they stumble onto what the trainer was after. Dogs approach responding to commands with a carpet-bombing mentality whereas we would prefer neat, precise "smart" bomb responses.

The only viable explanation for this is that inter-command discrimination is taxing to animals. You, the trainer, must therefore provide adequate incentive for the dog to attend to the content of the command as well. This is a specific and relatively long-winded training task, especially when the number of responses you have trained piles up. Dogs struggle much more with random order sequences of multiple commands. They get better at it with practice, but only if a standard is set that demands they get each command right the first time.

Kindergarten Stay

For either sit or down-stay, the first exercise is a repetition of the procedure described in the previous chapter for conditioning the no-reward mark. As soon as the dog is in the sit or down position, hold the treat a couple of feet away at dog height and snatch it away (just after you say "AH!AH!") at the first sign of movement. Repeating this forces the dog to switch strategies: to plan B, which is usually immobility. The first evidence of deliberate freezing must be immediately rewarded. The duration of the stay in this exercise is half a second or so for the first few trials, but can almost immediately be bumped up to 5-10 seconds by simply marking and removing the treat every time the dog breaks position. He learns that he can sit there and keep collecting at 5-10 second intervals provided he doesn't move. Be sure to hold the treat at dog height, rather than high and out of striking distance. The whole idea is to tempt him to move, so that you can mark this as an error and get a deliberate attempt to not move. This is playing devil's advocate and really grinds home the concept of stay.

The down-stay is somewhat harder than the sit-stay because many dogs tend to pop back into a sit when the handler himself goes upright. The dog assumes the exercise is a push-up, in other words. This is another case of inter-command discrimination, if you think about it. You wanted down-stay whereas the dog learned the pattern of sit-down-sit-down. "Sits always follow downs" is the dog's policy. This may give you an appreciation of how readily dogs learn patterns: he only knows two commands, and already it's a pattern. This tendency in dogs works against you every step of the way. The dog wants to learn the right order, but you want him to learn the right commands. The way out is through perseverance and exquisite timing: mark the instant the dog starts to pop into the sit (as opposed to when he has been sitting for a second or two) and click the first evidence of holding the down stay. Work up to 5-10 second down-stay, with the handler standing in a normal posture.

In any stay exercise, when the dog has stayed for long enough - he has made the criteria for reward, in other words - you may choose to release him from the stay, rather than clicking and rewarding and continuing the stay. The release is distinct from the rewarding of the stay. The reward is the click and treat. The release is a signal that the stay exercise is over, that the dog may now move again. Whether you reward a given stay or not, you must let the dog know when it's over ("you can stop staying now"). You may also wish to reward a stay in progress but not release it just yet. Many trainers presume that the reward-mark, the click, ends the trial, but in dog training, it is advisable to have a formal release word, especially to end long-duration behaviors like stays, attention and heeling. Quite often, reinforcement will happen along the way, but the behavior is expected to continue until release. Most dog trainers use the word "okay!" said with some enthusiasm, but some argue that this word comes up too often in everyday use. It doesn't matter what you employ as a release as long as you have one and know when to use it. The dog will be able to discriminate, with experience, a release signal from your use of the release word in everyday conversation: remember, getting dogs to generalize is the hard part.

When you perform this first stay exercise, you may use the word "stay" right off the bat because: 1) there will be no refining of the actual behavior - immobility is immobility, a very cut and dried criteria and 2) you are extremely likely to get good responses very early in the game. The sequence is, therefore:

1) command to sit or down
2) dog sits or lies down
3) praise
4) command to stay
5) dog stays or breaks
6) trainer rewards a stay or marks a mistake
7) if dog right, trainer releases stay or does another few
   seconds; if dog wrong, trainer repeats exercise

Be sure to say "stay" only once. Novice trainers tend to fall into a mantra-like chant of "stay...stay...staaa-aaay..." to "remind" the dog. This is sloppy training. Give commands once and then sink into your main role of feedback provider.

When you teach stay, you are also teaching the dog an exception to the targeting rule: the dog is now told he is wrong when he targets the treat. The word stay will provide a nice discriminative stimulus that will take on the meaning: "don't follow the treat." Until now in his training, it has paid off to do what is very natural: to target the treat or the hand (i.e. follow it wherever it goes). Now you are asking for a strategy shift. This is not just a different behavior but a new approach to finding out what the behavior is! Targeting was his strategy before. Now not targeting the treat is the way to win it. So, stay is a nice breakthrough command to widen the horizons of a dog's brain.

Practise this basic stay exercise in as many places as possible to get in some early generalization. Vary your position relative to the dog, vary the kind of reward, vary trainers and even try dropping the reward on the ground by "accident." When you play this last game of chicken, it is critically important that you are fast enough to prevent the dog from getting the treat when he breaks the stay to lunge for the food on the floor. Dogs usually fall apart when you drop the treat: not targeting food in your hand is one thing but not targeting an obvious freebie on the floor is much, much harder. So, be ready. As soon as you drop the food and the dog breaks, mark the mistake ("AH!AH!") and snatch up or step on the bait. Re-command the sit or down and repeat the same exercise until the dog freezes even when you drop the food on the floor. Reward this show of self-control immediately. The dog learns that the way to win even that piece of bait on the floor, once the word "stay" has been uttered, is to not move. When the dog is doing this correctly over and over, try it in a new location or with a different body posture or type of bait to get more generalization practice in. You can practise this exercise with every meal. Ask the dog to sit-stay before you put the bowl on the floor. The dog must hold position while you put the bowl down and wait until you give the release to begin eating.

Kindergarten Stand

As dogs stand up from a sitting or lying position, they almost invariably take a step or two forward. Your lure and, eventually, your hand signal will reflect this natural movement. The first step in teaching stand is, as usual, to obtain and reward as many instances of the behavior as possible. The dog is sitting and you have a food target in your hand. Hold the target near his nose and then move it smoothly away from him in a clean horizontal motion. What happens? In most cases, the dog stays. This is because you have been doing stay exercises and the picture for stand looks like another proofing variation. What's different is that you did not command stay. Part of stimulus control is the dog not performing the behavior in the absence of the cue: this is what you're grappling with when the dog offers stay on a stand prompt. Now you must get the dog to do another strategy shift: back to targeting. There are three ways to do this: a body prompt to stand, verbal prompting or simply waiting for the rewardable response. The body prompt is a gentle finger or two in the dog's groin area, gently lifting upwards. As soon as the dog stands, click and give a reward. Usually only a few physical prompts are necessary to let the dog know that this is not a stay exercise. A verbal prompt might be your release word or other encouraging noises to try to get him unlocked from staying. After a few repetitions, reduce the prompting and wait for the behavior, rewarding every instance until it is solidly installed.

All this will, naturally, make a temporary mess of your stay but don't panic: the dog will learn to discriminate a stand command from a sit or down stay and win a larger brain as a fringe benefit. To do this, you may want to oscillate between sit-stay and stand from a sit trials to improve the dog's discrimination between these two commands. Then do the same thing with down-stay and stand from a down.

Once the dog is standing readily from a sit for a food target, teach him to stand from a down. This is trickier than stand from a sit but is made easier by the fact that the dog has learned to stand from a sit already. Use the same prompts. When he's standing with great abandon from either a sit or a down, work to obtain this response for a hand signal only, just as you did for sit and down. The food lure goes back into your pocket or other hand. You may go back to physical and verbal prompting temporarily if the behavior falls apart. Reward every blank-handed stand until he's smooth at this. Then, put it on a schedule of 50%.

When the dog performs without mistakes or hesitation for an empty handed signal, you may start installing the verbal command. You will probably have to signal or prompt quite a few after giving your verbal command before weaning off these crutches. The sequence is:

    1) verbal command "stand," (wait one full second...)
    2) hand signal and/or food lure for stand,
    3) dog stands
    4) click and reward

Remember that stand from a sit and stand from a down are two separate exercises, so work on them separately. When the dog masters the stand with only a verbal command, put it on a reinforcement schedule (i.e. start rewarding it intermittently rather than all the time), and start working on three-way command discrimination.

High School Positions

A *Three-Way Command Discrimination* is an important foundation exercise in obedience training. Can the dog reliably, on the first command, perform a sit, down or stand from any position? Can he do it for verbal-only commands? The three-way exercise is harder than the earlier sit vs. down discrimination because in that exercise, when the dog is already in a down, the next thing asked for is always going to be sit. If he's already in a sit, the next command will surely be down. Dogs learn, in other words, to "do the other one." You can, in fact, avoid this by throwing in trick questions (commanding another down when the dog is already down). But it's much more efficient to simply add a third position. Adding that third position - the stand - changes everything. This is where dogs really get the concept that the cue means something very specific. And this is where the trainer gets good at acquiring stimulus control.

Practise sit, down and stand in random order for verbal commands, prompting with a hand signal when the dog does nothing or is incorrect. Reward only those responses which the dog guesses right first try, without the added hand-signal. By this point the dog can tolerate this regime. Note weaknesses. Typical weaknesses are: executing sit from a down, down from a stand and stand from a down. These particular changes often need to be drilled on their own: practise the same change over and over until it is performed smoothly and then re-integrate it into the random order exercise. This is fairly painstaking work but well worth it for the rewards you reap in terms of the dog's understanding of basic positions as well as the learning to learn effect. This puts you in good position for everything else you ever plan to teach your dog.

The basic recipe, when teaching basic obedience exercises like sit & down-stay, coming when called and heeling is the same at all levels, from kindergarten through to PhD. When the dog gets it right, there is a click and a reward. When the dog gets it wrong, the initiation of the mistake is given a no reward mark ("too bad!" or "AH!AH!"), and the exercise is repeated. When the dog starts getting it right over and over, the response is put on a reward schedule, and the standard can then be raised. If the dog gets it wrong over and over, the standard needs to be temporarily lowered to keep the dog playing the game. Variations on this basic recipe serve to refine your training. Knowing exactly when to do what variation is, again, an art that takes time to master.

Never be afraid to review more basic exercises whenever the dog falls apart. It is more important to keep the flow of training going than to hammer in any given exercise. You can always raise the standards again later. The dog should be playing you every second. If he's inattentive and not even trying, you've lost him, and your training is going nowhere. The prerequisite for training is that the dog is playing the trainer. Your ability to set appropriate standards as well as your timing and delivery will determine whether the dog plays you or switches his attention to other features in the immediate environment.

College: Positions at a Distance

The change in picture when the handler is farther from the dog causes massive generalization problems. We tend to do all our interacting with dogs, including training, at very close range. One of the key elements in the up-close package is that rewards are, quite naturally, transferred from trainer to dog up close. This repeated association, close to handler = high probability of reward, far from handler = low probability of reward makes dogs fall apart when you get more than a few feet away. Overcoming this obstacle is a major breakthrough in the dogs' generalization of any command he has learned. It's as though he has the revelation: "Hey! You mean sit works at 20 feet, too? Amazing!" Getting there is like any other training task: you must set a standard that the dog can already achieve sometimes (so he can win at the game right off the bat) and gradually crank it up, provided he continues to make progress. If you can get position changes at a distance, it paves the way for any subsequent tricks or commands you train. They will generalize to distance much more readily.

A good warm-up for this is to work up close but vary your usual command "picture." During training, dogs attend to more than commands: gestures, body language, the location of training, the trainer's demographics, distance, posture and orientation are all salient elements in what's called the stimulus package. Our goal is to vary everything except the command itself. So, make him do position changes while you sit in an easy chair, flipping him treats after the click, so he gets unhooked from the idea that being up close to you is necessary for reward collection. Practise position changes while he is in his crate. Practise with you lying on the couch or on the floor. Practise with your back to him, using a mirror to watch his responses. All of this helps the dog find out that regardless of how the "picture" changes, the command always means the same thing: doing the behavior earns him a reward. When you've got these in the bag, distance will come much more readily. When you practise changes at a distance, the dog will tend to creep forward. I strongly suggest you prevent this mechanically. There are a number of ways to accomplish this. One is to continue working him while he is in his crate. After each nice successful run of position changes you take one step backwards. The dog learns that he can make you approach the crate and reward him by executing correct changes on command. Putting him behind some barrier, like a baby-gate or fence, is equally effective. You can work with him at the top of a flight of stairs or other natural forward-movement inhibitor. You can put him on leash and tether him to a post. This affords you the added generalization bonus of the dog doing changes with the sensation of the constant pressure of the tether. A lot of dogs initially fall apart when you do this: "I can't possibly lie down with this tether on..." and, after some training: "well, hell, I guess I can." Bigger brain again.

Increase distance gradually and spend time working through any mental blocks, such as the tethering one. One wall you will hit usually occurs at around 8-10 feet, especially if you are working on hand signals as well as verbal commands. It could be that the signal looks different when you reach that particular distance, or it might just be the distance at which the training "gravity" loses its hold, and you are on truly novel ground. Who knows. Once you get past this, things seem to go more smoothly. The transition from 10 to 30 feet comes much more easily than the transition from 2 feet to 10.

Whenever he guesses right, go in and reward. When he guesses wrong or does nothing, approach immediately and do whatever command or prompt it takes to get the response. Try to reserve rewards for snappy, correct responses on the initial command or signal, unless you're really losing the dog. Avoid the habit of holding the signal or repeating the command as this will lead to chronically sluggish changes. Randomize the order of positions, so the dog can't latch onto a pattern, such as sit-down-stand-sit-down-stand. Don't try this exercise without the physical barrier until he is truly acing the changes without hesitation. If you allow creeping in early training, it gets stamped into the exercise and will give you grief for all your distance work further down the road. Keeping creeping at bay is hard enough without a good early-training imprint. Trainers are so eager to see what looks like a finished product that they shoot themselves in the foot with this exercise all the time.

Elementary School Stays

The goal is that the dog will hold a sit or down stay for up to 20 or 30 seconds while the handler walks in circles around the dog. The message to the dog is that he must remain seated or down even if the trainer is moving. To start training this, command sit or down, then command the stay as in the kindergarten exercise and take a small step to one side. Keep your eye on the dog. Try to time your no-reward mark to the instant his butt starts to come off the floor. If he holds position, pivot back in front of him and reward. Then try two steps to the side. If he breaks the stay, mark the mistake, get him back into a sit and then try one step again before attempting two. Beginner dogs are fragile little learners; they need to win the game fairly often.

With a dog who is more experienced at learning, the trainer would probably take another stab at two steps after the dog's boo-boo rather than giving him an almost guaranteed success on the very next trial. More experienced dogs tolerate dry spells between reinforced responses better than greenhorns. When your dog is hooked on obedience, you can be more time-efficient in your training. For now, err on the side of being too generous and gradual. This is especially the case if your dog's attention tends to wander.

Work gradually up to the level where you can command sit stay or down stay and on the first trial, every time, walk around the dog without him breaking the stay. He is allowed to follow you by rotating his head, but body rotations or position breaks are no good. Many dogs find it disconcerting to have you move behind them while they hold a stay, so always be prepared to temporarily drop standards and reward a couple of easier reps if things bog down. For instance, if you have worked up to five or six steps to almost behind the dog, but the dog breaks the stay whenever you take that seventh step to directly behind him, go back to the rewardable five or six step exercise often enough to keep the dog playing the game. You may also insert an intermediate step like six steps plus a lean toward the seventh. If he can do that, reward it a few times, and then try a half step after number six. And so on. Dogs fall apart because trainers lack the discipline to train gradually enough: we set arbitrary criteria, in other words. It is extremely presumptuous, if you think about it, to want to dictate what another being, let alone a being from another species, is going to find easy or difficult. You must always select something from the sample of responses the dog is already giving you.

When he can hold a stay while you parade around him, put it on a schedule, and try it in new locations to get some generalizing in. Expect the dog to regress in each new situation. People take it very personally when dogs regress or fail to generalize. They start searching for a reason: over-excitement, lack of exercise, malice, revenge, spite, stubbornness, breedism. These are usually irrelevant. The reason is likely to be failure to generalize. Simply re-train from scratch. The re-training will go more quickly than the initial installation, often with one trial per increase in difficulty (dog: "oh yeah, this again"). For now, avoid locations with excessive ambient distraction (e.g. running squirrels). You can try those later.

High School Stays

The goal is that the dog will hold a stay for a minute or two with the handler 30 or so feet away. There are two parameters here: one of duration (the minute or two) and one of distance (the 30 feet). These must be perfected separately and put on a schedule before combining them. So, first, while remaining at very close distance, start increasing the length of the stay. From 30 seconds go to 45 then 60 and so on. If, at any duration, the dog falls apart, re-attempt it for several repetitions. If he keeps breaking, be sure to do a few shorter stays so he succeeds before ending the training session. It may take a few sessions to get him up to two minutes or more in any location. When he is reliably doing a couple of minutes without breaking, put it on a schedule and tackle distance.

To train distance while keeping duration short, you will practise "bungee" stays. Pretend there is an elastic cord between you and your dog. Move away from him to an initial distance of, say, six feet. When you reach the six foot mark, immediately bounce back in to reward the stay. If the dog breaks at any point, mark the error and try again. If the dog breaks again, do an easier one, i.e. shorter distance. You are going to attempt stay at the same level of difficulty twice before lowering your standards. If you lose the dog, i.e. he loses interest and stops even trying, you need to drop standards faster, in this case after one mistake. Whenever you're cranking up the level of difficulty, be very sensitive to the animal's attitude to the training: his quitting or excessive frustration mean you're going too fast. Learning will always be somewhat stressful. Your job as trainer is to keep the dog playing the game and to maximize progress in the particular exercise, all the while cultivating his growing addiction to the game itself. Making the game too easy or using bland, continuous reinforcement schedules will also be detrimental, resulting in a minimalist approach from the dog. They don't get addicted if it's too easy to win.

The reason you can't initially combine the parameters of distance and duration is that both you and the dog need to agree on the criteria for reward at any given moment in training. If you attempt twenty feet for one full minute right off the bat and the dog actually stays for 40 seconds and then breaks, he missed the duration aspect but nailed the distance: is it rewardable or not? This is very confusing and demoralizing for animals until each element has been separately trained. Then, no-reward-marks will be more likely to hit accurately.

You may start to combine the criteria of duration and distance when the dog is good at each of the above exercises. When you do this combining, start moderately with something like 10 feet for 10 seconds, then 20 feet for 10 seconds, then 10 feet for 20 seconds. Crank the standard up gradually by raising one element and then, if successful, the other. Again, be prepared to drop the standard if you hit a snag.

When the dog does two minutes at 30 feet, put it on a schedule and take it on the road. Each location will, once again, probably cause a regression which you will take in stride by dropping standards to get rewardable responses and then cranking up the volume. Once you've got it in four or five varied locations, you graduate to College where you get into heavier distraction proofing.

College Level Stays

The goal now is for the dog to hold a stay in the presence of distractions such as other dogs milling around, a squirrel or tennis ball zipping past, a wiggly child patting the dog's head. Each distraction needs to be worked separately and with distance and duration minimized at first. So, you will go back to working up close to the dog and rewarding after each and every distraction refusal. It's important to understand what a distraction refusal is, because this is the rewardable response in distraction proofing. A lot of people beaver away at manufacturing distraction refusals with gradual increases in intensity and beautifully timed no-reward marks but then miss the magic moment when the dog refuses to take the bait. Have the criterion clear in your mind before you start presenting distractions and reward without hesitation when he makes the grade. In stays, this is difficult because the rewardable response is a non-event: the dog does nothing but hold his stay. This is a classic example of why you must think in advance about criteria.

Begin with some simple handler-movement distractions. Jump in the air a few feet from the dog. If he holds the stay, go back and reward. If he breaks, mark it and repeat. If he breaks again, assess. Was it a major break or was it an almost-stay. If the former, back off and do something easier. If the latter, try one more time. Needless to say, at every moment during distraction training, you will have your full concentration on the dog. It is critical that you catch the instant when your dog begins to break his stay. There is a saying: a mediocre trainer catches the dog after he gets up on a stay exercise, a good trainer catches the dog as he starts to get up, a great trainer catches the first muscle contraction. In distraction training, timing is even more critical because your only hope of stopping the dog from going flat out for a really attractive distraction is to interrupt early in the sequence. Try, for instance, a no reward mark on a dog chasing a fleeing squirrel at the moment before his jaws make contact with the squirrel some 50 yards away from you. Now, try a no reward mark when he leaves your side and takes the first step towards the squirrel. Which offers some chance of success?

If the dog gets a couple right in a row, escalate the distraction. Try a jumping jack. Try a twirl. Try Flamenco dancing. Try the twist. Try crouching down. This last one is tricky because, for a lot of dogs, crouching is a recall prompt. It is not, however, a command, so it's fair game for stay proofing. The dog will start to learn that the only thing that can end a stay is another command or a release. Try faking a sneeze. Try drumming on the floor. Whenever he refuses a distractions by holding the stay, go back and reward him. If he cracks, mark the mistake and repeat. Never escalate until you've had at least two perfect responses in a row with the same distraction. Try lying on the floor. Try rolling around on the floor. Try bouncing a ball. Try rolling a ball. Try throwing a ball. Try throwing several at once.

Now try touching the dog while he is staying. For a great many dogs, this is a whole new ballgame. If your dog is jittery or explosively friendly when people approach or touch him, this "sit to greet" will prove tricky but is worth cultivating. Start doing a series of approaches and head touches yourself until the dog is sitting solidly trial after trial. Then try swishing him all the way from head to tail. Then do simulations of how people pat dogs. These will include the up and down pat-pats on the head as might be delivered by a young child and the two-handed grasp around the ears with deep scritching that many adult dog lovers administer.

When you can't get him to break the stay anymore, you will start getting other people to administer the pats while you watch and supply feedback in the way of rewards and marks. Start again with approaches and light head touches. It is critical that you do multiple repetitions, i.e. series of touches, rather than just one or two. Remember troubleshooting? This is similar. Please note: if your dog is not socialized to people, do not do this until he has had some remedial socialization, described in chapter 3. When the dog is solidly sitting for head touches, try the full length swish by the same person. When this has been solid for several trials in a row, start with increasingly more difficult variations.

Stick with the same person until the dog will tolerate any and all kinds of contact without breaking the sit-stay. Only then will you start off a new person with small head touches. Be prepared for the dog to fall apart temporarily each time you introduce a new person. The magic moment is when you introduce a new person and whiz through the progression without any mistakes at all. This may be on person number three or person number twelve, but it will eventually happen. Make sure you've covered the major demographics, especially kids. When this is done, you have a nicely proofed sit to be patted.

When he will hold position confidently as you throw balls and squeaky toys all over the place and as he's manhandled by any person, take your distraction training on the road. Each new location will compound the distraction problem with its unique combination of ambient distractions. This is above and beyond the fact that all new locations evoke a failure to generalize. It will probably be necessary, therefore, to drop the standards and re-build the sit-stay for each distraction. Take comfort in the fact that each subsequent re-train of obedience exercises will go faster and faster, culminating one day in a dog who you can teach even brand new exercises in highly distracting environments and who will almost instantly generalize that training to all novel locations. Such an educated dog is simply a product of extensive training, rather than some genetic endowment of either dog or trainer. Luckily, training is fun, so get involved with the process rather than obsessing about the product.

Come When Called

Coming when called is high on the priority list for any pet dog to learn yet is usually mangled by the trainer if it is taught at all. The critical mistake, in many cases, is the attempt to use the command before it has been installed. This premature use of the command actually serves to de-condition the behavior and undermines future attempts at training. The typical premature use of "come" scenario is one in which the owner calls the dog over and then does nothing or else inadvertently initiates unpleasant activities or end pleasant activities. The command was presumed "known" because the owner had witnessed correct responses in the past. The command, sooner or later, falls apart utterly and completely, and the owner blames the dog. Underneath all this is the dangerous assumption that the dog will be "naturally" obedient. Let's look in some detail at what's happening.

Puppies have a natural tendency to approach when you call them, crouch, clap your hands or make enticing noises. They are compulsive greeters. They are also, and this is important, perfectly obedient to the laws of learning. If you capitalize on this natural inclination for the puppy to rush at you for these prompts and then fail to reward these beautiful responses or, worse apply either a positive or negative punisher, the puppy's days of coming will be numbered. The subsequent disobedience has nothing to do with rebellion, testing of authority or spite, but merely represents the cumulative effect of any and all deliberate and inadvertent training to date. What are the consequences to the dog of coming? Let's look at an example.

New puppy, Buffy, comes home to her new family. For weeks, Buffy toddles enthusiastically up to anyone who calls her, wagging and wiggling. The whole compulsive greeting thing. Buffy's owners presume that Buffy understands to come when she is called. She is, after all, doing it every time. She is also, by the way, endowed with a brain-stem and spinal cord, the minimum requirements to make her subject to the laws of learning. For their part, incidentally, her owners think Buffy is a Rocket Scientist.

After a few weeks, Buffy occasionally does not immediately rush to anyone who calls, especially if she is otherwise occupied, but this is not considered a big deal because she comes "most of the time." Her owners routinely call her over to give her affection, to come in from the yard outside when she has been let out to have a pee, to interrupt her when she is getting into something she shouldn't be doing, to groom her, to put her into her crate when they leave and occasionally, to reprimand her for leaving a puddle on the floor or for chewing the baseboards. What is the cumulative effect of all this?

Sometimes Buffy gets rewarded for coming by the attention and affection. The rest of the time, the words "Buffy!" or "Come!" are associated with either the initiation of an aversive (punishment for past transgressions, grooming or being crated) or the ending of something she likes (being in the yard, getting into stuff she "shouldn't" be getting into). When she is old enough, Buffy is taken to the park or dog run for exercise and called when it is time to go back home. The sequence used is 1) command "come," 2) dog comes, 3) leash put on/freedom ended. She comes the first couple of times but then starts refusing to come. One day, when her owner is late for work, Buffy does not come at the end of her morning romp and plays keep-away for 30 minutes. The owner calls an obedience school that evening and announces that Buffy is "stubborn." After all, she "knows" what come means and yet refuses to comply. But what does "come" really mean, to Buffy?

Buffy has learned, first and foremost, that "come," clapping and bribes very often mean the end of fun or the start of something yucky. She learns, as any normal animal would, to not approach when she hears that word or sees that picture. This is not specific to Buffy or to some rebellious flaw in her particular personality. This is important to understand. If I said to you, for instance, "approach for something unpleasant..." how compliant would you be? That's what "come" is to Buffy. The fatal flaw in the thinking of most owners is that they imagine the dog is a moral being who understands the owner's authority and is susceptible to guilt. When the owner demonstrates disapproval of the dog for not coming, this is presumed to be sufficient motivation to overcome the obvious animal learning implications: the initiation of aversives or ending of reinforcers for the dog. Dogs are, however, amoral and completely selfish. If they have a concept of the word "should" it would tie closely into their pure sense of self-interest and perfect obedience to learning laws. In dog culture, when someone calls you, you should absolutely not come if that picture is associated with the ending of fun or initiation of something you don't like.

The first mistake Buffy's owners made, long before punishing scores of recalls, was to presume that the dog was "obeying" a prompt: the calling and clapping. Prompts are merely elicitors. They tend to make behavior happen, all other things being equal. But these antecedents quickly take on the more powerful role of conditioned stimuli when they are paired with events of relevance to the animal. The consequences of coming make all the difference. The prompt, in the case of Buffy, wore out pretty quickly when "come" started to mean bad news. This is why a prompt might appear to work for a while and then cease to work anymore.

The way out of this common predicament is to bite the bullet from the outset and not only accept but also actively exploit those laws of learning to which the dog will be perfectly obedient. Train in harmony with the principles of how animals learn. Stop trying to fight it. Each and every time the dog approaches, systematically reward him with affection, play and food treats from your pocket. Reserve the dog's name and the word "come" as sacred utterances. Never follow them with something the dog will not like or with the cessation of something the dog is enjoying. Have regular recall conditioning sessions, as you did for sit, down and stand. When in the park or dog run, teach the dog that come is simply a check-in break most of the time: the dog comes, gets a pat and food treat and then is told to go back and play. Teach the dog that failure to comply, in the heat of fun, results in the ending of that fun. Stack the deck in your own favor. Here are some basic recall exercises.

Kindergarten Recall Exercise

Two or more family members take turns calling the puppy (or untrained adult dog) back and forth in the kitchen or down a long hallway. Every time the puppy comes to someone, he is told to sit, taken by the collar and then given a food treat from the caller's pocket or given a fast round of a tug game with a toy from the caller's pocket. When the puppy does this perfectly every time, the food treats or tug games are gradually reduced to about half the time. You may, once again, be selective once the schedule is in place: why not pick the best efforts since you're only rewarding half of them anyway?

A variation on this exercise is hide and seek: the dog is held by one person while the other hides somewhere in the house. The dog is released after the hidden person yells "Buffy, come!!" The dog is now on a search and rescue mission. When the dog arrives, a greeting celebration ensues, and a tug game is initiated. During this time, the other family member hides. The dog is then sent, on that person's command, to make another find. The dog's impression of the word "come" shoots way up. You can also practise "random" recalls, for which you only need one person. Call the dog over at random times and reward him with a treat or play session. In fact, why not precede all enjoyable activities with a recall so that the best predictor the dog has that something good is about to happen is the word "come."

When practising recalls, the initial sequence of events should be:
1) command to come
2) prompts: hand clapping, luring, squealing noises etc.
3) dog approaches
4) dog praised enthusiastically during approach
5) dog told to sit when he arrives
6) dog sits
7) handler takes dog's collar in one hand and
8) reaches into pocket with other hand to give dog a food treat or tug toy

When the dog has had several brief sessions like this and thoroughly enjoys the game, phase out the prompting (#2) and "getting warmer" feedback (#4), so that the dog performs the behavior for the command only. When this is accomplished, put it on a reinforcement schedule, selecting the best efforts for reward. Try to practise in at least three or four different locations.

Elementary School Recall Exercise

If the recall command was a wall that you are building, you have, with this kindergarten exercise, laid down the first row of bricks. You've started a foundation. To lay down the second row of bricks, you will teach the dog a controlled distraction exercise. For this you need two people. One is the handler, the other takes the role of distracter. The handler has nothing on him: no treats, no toys, nothing. The distracter has all the rewards the dog likes: liver, cheese, the dog's tug toy. The distracter shows the dog that he has possession of all these things but without letting the dog have actual access. The handler, who has shown the dog that he has no rewards with him, goes a short distance away and calls the dog. In most cases, the dog will ignore the handler and "play" the distracter, the obvious slot machine at that moment. The distracter will simply ignore the dog's efforts. These might include pawing, jumping, whining, performing beautiful sequences of sit-down-stand, barking etc. The handler will keep trying to call the dog at frequent intervals. There is no rush here because the rewards are well controlled. The dog is not winning anything but simply wasting his time with all his behavior directed at the distracter. He just does not know this yet.

Sooner or later, the dog will experiment by moving towards the handler who is calling. The handler will praise with enthusiasm as the dog approaches. When the dog arrives and sits at the handler's position, the distracter immediately runs over and relinquishes one big treat or gives the toy to the handler for a nice round of tug. Then the distracter goes away again, more than likely followed by the dog, and the exercise is repeated. The dog learns, over time, that the way to get what the distracter has is to do what the handler is saying. Obedience is the answer! Be advised: this takes time and patience the first few trials.

If sessions of this exercise are done repeatedly, you end up with a dog who will fly off the distracter in order to respond to the handler's command to come. You may also get variations, such as the dog coming to the handler before he has given the command. Simply ignore this. Repetition is the key with this exercise. Some dogs catch on more readily than others. This has less to do with learning rate than it does with how impulsive or emotional a dog is, as well as how well the dog has been primed with the basic, kindergarten recall exercise. It is a good idea to alternate roles of handler and distracter so the dog learns that the command "come" is the key thing to attend to, not a specific person. Always rule out what's irrelevant. Be sure to take the exercise on the road when the dog nails it every time in the house. Besides varying location, you may also want to experiment with different flavors of distraction: novel food, another dog's smelly toy etc. will initially trigger a failure to generalize.

High School Level Recall

When the dog is an ace at the controlled distraction recall exercise (elementary school), it is time to bump the motivation up another notch. You will now teach the dog the game of running through your legs after a thrown ball or tug-toy. This is putting the dog's predatory drive to work for you rather than having it as a perpetual competing motivation. At first, use no commands. Simply get the dog interested in the toy by playing a quick round of tug or teasing him with it. Then, with your legs apart, lure him in close and, when he's focused on the toy, lob it through so that the dog goes through as well. Repeat this over and over to get the dog used to going through your legs. Some dogs are deeply suspicious about doing this. Big dogs will have to flatten themselves somewhat. All dogs can learn to do it, and it is well worth the effort.

When the dog is going through your legs without hesitation, put him in a sit stay eight or ten feet away, set yourself up and on the command "come," send him through for the throw. Delay throwing the object until you are sure he is going to go through. Dogs quickly get into the habit of going around rather than through if the trainer allows a few of these scoot-arounds to be rewarded by throwing too soon. If the dog attempts to go around, withhold the throw. He must learn that he has to go through in order to get the toy. Keep your throws as level as possible (rather than throwing upwards) to maximize the flat-out chase aspect. After each throw, have a fast round of tug-of-war. This makes the game even more interesting to the dog as well as giving him a reason to get the toy back to you as soon as possible after he catches it.

As he gets better at it, increase the distance between yourself and him. Do plenty from a sit-stay but also do it out of context of formal training sessions. Spring "come" on him when he is least expecting it (have your tug-toy hidden on you). This can be the initiation of your daily tug/retrieve session with him as well as part of the obedience breaks during tug. The more the dog does this exercise, the more he learns to charge you with great intensity on the word "come." Making use of predatory aggression is making use of one of the most potent motivators around. For many dogs, it far outranks straight food rewards (the theory behind this is interesting: free food feeds him for now, whereas honing hunting ability feeds him for a lifetime. Also, moving "food" is fresher). When the dog will charge you at top speed from 30 feet away and reliably go through your legs every time, simply ditch the prompts.

Up to now, you've been standing with legs apart and tug toy in hand. This picture is an important signal for the dog. It predicts what follows. What the dog must now learn is that the word "come" by itself is as good a predictor as that picture. The way to do this is to, first, hide the tug toy up your shirt or in your pocket, somewhere the dog can't see it, but where you can quickly access it at the key moment. Put the dog on a sit stay and leave him to set up a recall as usual. When you get 30 feet or so out, stand normally, legs together and arms by your side. Tell the dog to come. What you will probably find is that the dog does not charge you with anywhere near the same zeal he did when you were doing the previous through-the-legs exercise. That's okay. When he gets halfway to you, whip the toy out from its hiding place, open your legs and do the recall throw as usual, just before he gets to you.

In a few repetitions, the dog will start charging again, even though you are standing normally. This is because your normal posture has started to predict the picture he has come to know and love, that of you with legs apart and toy in hand. You will work now to gradually delay the leg opening and toy appearance until the last possible instant. The goal is for the dog to learn that your regular recall command and posture predicts the game as reliably as the open leg posture did before.

When the dog charges his recalls with you standing upright, it is time to restore the sit, at least some of the time. The goal now is for the dog to delay his decision on whether to sit or run through until the last possible instant. The way to accomplish this is to sometimes send him through and sometimes ask for a sit. You ask for a sit by keeping your legs together and commanding a sit. The first time you spring the sit on him after he has done scores of through-the-legs drills, be sure not to lock your knees or you may be literally knocked over. A good idea is to command the sit well in advance on this first occasion, when the dog is, say, 10 or 15 feet away. Use a verbal command as well as a broad hand signal. Practise a few sits in a row until he seems to anticipate the sit. Then send him through the legs a couple of times. Then go back to sit. The idea is to keep him guessing so that his policy becomes to charge at top speed and then evaluate when 10 feet away. This way you retain maximum motivation with deceleration delayed until just before recall completion. That's good juggling of the speed and sit elements.

On those recalls where a sit is the final product, you can always whip the toy out from under your shirt and play tug anyway, after he sits. You must reward the sits occasionally. Perfection of this exercise lends tremendous distraction-proofing to your recall by placing it at the top of the reward hierarchy in virtually any situation. After all, the reason that dogs would rather play with dogs or chase squirrels or sniff through the underbrush rather than coming when called is that these activities are fun and exciting whereas coming is not. Your job is not to lament this, but to make use of the dog's addiction to fun by making recalls the most fun and exciting activity your dog gets to do.

College Level Recall

If you have successfully installed the High School speed-drill exercise, described above, you may find you don't need the College level exercise. In other words, the dog has a near-perfect recall in all situations. That is the power of predatory aggression. If you weren't instantly successful with that exercise, don't be tempted to give up early and try the next one in the hopes that it will fix competing motivation problems. Try harder to cultivate a speed-drill. Some dogs take longer to catch on than others. These are the unkeen retriever types, typically. It's worth loosening them up in any event, so I would encourage you to persevere.

The college level exercise is designed to interrupt the dog and coerce the recall in those situations where the dog fails to come when there's competing motivation. Typical competing motivation is the dog interacting with another dog, deeply embroiled in some smell on the ground or pursuing a fleeing object like a cat, squirrel or car. Please note that if you have a dog who is not conditioned, i.e. you have not diligently done the kindergarten and elementary school recall exercises to the point of reliability in a variety of locations, you have no business trying what follows. It's not a band-aid to fix your "stubborn" dog who door-dashes every chance he gets or won't come in from the yard. No skipping ahead. There are no quick fixes here. You must pay your dues first.

The first step in the College level recall is to get the dog to come when in mid-chase in the opposite direction. You will start training this in the middle of an ordinary retrieve game with your dog. Throw the ball or toy as usual and, after the dog initiates the chase, give your recall command. The dog will almost certainly ignore this. Immediately spring into action, loudly giving a continuous no-reward mark ("AH!AH!AH!AH!...") while you charge after the dog. Really rain on his parade. Physically prevent him from taking the toy or remove it from him if he has already grabbed it. The aim with this mild punishment is to create some inhibition for the next trial. Then try again. If the dog is not slowed down at all on the second trial, you need to be more dramatic with your interruption. Act as though it is a real emergency. What would you do, for instance, if your dog were running towards an expressway? Your goal is to be able to stop the dog dead in his tracks in mid-chase if necessary because, one day, his safety could in fact be at stake.

Practise until the dog responds to the recall command. This response will be an extremely tentative and shell-shocked looking one. That's okay for now. As soon as the dog stops or turns around after the command, praise very enthusiastically and encourage the

Walking away

Meggie, Come!

Full speed

Through the legs

Reward time

Start again

dog towards you with every prompt in the book. Clap, crouch, hold a food lure and talk baby talk. This exercise is difficult and stressful. The dog needs to know he is on the right track. When he gets to you, praise lavishly, click and reward with a really special food reward or tug-game with a toy from your pocket. Then do it again.

At some point, you will probably run into the following snag. You throw the toy and the dog, having experienced a couple of confusing and aversive interruptions from you, now does not chase the toy at all. Simply jolly him back up with a couple of retrieve throws without interruption to build back his confidence. Dogs do not instantly learn that it was the failure to respond to the recall cue that was the problem: many think it is now dangerous to chase their toy. You must tease this out by alternating normal throws and ones that you interrupt with the recall.

Your goal is a dog who will stop on a dime on your "come" command, whirl around and confidently come to you. But he will also retrieve with the same zeal as before you installed this exercise. The only way to get there is with solid, carefully executed work. Carefully executed means you must monitor the dog's attitude every step of the way, always building up if necessary, then inhibiting more if necessary. You must walk a fine line.

A good policy, when you get those perfect responses, is to have as reward a command "GET IT!" which means he may now re-attack, with gusto, the object he was called away from. He now understands that his failure to comply with the recall command terminates the chase, whereas complying with the command means that you permit him to get the toy. When he has this exercise down, vary the thrown object to start getting generalization. Do balls, toys, food, Frisbees, whatever he will chase. When this is done, take it on the road for some location generalizing. Vary the point in the chase at which you give the recall command, bearing in mind that the further the dog is from you and the closer he is to the object, the harder it gets. You are trying to get the dog to turn on a dime with any object in any place at any point in the chase. This exercise primes the dog for a recall away from other distractions such as dog play or fleeing squirrels. The principles are the same, but you don't have the luxury of repeated trials in most cases. Therefore, before even attempting recalls in these circumstances, be sure you have perfected the recall off a chased object with generalization of both the object type and location.

Pulling On Leash

Dogs naturally pull on leash. There are a couple of reasons for this. One is that the pulling is usually reinforced by the owner in the form of forward movement. The dog pulls because pulling works. He never finds out that not pulling would also have worked because the natural pace of most dogs is faster than the natural pace of the owner: the dog hits the end of the leash immediately and thus, self-teaches to pull. This is not a rank thing: extremely submissive dogs pull on leash with as much abandon as middle ranking and dominant dogs. The other reason dogs pull, even to the point of gasping for breath in obvious discomfort, is that dogs have what is called an opposition reflex. As soon as they feel pressure against their necks or chests, they reflexively lean into it. This is part of the reason Huskies and Malamutes, as well as a lot of other breeds, love pulling in harness. It is intrinsically rewarding.

So, given what you're up against, it is prudent to begin anti-pull training from day one, rather than waiting till the dog has an entrenched pulling addiction. The main pull prevention exercise, for puppies or dogs who do not already have a strong habit, is the red-light/green-light game. The rule of this game is that, while on a walk with the dog, you may only move forward if the leash is loose and jangly. As soon as the dog tightens the leash, you will freeze dead in your tracks. The loose leash is the green light - handler moves forward; the tight leash is the red light - handler stops. Moving in the direction the dog wants to go is a potent reward which you must never give for pulling on leash.

The first time you play this game, the dog will do a bit of lunging and straining when you put the brakes on. Simply wait until, eventually, by chance, he slackens the leash. Then start moving. As soon as you do so, he will re-energize and, no doubt, hit the end of the leash, causing you to stop again. The dog requires some repetition to see the trend: tightening the leash grinds the walk to a halt every single time, slackening the leash makes movement happen. The dog does not learn to walk on a loose leash in one shot. What you get, rather, is a gradual decrease in attempts at pulling. So, keep it up. When he gets the religion, you are on the way to a lifetime of smooth sailing.

If you have an already existing pulling problem, you will probably have to use heavier artillery, training-wise than the red-light/green-light game. Your options are to 1) try the red-light green-light game anyway, 2) play the game but with active corrections and/or penalties, 3) change equipment.

Playing the game with active corrections means that, rather than simply stopping when the dog starts pulling, you warn him with a word such as "easy" or "steady" and then, if the dog doesn't back off, you stop moving and give a sharp jerk and release motion on the leash. The dog learns that the warning predicts the leash jerk if he continues to pull. This "leash correction" is a punishment. Its purpose is to buy you a few seconds of no-pull behavior which you must then praise and reward with forward motion or food from your pocket. If the dog already has a strong pulling habit, be prepared to warn and correct virtually ad infinitum. Usually, this method will simply keep pulling at bay, making walks more tolerable. It also relies heavily on the use of punishment. Not only does this put you repeatedly in the role of bad guy, but many dogs desensitize to the correction. I describe it, in spite of its shortcomings, because it works like a charm on the occasional dog.

A better way to beef up the red-light/green-light game is to give the dog distance penalties for pulling, such as a "one yard penalty" or a "three yard penalty." When the dog starts to pull on leash, he is warned, pulled back and then you retreat some distance to make the dog cover the same piece of ground again. A good motto is "we'll keep doing this patch of sidewalk until you do it without pulling." The first few times out, the dog will likely have to do the same piece of ground many times in a row before he figures out that it's his pulling which is giving him the penalty. You can make this clearer by marking the initiation of pulling with "Too bad!" or "AH!AH!" which signals him that you are about to remove a reward: progress forward. When you retreat to re-try a piece of ground, make sure the leash is slack before commencing another stab at forward walking.

Industrial strength pullers can actually injure their human companions. If pulling has been allowed to blossom to this point, these dogs usually need new equipment. There are several "power steering" options available now. Probably the best of these is the dog halter, which looks and works very much like a halter or hackamore does on a horse or pony. The idea is to move the leverage point from the neck to the muzzle. Now when the dog tries to pull, there is nothing to lean into: the dog's head simply turns around. These sorts of devices allow people to control half-ton horses, so it's not surprising that they can give you a lot of control of an 80 pound Labrador. Halters for dogs are put out under a few different names, like "Gentle Leader" and "Halti."

The advantages of halters are: 1) they dramatically reduce pulling on leash in most dogs, 2) they work without employing pain and 3) they require very little expertise. The disadvantages of halters are: 1) most dogs fight them initially (there is an adjustment period), 2) to the untrained eye they resemble muzzles and 3) the effects do not generalize well to when the dog is not wearing the device.

By giving the handler control of the dog's head, halters are also good tools for controlling lungy, aggressive dogs. They have not caught on, in spite of their obvious efficacy because of those first two disadvantages: people don't like the look and they don't like seeing their dog so obviously hating it the first few times it's put on. People who use them are asked over and over by passersby why their dog is wearing a muzzle. Halters are far from muzzles: while good control of the head and jaws is achieved, dogs can pant, drink, retrieve a ball and bite while wearing one. I personally think the look is cute. Dogs wearing halters look like little ponies. The adjustment period is over with quickly if the owner handles the first few experiences properly. This means not giving in and removing the halter if the dog throws a tantrum. Raise the dog's head every time the dog lowers it and paws at the halter. Provide lots of praise and treats when the dog tolerates the halter.

Another option is an anti-pull harness. This is not to be confused with a pulling harness which is used for sled racing and draft work. The original anti-pull harness is the Sporn Harness, named after its patenter. Another brand, the Lupi, is put out by the company which sells Halti brand halters. The anti-pull harness, according to product literature, works by converting the forward pull of the dog into upward thrust. I honestly don't know how it works. Perhaps there's some aversive being applied. Suffice to say that, for some dogs, it works a veritable overnight miracle and, for others, it makes a small dent, if any, in their pulling. Prospective users should test drive one on their own dog before buying.

The advantages of this device are: 1) when it works, it works very well, 2) it is safe and seems to work without employing pain, 3) it takes no skill to use and 4) dogs usually accept it right away. The disadvantages are: 1) it does not work on every dog, 2) the effect does not generalize well to when the dog is not wearing the device and 3) the original brand is fairly pricey.

These two products, halters and anti-pull harnesses, represent the evolution of anti-pull training. However, most people address their pulling on leash difficulties with another device, the choke or strangle collar. As its name implies, this collar is designed to strangle the dog. It is the most widespread tool in dog training. There are chain link strangle collars, ones with wider links to preserve the dog's coat (not his trachea, mind you, his coat), fabric ones, ones with limited strangulation capacity and ones with enhanced strangulation capacity which clip on and sit higher on the dog's neck to increase the ability of the collar to cut off the dog's air. It is pretty amazing how much time and energy has been devoted to the design of strangulation devices for man's best friend. People avoid halters in droves because the dog "doesn't like it" but think nothing of digging metal or a thin cord right into their dog's windpipe.

One problem with strangle collars is that the aversive delivered is mild to moderate for most dogs. It doesn't hurt that much. The effect is thus marginal on most dogs' behavior. Rarely does one or two punishments with a strangle collar work: a virtual lifetime of leash correction is in store for dogs whose owners opt to use chokers to train. But while a strangle collar's capacity to hurt is iffy, their capacity to harm, i.e. to damage the dog acutely or cumulatively, is considerable. This is what is so insidious: it seems to have very little effect, so owners escalate the number and force of leash jerks or switch to a more dangerous model, in the meantime desensitizing the dog gradually to the jerks. All the while, the dog's windpipe is being bent.

Another problem with a choke collar is the strength and co-ordination required to deliver an adequate leash correction. Many people are physically or psychologically unable to do the technique correctly. They end up simply putting on a choker and hoping it will do the work itself. The result is a dog straining on the end of a leash with its tongue turning a more obvious shade of blue.

So, why are they so popular? The answer lies partly in the historical traditions of dog training. The original trainers were military men training German-bred German Shepherd Dogs. This combo did okay with strangle collars though, I would argue, not half as well as they would have done with clickers and sliced hot dogs. But they got away with it. These were the prototype trainers whose methods trickled down to people who, after W.W.II, joined the first organized community obedience classes with their family pets. It sort-of-kind-of worked on enough dogs that, without critical scrutiny and without alternatives around, the method stuck for decades.

The other part of the answer is probably our punishment-oriented mentality. These collars give the handler power to deliver punishments with all the resulting frustration displacement and temporary suppression of behavior (and eventual global suppression of behavior). We do so love violence.

The last option for reducing pulling on leash is the prong or pinch collar. This looks like a medieval torture device, with double rows of blunt teeth which, when the dog pulls, dig into the dog's neck. This design makes it much more aversive than a strangle collar. Ironically, in spite of its fearsome appearance, it is self-limiting by design and therefore a much safer piece of equipment than a choker. Because of the increased aversiveness and decreased risk of harm, it is an infinitely better choice than a choker. It is therefore, arguably, a reasonable option to prevent pulling. However, in light of the availability of halters and Sporn harnesses and of good, early training on plain buckle collars using red-light/green-light technique, prong collars are harder to justify. They can never be justified as tools to teach sit, stay, come or anything else apart from walking on leash.

Kindergarten Heeling

Heeling is defined as the dog walking at your left side (or right side, it doesn't matter unless you plan to compete in obedience trials) with his head or shoulder at your pant seam, never deviating from this position and sitting automatically whenever you stop. Kindergarten level heeling is simply teaching the dog to continuously follow a moving food target. The target is held against the left side of your body, so the dog also learns to follow your body while he follows your hand. First, fill your pockets with treats. Put one treat in your hand, show it to the dog and then move the target to the side of your body at your dog's height. Large dogs will end up with a target at hip level or higher and smaller dogs will need a target around knee level. This means, for the initial few training sessions, you will have to bend if you have a little dog. You can use your right or left hand for this, depending on how you are most comfortable.

If the dog is attending to the target, start moving forward. It is a good idea to encourage the dog to follow you with verbal chatter at first. Take a few steps and halt. As you halt, give your hand signal for sit in a backwards direction, as though pushing the air directly backwards. Click and reward the dog when he sits. You are trying to get the dog to sit straight, i.e. on a parallel track to yours and not turned inwards. Dogs will tend to turn in towards your body because this orientation has, up until now, been the one associated with rewards. Your goal in initial heel training is to get the dog to associate the rewards he will be earning not just with the following but with the view he has of you from heel position.

You can do some reinforcing of just this "view" by simply standing there with the dog sitting in heel position and having him visually track a target from his nose all the way up the side of your body. After praising him for watching for a couple of seconds, give him the reward. You can even drop it to him: he'll enjoy learning to catch. When you do this "picture" associating, make sure you keep your shoulders straight and not turned towards the dog at any point. Shoulder turning changes the view to exactly the one you don't want.

When the dog is following eagerly, practise turning in all directions: right, left and 180-degrees. When you turn 180 degrees, do so with the dog on the outside track. This means that if the dog is on your left, whirl around to your right. If your eventual aim is to compete in obedience, keep your left and right turns as square and military as possible and single track on your about-turns. This means that, when you do the 180, you are walking the same line in both directions before and after the turn, rather than executing a U-turn which would put you in another lane. You will also have to learn smooth pace changes and decent footwork if you want to look nice in the competitive obedience ring, so be sure to get yourself into the hands of a good, qualified instructor who can polish these things if and when the time comes. For now, you just want to get the dog following reliably and turning as tightly in position as possible. This takes practice. Reward as often as it takes to keep the dog targeting the lure.

Heeling vs. Walking on Leash

You will need to practise this and other heeling exercises for a long time before the dog will heel with any skill on a real walk, but in the meantime, it is important that he have some idea of how to walk on leash. Make sure that you have solved your pulling problems with the red-light-green-light technique or by changing equipment, as described above. Teaching heeling and walking on a loose leash are two separate endeavors. Heeling is a complex behavior which will take many months of practice before it is precise and reliable. Getting this behavior generalized from your living room to the great outdoors takes even more time and patience. Make sure it's well conditioned indoors before taking it outside to practise during actual walks. And, because heeling is harder for the dog, don't expect it in endless quantities while on a walk, especially when your dog is only initially learning to heel outdoors. So when you do introduce heeling on actual walks, ask the dog to heel for short bursts at first, all heavily rewarded.

Eventually, you may ask for heeling of up to several minutes' duration while, for instance, going through crowded areas or crossing streets. The rest of the time, I suggest you teach your dog to simply walk on a loose leash or use a halter or Sporn harness if the pulling is severe, as described earlier. This way he has some freedom of movement to sniff the ground, the main highlight of walks for most dogs. Dogs need to investigate the urine and droppings of other dogs to gather important dog social data. They can't do this if they're heeling. The most important thing to remember is that walking on a loose leash and heeling are two separate enterprises. The heeling you will bring up to speed in training sessions before introducing it during walks, whereas walking on a loose leash will be trained on walks from day one.

Elementary School Level Heeling

The aim now is for the dog to heel with a faded target, sit automatically when the handler stops and keep attention fixed on the handler at all times. Before trying these exercises, be sure you've practised plenty of lure following as described in the kindergarten heeling exercise. The dog needs to be a rabid targeter because this will ensure sufficient momentum for the fading and occasional removing of the target which you will be initiating now.

In a low distraction environment, warm the dog up by having him follow the food target held against the left side of your body. Stop often to command a sit and reward the dog. Now, choose a moment when he is following well and do the following: for a second or two move the target up and away slightly, from your hip to your chest for instance. When you do this, chat the dog up enthusiastically. You want to convey to him that moving the lure further away is a Good Thing. After a couple of seconds, if he continues following closely as before, make it an actual good thing by giving him the reward. Then, start off again with the lure in its original position. When he's following well, move it away again, keep him with you using enthusiastic chatter for a couple of seconds and then give the reward. You are rewarding on the fly now rather than asking for a sit. The criterion you are isolating for reward is his following for a faded prompt: the more distant lure.

Do the prompt-fade over and over just before giving rewards. Done sufficiently often, the fading of the food target becomes an event the dog relishes: he learns that the removal of the target means the reward is coming soon. If you fade the food target and the heeling falls apart immediately, it means you have not done enough basic target-follow conditioning. Go back to kindergarten and practise some more. Then try fading again. Make sure, also, that you are propping up the heeling with the praise when you fade the target in this early transition phase of training.

When he's no longer falling apart as you fade the target, the next thing to do is to extend the duration of the heeling for the faded prompt. Go for three seconds, then four, then five. As usual, drop the standards and go for shorter bursts if the dog falls apart and starts performing badly. This falling apart and being rebuilt is an inevitable process for the dog in training. And it is sure character-building for the trainer. In a few sessions, you will be able to heel the dog for a food lure held much more discreetly than before and for longer stretches between rewards. When he can do this, start working on automatic sits.

The most efficient way to install automatic sits is to heel the dog with frequent halts. For the first while, the sequence is as follows: 1) you stop walking and 2) you hand-signal the dog into a sit, as much in heel position as possible (of course, you click and reward nice responses as usual). Your eventual goal is for the cessation of walking to become the sit command. This is why it comes first. Avoid the common error of prompting or signaling the sit before you halt or as you halt. If you do this, the known hand gesture will block the event you are trying to establish as a command: your coming to a halt. This is because, when done at the same time as or after the sit command, the stopping provides no new information.

The correct order of events - halt then hand-signal - may cause the dog to continue past the point at which you stopped. Don't panic and fall into the trap of pre-emptively commanding a sit before halting. It is tempting to do so, because it seems to solve the problem. It is actually merely postponing the problem to the inevitable day when you want the dog to sit for cessation of walking alone. Cessation of walking must, therefore, come first in the sequence if it is to ever be established. So, the solution is to get your prompt in with some urgency as soon as you have stopped walking, to reduce the dog's overshooting. You may also selectively reward those sits which are more in position, once the dog is sitting every time and for intermittent reinforcement. Shaping comes to the rescue again.

When the dog is no longer overshooting on halts and his sits are relatively well positioned, you will start fading the signal. Start off with a series of halts and signals as usual, rewarding the nicest sits. Then, after halting, try a smaller hand signal for sit and see if you get one. If you do, reward it. If you don't get a sit, give your broader signal but fail to reward the sit thus produced. Then repeat the exercise. If the dog is consistently failing to sit for your faded signal, try a less faded signal, something between what works and what doesn't. You are searching for a new standard. As soon as you get a level of hand signal which works most of the time and is faded from your previous signal, work on this until the dog is sitting every time. Put this response on a variable schedule and then fade the signal further. The goal is to fade the hand signal to nothing. A lot of dogs pick up automatic sits very readily, partly because sit is such a strong behavior to start with. If the dog doesn't catch on quickly, you will systematically fade the prompt, always putting a nice response on a schedule before making the exercise harder by fading it even more. At some point, you may go to a whispered verbal command if the dog is having a hard time getting unglued from the hand signal. If he starts overshooting again or sitting excessively crookedly, you may have to perform a repair job on sit orientation as a separate enterprise. This is why dog training is so much like juggling: as soon as you focus on one thing, something else falls apart. Getting and keeping everything polished up is a juggling act of great skill.

High School Level Heeling

The goal now is to get heeling of up to a minute in duration with verbal prompting but no food target whatsoever. This is achieved by continuing the prompt-fading process we began in elementary school. Now, rather than fading the target a little, you will try removing it altogether for a couple of seconds before giving the actual reward. When doing these kinds of exercises, try to be choosy about the moment you select for the actual reward. In a long duration behavior like heeling, there is a lot of choice of when to click and treat. Trainers quickly fall into the trap of thinking they are rewarding the heeling as a whole when they click and treat, but in reality, the click is selecting a particular moment of heeling much more than the seconds or minutes of effort that came before that instant. This is particularly troublesome when one pushes the dog past the point of destruction: the dog's performance starts to deteriorate, and the trainer clicks and rewards to regain the dog's interest. This common error results in reinforcement going to exactly what you don't want: poorer heeling. Get in the habit of clicking the nice instants and hitting the deterioration with no reward marks ("Oh! Too bad!") If there are no nice instants, you are simply setting the standard too high. Your responsibility as trainer is to keep the task easy enough to maintain the dog's interest and provide you, the trainer, with plenty of rewardable responses.

Juggle the two criteria, the duration of heeling and the degree of prompt-fade, carefully. This means keeping one on the easy side whenever you turn the screws on the other. For example, if the dog can heel nicely for 30 or 40 seconds for a target held in a closed hand at your stomach with lots of verbal prompting, what would you do with the duration when you decide to remove the hand target part altogether? Right. Reduce it to a couple of seconds rather than asking for the 30 or 40. After several successful trials like this, then start gradually increasing the time between rewards until you're back up to 30 or 40. Breaking obedience exercises down this way is the cornerstone of good training. Combine criteria only when the dog is proficient at each separately and combine with close attention paid to the level of difficulty of each. Failure to do so is a classic error which makes dogs fall apart all the time.

Now heel the dog in a variety of locations, not just in your house. Always be prepared for the dog to regress substantially every time you try a new location. Drop the standard to whatever the dog can achieve, so that his experience in each place is a good, rewarding one. Then, gradually crank the standard up until he will heel in several different places as well as he does at home. This regression in new locations is a predictable part of training for all commands, but is usually exaggerated for heeling because heeling is such a multi-dimensional task for the dog (read difficult). You may even have to temporarily go back to food luring if necessary.

Location generalizing is frustrating for beginner trainers because the behavior which works so reliably at home seems to suddenly disintegrate. What was strong is now very feeble. There's a powerful temptation to ascribe the dog's failure to respond to some individual or breed defect rather than to a mundane animal learning phenomenon. But this effect is the rule rather than the exception. The good news is that the more behaviors you train and generalize, the more quickly the dog will get to be at the process. Remember, this can culminate in a dog who can generalize newly acquired behaviors and commands with no perceptible lag, even in quite difficult locations. This is part of the "learning to learn" effect which comes with sufficient volume of education of any animal.

College Level Heeling: No Prompt

When the dog heels nicely for at least a minute for verbal encouragement only and no food target, the next task is to fade the praise. This is an optional step if you do not intend to compete in licensed obedience trials. In these events, the dog is expected to heel for durations of around a minute at a time with no feedback from the handler. The way there is no secret: gradually fade the verbal coaching, selectively rewarding after increasingly long stretches of good heeling without this prompt. Then take it on the road to proof location changes and various flavors of ambient distraction.

If your goal is to compete, be sure to use obedience fun matches as one of your main training locations. Not surprisingly, fun matches afford the best simulation of the location where you will most want nice responses: obedience trials. This doesn't mean you necessarily have to enter, simply hang out and train. The main goal is for the dog to learn that this location predicts the usual contingencies of reward and marks.

A frequent error is prematurely entering obedience trials where the rules forbid feedback from handler to dog. If there are small (or, worse, large) imperfections in the dog's performance, the dog will learn in one or two trials that, in that particular context, there are no consequences. This also can happen if the dog is not on a thin enough reinforcement schedule: if rewards don't come when expected, the dog asks the old question, "what's different?" and the inevitable answer is "this context" which, no doubt, includes elements like the presence of other dogs, nervous people milling around, and people with corsages who are carrying clipboards barking out commands like "forward!" etc. Dogs discriminate environmental differences with great ease and the context of a dog show will quickly come to equate "no contingencies in effect" if the dog has an imperfect routine or is still on a continuous reinforcement schedule for any of the required behaviors.

Competitors label dogs like this "ring-wise." Many assume some malicious intent on the part of the dog, rather than accepting the predictable, inevitable and mundane learning phenomenon of operant discrimination. The contingencies are, indeed, different in an obedience trial, and the dog, perfectly obedient to the laws of learning, will perform accordingly. That is, unless he is never allowed to perceive the lack of contingency. This means 1) lots of training, (training, not performing) in this context and 2) entering trials only when the dog's performance is extremely tight and on a thin enough reinforcement schedule that minimal damage will be done to the behaviors by the feedback-free experience. Obedience trials can be very damaging. The worst thing is that, once the dog has learned that the obedience ring is a place where rewards and no-reward marks don't happen, all subsequent work will feel this imprint even if the existing errors are corrected outside the ring. This goes for any performance situation where the feedback density changes, not just obedience trials. Dogs discriminate context variations and their associated contingencies brilliantly. You can make this work for you or against you.

Tug Toy Motivators

College level heeling is a good point at which to introduce tug-toy motivators. The dog has a good understanding of how the game of training works and you have good skills. So, experiment with varying the reward: rather than giving a food reward after the click, produce a tug-toy from your pocket and engage in a brief round of tug of war. Keep it brief. This means a few seconds only: the idea is to keep him ultra-motivated. Longer tug sessions are reserved for two occasions: when the dog really hits the jackpot with some wondrous response or when you're ending the training session, always a good time for an extra large reward. (When you end sessions, by the way, try to finish up on some decent response rather than after some big regression or series of poor responses. If necessary, drop the standard to achieve a successful ending response which will merit the jackpot reward.)

The reasons for using tug-toy motivation are:

1) varying the reward is always a good idea
2) many dogs work more enthusiastically for tug-toys than for bait
3) the interactive game provides good bonding in the form of cooperative killing
4) it's a great energy burner for the dog
5) it provides an opportunity to improve control of your dog, especially his jaws, when he is in an excited state

Before using tug motivation in obedience, read or re-read the tug-of-war rules of engagement in chapter 2. Tug-toy motivation is especially useful when speed and enthusiasm of response need to be bumped up. Food is a better reinforcer for achieving precision.

Competing Motivation

A dog who has a strong and well generalized response to a particular command and who is normally very motivated by the reinforcers he intermittently receives - food and tug-games for instance - may fall apart under certain conditions. Illness and severe stress can make behavior fall apart. A much more common interference is competing motivation. The dog hears and understands the command, but something else in the environment is potently reinforcing an alternative behavior. Your bait and tug-toy are losing out to dog-play or the trail of a rabbit in the woods. What do you do? The first line of defence is to make the behaviors you want strong: recalls, downs, stays etc. and to rehearse them in areas with gradually increased ambient distraction. The next line of defence is to recognize that there is always a reward hierarchy. The most potent reinforcer wins out over the less potent which in turn wins out over the weakest. If, when in the woods, the dog would most like to follow rabbit trails, followed by playing tug, followed by cheddar cheese cubes, followed by sniffing novel dogs, followed by freeze-dried liver, followed by swimming in the pond, be advised that if you are trying to obtain come using freeze-dried liver but a nearby dog is offering a greeting ritual and the forest is offering rabbit trails, the forest will win. If the forest wasn't there, the dog would win. Enter the Premack principle.

The way you can always win is to take control of the dog's access to everything in the reward hierarchy. Give names to all these good things: "find rabbits" and "go see the dog." These become reward-commands, just like clicks came to mean food and tug. The way the dog gets you to give these reward-commands is to first obey other commands such as "come" or "sit." His access to rabbit trails, dog playmates etc. is contingent on his snappy response to obedience commands. Dogs fail to comply around competing motivations because they think the best way to get the things at the top of the reward hierarchy is to try to access them directly. The commands you are giving would get in the way. This is where you must prove them wrong. Not only does coming when called not interfere with the dog's access to the rabbit trails, it becomes the only way the dog may obtain access to rabbit trails.

You must, therefore, resolve to interrupt him and, if necessary, physically prevent him from obtaining these rewards unless he has earned them. If you say come and the dog ignores you and carries on sniffing or running towards another dog, you must explode into action. Charge, cursing and sour-looking, to the scene of the crime ("cut him off at the pass") and prevent or cut short any collection of those "top rewards." Failure to do this means the dog obtains the item at the top of the hierarchy for disobeying you. This is not good. Time to drill a few recalls until you get a nice one. Then and only then, say "go see the dog" or "find rabbits." When he's in mid-sniff, try calling again. If he ignores you again, go in and rain on his parade. If he starts playing keep-away, get really grim: rain harder on the parade until he gets worried and backs down. As soon as he gives up, lighten up your demeanor. He made it better for himself by letting you catch him. Drill some more recalls, on line if necessary. When he does a nice one, say "find rabbits" and let him off leash again. Same regime if the dog wants to greet a person or dog and ignores a command to sit while out on a walk. The dog has to sit or no patting, no dog. Simply be prepared to put your money where your mouth is. If the dog simply wiggles and pulls, say "too bad" and walk away in the other direction. You don't have to let him do anything, including greet people or dogs. A troubleshooting session, where you drill the same scenario over and over (described in chapter 4) is a good idea when emotional responses like appeasement and greeting are present.

If you rehearse this enough, the dog gets the picture. No anger, no frustration, just a simple rule: comply with commands and you will get the good stuff dogs like. Don't comply and you don't get them. Dog's choice. If you give the dog this choice, he will always comply, no matter what else is out there because you are exploiting rather than competing with the reward hierarchy. You are using the laws of learning to which he is always, without exception, perfectly obedient.

PhD Suggested Dissertations

If you have trained up to this point and want a greater challenge, here are some suggested "post-graduate" projects, the nuts and bolts of which you may work out for yourself based on the principles you have learned.

*Random position changes at 30 feet for verbal only command in a distracting environment

* First-command discrimination of 10-20 verbal cues

*10-minute sit or down-stay with handler out of sight (spying) and heavy distraction

*Heeling with no food or verbal prompts through heavy distraction environments

*Recall with automatic sit from mid-chase or mid-dog play in novel location for one verbal command

Final Note

If you have not already done so, please spay or neuter your dog.

Recommended Reading

Bailey, Gwen: *The Perfect Puppy.*
Reed International Books, London 1995

Dunbar, Ian & Bohnenkamp, Gwen: Behavior Booklets.
James & Kenneth, Oakland 1985

Dunbar, Ian: *How To Teach A New Dog Old Tricks.*
James & Kenneth, Oakland 1996

Dunbar, Ian: *Sirius Puppy Training* (video).
Bluford & Toth Productions, New York 1987

Fox, Michael: *Understanding Your Dog.*
St. Martin's Press, New York 1972

O'Farrell, Valerie: *Problem Dog.*
Methuen, London 1989

Pryor, Karen: *Don't Shoot the Dog!*
Sunshine Books, North Bend 1984

Pryor, Karen: *A Dog and a Dolphin.*
Sunshine Books, North Bend 1985

Reid, Pamela: *Excel-Erated Learning!*
James & Kenneth, Oakland 1996

Singer, Peter: *Animal Liberation.*   Avon Books, New York 1975

Sternberg, Susan: *Inducive Retrieve.*   New York 1990

Tortora, Daniel: *Help! This Animal is Driving Me Crazy!*
Fireside, New York 1977

Voith, V. & Borchelt, P.: *Readings in Companion Animal Behavior.*
Veterinary Learning Systems, Trenton 1996

Wilkes, Gary: *The Click and Treat Starter Kit* (with video).
Sunshine Books, North Bend 1995

Jean Donaldson is the owner of Renaissance
Training in Montreal, where she lives with
Meggie (left) and Lassie (right).